W9-DIT-686

DUKE · UNIVERSITY · PUBLICATIONS

CHURCH-STATE RELATIONSHIPS IN EDUCATION IN NORTH CAROLINA SINCE 1776

Church-State Relationships in Education in North Carolina since 1776

By

LUTHER L. GOBBEL

DUKE UNIVERSITY PRESS
Durham, North Carolina
1938

A DUKE UNIVERSITY CENTENNIAL PUBLICATION

This book, by an alumnus of Duke University, is one of a group published in connection with the Duke University Centennial, celebrating in 1938-1939 the anniversary of the origins of Trinity College from which Duke University developed.

PRINTED IN THE UNITED STATES OF AMERICA, BY
The Waverly Press, Inc., Baltimore, Md.

TO MY WIFE

MARCIA RUSSELL GOBBEL

INTRODUCTION

THE SHARP emergence, under stress of totalitarian pressures, of the issues involved in the relations of church and state, is one of the surprising phases of this present strange and difficult period in human history. Pagan mythologies are being resurrected, the worship of state or ruler is demanded, education is replaced by propaganda, and freedom of speech is denied.

If we are free from this sort of thing in America, it is because of two principles that are well rooted in our life: the principle of religious freedom, and the principle of public responsibility for education for citizenship in a democracy. In some respects these principles agree; in other respects they are complementary, and each serves to offset the extremes to which the other may be carried. The relations of church and state call particularly for a spirit of mutual respect and conciliation as they deal with education, in which both are so vitally interested.

The history of church-state relationships in education in North Carolina is most interesting and in some respects unique. North Carolina was the first state to open a state university. It had no denominational college until the fourth decade of the nineteenth century. In its struggle to secure a free, tax-supported system of public schools, the churches were not opponents, but advocates of the democratic system. Though there was sharp conflict from time to time between the state university and some who spoke in the name of the churches, there has been no such bitter war between secularism or atheism and Christianity as was waged in some other areas. The outcome has been an era of conciliation and co-operation in which the schools and colleges and universities of North Carolina have grown increasingly to command respect.

President Gobbel tells this story concretely, yet with objectivity and restraint. This volume should receive a wide reading; it will help American citizens generally to understand more fully the principles which underlie the successful co-operation of church and state in that most important of all things that we desire for our children—adequate education.

LUTHER A. WEIGLE

Yale University
March 14, 1938

FOREWORD

In this study are traced the relationships between the church and state in education in North Carolina from the beginning of the commonwealth in 1776 to the present time. The results of the study show how and why, in the beginning, the state assumed responsibility for higher education, the part the churches played in the founding and formative years of the State University, what the churches expected of it, and why certain denominations turned away from state institutions to found their own colleges.

Following an explanation of the denominational college movement, this study shows the difficulties encountered by the denominations in connection with their charters, early examples of co-operation and conflict between church and state agencies and institutions of higher learning, and efforts of friends and leaders to defend the policy of the University.

The second chapter reveals the factors responsible for the closing of the University following the Civil War, the opposition of the churches to its reopening, their criticism of it in the years immediately following its reestablishment, and the University's methods of dealing with its critics.

The terrific contest for the first state appropriation, the struggle to secure increases, and efforts to raise the educational standards of the University are shown in the third chapter. A forecast of the bitter crisis resulting from the accumulation of conflicts in higher education is here brought out; and in the following chapter the crisis is discussed in detail. The demands of the church group, the methods and maneuvers of both sides, and a summary of their arguments, reveal the intensity and bitterness of the long, hard road leading to the establishment of the principle of state aid to higher education, the recognition and support of the public school system, and the secularization of the control of state educational institutions.

The study of relationships in the realm of elementary and secondary education reveals an absence of the rivalry, bickerings, and battles encountered in the field of higher education. The church's fight was to get the state to support common schools. The churches held the line, after a fashion, until the state was ready to accept the obligation.

By the beginning of the twentieth century church and state had learned how to get along together in educational matters. The present century, therefore, has been, with a few exceptions, an era of conciliation and co-operation. The study closes with a brief analysis of the present *modus vivendi*.

L. L. G.

ACKNOWLEDGMENTS

THE ARDUOUS and almost endless task of searching the records covering over a century and a half of North Carolina educational and ecclesiastical history and of assembling the material for this study would have overwhelmed the writer but for the inspiration, advice, and cooperation of many persons whose timely assistance I wish now gratefully to acknowledge.

So numerous are they to whom I am indebted that it is impracticable here to name all of them. In the footnotes and the bibliography appear names of those whom I have quoted and of some from whom I have obtained ideas, suggestions, or other aid. There are others to whom I am obligated in a special way, to whom I now refer.

To the librarians and library staffs of Yale University, Duke University, the University of North Carolina, Wake Forest College, Davidson College, Greensboro College, the North Carolina State Historical Commission, the North Carolina State Library, and the Presbyterian Library at Montreat, North Carolina, who not only gave access to valuable records, but guidance in the discovery of pertinent sources, I owe a debt of gratitude.

To Dean Luther Allan Weigle of the Yale Divinity School I am obligated not only for aid in limiting the scope of the study, but also for timely and kindly suggestions at various stages of its progress. Dr. John Siler Brubacher, who shared with Dean Weigle responsibility for supervising the study, Dr. Clyde Milton Hill, chairman, and other members of the Department of Education of Yale University, gave valuable assistance, which is gratefully acknowledged.

In its original form this study was presented to the Faculty of the Graduate School of Yale University as a dissertation in candidacy for the degree of Doctor of Philosophy. With minor revisions it is being published in the present form.

Mrs. Gobbel, whose inspiration has been felt at every stage of its progress, and the late Dr. William Kenneth Boyd, of Duke University, have assisted in a critical reading of the manuscript in preparation for its publication, but should not be held responsible for any errors or omissions found in the study.

LUTHER L. GOBBEL

Greensboro, North Carolina
March 14, 1938

CONTENTS

CHURCH-STATE RELATIONSHIPS IN EDUCATION IN NORTH CAROLINA SINCE 1776

I

The Beginnings of Controversy between Church and State in Higher Education

The State Assumes Responsibility for Higher Education

THE State of North Carolina from the very beginning assumed, theoretically, responsibility for encouraging and promoting higher education. The framers of the Constitution, meeting at Halifax, December, 1776, put into the fundamental law of the state a clause providing

> That a school or schools be established by the Legislature, for the convenient Instruction of Youth, with such salaries to the Masters, paid by the Public as may enable them to instruct at low prices; and all Useful Learning shall be duly encouraged and promoted in one or more Universities.[1]

Immediately following the close of the Revolutionary War the state legislature, in 1789, chartered the University of North Carolina.[2] This institution opened its doors in 1795 and now holds the distinction of being the oldest state university in America.

The establishment of the University of North Carolina is a phenomenon of history which calls for investigation and explanation. Here is a commonwealth assuming responsibility for and taking the lead in promoting education, whereas, in colonial times, almost without exception, efforts to promote education were made by the church.[3]

The churches founded no college or university in North Carolina until near the beginning of the second quarter of

[1] *Colonial Records*, X, 1012. Article 41, Constitution of 1776.

[2] K. P. Battle, Sketches of the History of the University of North Carolina, in Addresses and Papers of K. P. Battle, pp. 2–3.

[3] R. D. W. Connor, *History of North Carolina*, I, 204.

the nineteenth century. Except for a few church and private academies, which did very little, if any, work in the higher branches of learning, the state was in entire, although not altogether undisputed, control of the facilities for higher education in North Carolina for the first fifty years of the state's history.

This study concerning the relationships between church and state in education in North Carolina leads one to ask: 1. What were some of the conditions and considerations which led the state to undertake higher education? 2. What part, if any, did the churches play in the founding and formative years of the State University and in any other educational enterprises under state auspices? 3. What did the churches expect of and hope from these institutions? and 4. What were the conditions and factors which led certain denominations to turn away from the University and establish institutions of their own?

1. Our first task, therefore, is to inquire, Why did this young commonwealth, emerging from its colonial estate, decide to go into the business of higher education?

In the first place, the churches were poorly organized and very weak, indicative of a low state of religion. The American Revolution, like most wars, proved an impediment to the progress of the church. During the Revolution there was a disastrous interruption of all organized religious activity in North Carolina.[4] There were no general church organizations covering the whole state. The Baptists had their Sandy Creek and Kehukee associations, and the Presbyterians their Orange Presbytery. But these could hardly be considered state-wide in scope and influence. The Baptists did not form their state-wide organization, the North Carolina Baptist State Convention, until 1830.[5] Not only were the Baptists divided organically; but they were also divided on the significance of education for the church.[6]

[4] John Wheeler Moore, *History of North Carolina*, I, 404.

[5] G. W. Paschal, "History of Wake Forest College," *Wake Forest Student*, July, 1925.

[6] *Ibid.*

One wing of the Baptists, which split off about 1830, did not believe in education for the masses or even for the ministry.[7] Their ministers of this period, we are told, were not well enough educated to teach school, as did the Presbyterian ministers of the state.[8]

As to the smaller sects, such as the Episcopalians, Quakers, Moravians, and others, they were too small, too scattered, and too disorganized, not to mention other difficulties, to undertake to establish institutions of higher learning.[9] For example, the Episcopal Church (the Established Church in colonial times) never was strong numerically in North Carolina; it was "reduced by that great event [American Revolution] to a state of actual silence."[10] In 1776 not more than six Episcopal clergymen were to be found in the state.[11] The political independence of the state cut off this church from the English episcopate, leaving the Episcopalians with no bishop of their own and no way of ordaining one. The Society for the Propagation of the Gospel ceased its financial support, and disestablishment deprived the Episcopal Church of property and accustomed revenues.[12]

[7] Lemuel Burkitt and Jesse Read, *A Concise History of the Kehukee Baptist Association*, p. 70.

[8] G. W. Paschal, *History of North Carolina Baptists*, I, 360.

[9] Moore, *op. cit.*

[10] *Journal of Annual Convention of the Protestant Episcopal Church, 1825*, p. 23.

[11] Francis-Xavier Martin, *History of North Carolina*, II, 395. Concerning the religious situation of this period, in general, Martin says: "Religion was at a low ebb; notwithstanding the provision made by law for one clergyman of the established church in every parish, there were not more than six ministers, settled in the province. The Presbyterians had nearly an equal number. The Quakers had religious establishments in the counties of Perquimans, Pasquotank, Orange, Guilford, Johnson, and Carteret. The Moravians or united brethren had six settlements, Salem, Bethabara, Bethania, Friedberg, Frieland, and Hope, and the number of persons under the care of this church, in all there was about five hundred. There was no regular establishment of any other denomination of Christians; though the counties were visited by itinerant Baptist and Methodist preachers."

[12] L. A. Weigle, *American Idealism*, p. 155. The *Journal of the Annual Convention of the Protestant Episcopal Church, 1825*, p. 23, records the Episcopal Bishop as saying: "Political feelings were associated with its [Episcopal Church's] very name, which operates as a complete bar to very useful or comfortable exercise of duty, by the very few clergymen, perhaps not more than three or four, which were left."

The Methodists entered the state late. Their first circuit was organized in 1776. Their interest centered largely in the poorer classes, and their method was largely evangelistic. They prospered during the period of the Revolution and after;[13] but it was not until 1837 that they split off from the Virginia Conference and formed their own Annual Conference. For fifteen or twenty years thereafter they sent their ministerial candidates and others to Randolph-Macon College in Virginia.[14]

The period immediately following the Revolutionary War, in North Carolina, as in the rest of this country, was one during which the moral and religious life touched its lowest ebb.[15] Of the Presbyterians, whose leadership in educational matters before and after the Revolutionary War is discussed elsewhere, it may be said here that "The pastors shed tears over departed worth," but "grieved most over the living who had renounced the religion of their fathers."[16] The total membership of all churches at the close of the eighteenth century in North Carolina was approximately 30,000 out of a population of 363,751.[17] No denomination

[13] M. L. Wood, *History of Methodism in the Yadkin Valley*; W. L. Grissom, *History of Methodism in North Carolina.*

[14] A letter written by Joseph Caldwell, undated but apparently written about November, 1796, soon after his arrival in Chapel Hill from Princeton to take up his duties as a member of the faculty of the University of North Carolina, reveals a great deal concerning the state of religion. He says: "The state appears to be swarming with lawyers. It is almost the only profession for which parents educate their children. Religion is so little in vogue, and in such a state of depression, that it affords no prospects sufficient to tempt people to undertake its cause. In New Jersey it has the public respect and support. But in North Carolina and particularly in that part of the state which lies east of us, everyone believes that the first step which he ought to take to rise into respectability is to disavow as often and as publicly as he can all regard for the leading doctrines of the scriptures. . . . One of the principal reasons why religion is so slighted and almost scouted is that it is taught only by Methodists and ranters with whom it seems to consist only in the power of their throats, or wildness and madness of their gesticulations and distortions" (Letters, University of North Carolina, 1795–1835).

[15] L. A. Weigle, *Religion and Secular Education* (a tract), p. 13.

[16] W. K. Boyd, *History of North Carolina* (*The Federal Period*), II, 186. See footnote 42.

[17] Drake, *op. cit.*, p. 154.

could establish its own institution of higher learning, and apparently had any thought or disposition to co-operate with the other denominations.

With the church in eclipse, the secular state gained the ascendency. The spirit of the times, inspired by the French radicals who were popular in North Carolina as well as in America generally, was chilling to religion; there was but little regard for religious institutions. The writings of Voltaire, Helvetius, Bolingbroke, Hume, Paine, and Rousseau were among the books in the libraries of the principal families of the state.[18] In the words of William Hooper, the French classics had "a factitious importance and popularity from the recent splendor of Voltaire, from our late obligations to the country of Lafayette, and from the overwhelming interest excited by the first French revolution."[19]

Then, one of the most potent factors which almost forced the state into education was a very practical, utilitarian one —the recognized need for education in a democracy. If the laws were not to be misinterpreted and corruptly used, the state must have trained men for public office, restrained by an educated public opinion.[20] Perhaps "A Citizen," writing in the *North Carolina Journal* in 1796, stated the aim correctly when he pointed out that, although until lately education was supplied outside the state, now at the University of North Carolina "enlightened sons of North Carolina will soon be qualified to fill all the public offices in the government, and likewise to exercise with capacity and reputation all the public and learned professions—as well as to discover and oppose successfully every latent measure tending to tyranny and oppression."[21] Governor Martin, twelve years earlier, in addressing the legislature of 1784, had called attention to need for the education of youth and pleaded for "seminaries of learning . . . where

[18] William Hooper, *Fifty Years Since*, p. 41.

[19] *Ibid.*, p. 17.

[20] J. H. Randall, *The Making of the Modern Mind*, p. 324.

[21] *North Carolina Journal*, April 6, 1796, p. 1.

the state may draw forth men of abilities to direct her councils and support her government."[22]

2. There is evidence that the churches, particularly the Presbyterian, played an important part in the founding and in the formative years of the University of North Carolina.[23]

In the constitutional convention itself the Scotch-Irish Presbyterians were prominent. The Mecklenburg delegation[24] carried with them to the convention not only instructions to use all their endeavors for the establishment of a university,[25] but also an educational background and a series of experiences in dealing with the British Crown, which put them on tiptoe for education in general and for higher education in particular. C. L. Smith, C. Alphonso Smith,[26] R. D. W. Connor,[27] and other writers agree that it was largely through their influence that the clause providing for a university was inserted in the initial constitution of the state.[28] The *Presbyterian Standard*, looking back one-hundred and twenty-eight years, gave expression to the feeling that but for the high educational spirit and great influence of the Presbyterians there would not have been a University of North Carolina.[29]

The refusal of George III to ratify the charter of Queen's College (sometimes referred to as Queen's Museum) under the supervision of Orange Presbytery, it is claimed, played an important part in fanning the educational zeal of the Presbyterians to white heat and perhaps prompted the

[22] *State Records*, XIX, 498.

[23] Cornelia Shaw, *Davidson College*, p. 6.

[24] Members of the delegation were: John Phifer, Robert Irwin, Zaccheus Wilson, Hezekiah Alexander, and Waightstill Avery.

[25] Battle, Sketches of the History of the University of North Carolina, p. 2, in Addresses and Papers of K. P. Battle.

[26] C. Alphonso Smith, *Presbyterians in Educational Work in North Carolina*, p. 23.

[27] Connor, *op. cit.*, p. 201.

[28] C. L. Smith, *History of Education in North Carolina*, p. 52. Also C. Alphonso Smith, *op. cit.*

[29] *Presbyterian Standard*, Feb. 5, 1908, p. 2.

provision in the constitution of the commonwealth for one or more universities.[30] The charter, granted by the colonial legislature in 1770, was immediately annulled by the king. A second charter, secured by the Presbyterians in 1771, also was repealed by royal proclamation.[31] Although this twice-repeated action of King George was quite in line with the established policy of the Crown concerning education in North Carolina,[32] the Presbyterians of Mecklenburg were not happy over the royal proclamations and, in spite of the royal disallowance, continued to operate the institution without a charter until the overthrow of the British rule. In 1777 Queen's College was chartered by the legislature of North Carolina as Liberty Hall, which was continued until 1780 in Mecklenburg and then was moved to Salisbury,

[30] Frank W. Blackmar, *The History of Federal and State Aid to Higher Education in the United States*, p. 193; Drake, *op. cit.*, pp. 45–46; Foote, *op. cit.*, pp. 513–514; Shaw, *op. cit.*, pp. 1–4; Connor, *op. cit.*, pp. 201–204.

To Benjamin Franklin much credit is sometimes given for the educational clause in the Constitution of North Carolina. It is said that in July, 1776, following a trip to France, Franklin aided in drawing up and supervised the final writing of the Pennsylvania Constitution, in which first appeared the educational clause just referred to, and that this clause was thus, in part, if not wholly, the work of Franklin. There are those who think that the words "low prices" almost mark it as his own. To the Scotch-Irish of Mecklenburg County may belong a part of the responsibility for this educational clause. And as to the words "low prices," there seems to be as much ground for crediting them to the Scotch-Irish as to Franklin. If Franklin originated them, the Scotch-Presbyterians no doubt found it easy to adopt them.

[31] *Colonial Records*, I, 596; Connor, *op. cit.*, p. 204.

The Board of Trade, which advised the king in this matter, doubted whether the king should "add Incouragement to toleration by giving the Royal Assent to an Establishment, which in its consequences, promises great and permanent Advantages to a sect of Dissenters from The Established Church who have already extended themselves over that Province in very considerable numbers."

The chief patronage and support for Queen's College came from the Presbyterians, and all the incorporators except two were Presbyterians. Although the charter provided that the president should be a member of the Church of England, "no compliment to his queen could render whigs in politics, and Presbyterians in religion, acceptable to George III" (Foote, *op. cit.*, p. 513).

[32] *Colonial Records*, XXIII, 823. The laws of 1770 vested the schoolhouse at Edenton in trustees and provided that "no Person shall be admitted to be Master of said School, but who is of the Established Church of England."

where it soon fell by the wayside.[33] Although it never became a state-wide denominational institution, its history is significant, not only as a daring attempt to promote education under discouraging circumstances, but also as one of a series of efforts by the Presbyterians of Orange Presbytery to establish an institution of high order, on Christian principles, and under Christian influences.[34] It is significant for this study because it helps one to understand the impulse which prompted the Scotch-Irish at Halifax to favor so strongly higher education and the powerful influence which the Presbyterians were destined to have in the educational affairs of North Carolina.

In the years immediately following the convention and the Revolutionary War, Dr. Samuel F. McCorkle, a staunch Presbyterian preacher and teacher, influenced tremendously the curriculum, the faculty, the trustees, the policies, and, therefore, the history and development of the University of North Carolina.[35] His influence, and that of the religious group which he represented, may best be understood against the background of another man prominent in the early history of the University. This other person was William R. Davie, a deist and spokesman of eighteenth-century rationalism.[36] These two men typified the conflicting currents and viewpoints clamoring for recognition in the early days of the University. They clashed at several points and

[33] Shaw, *op. cit.*, p. 4.

[34] C. L. Coon, *North Carolina Schools and Academies, 1790–1840*, p. xix.

[35] Dr. McCorkle was an active trustee of the University, organizer of its first "Plan of Studies," strong proponent of the doctrine of revelation, and spokesman for the conservatives.

[36] Davie, an Englishman by birth, a graduate of Princeton in 1776, a major in the Revolutionary War, represented North Carolina in the National Constitutional Convention in 1787, in the lower house of the state legislature of 1789, and in the North Carolina Convention for the ratification of the Constitution of the United States. He introduced the bill and successfully championed the chartering of the University by the legislature. He became one of the first trustees of the University and proved himself to be one of the most influential (see W. H. Hoyt, *The Papers of Archibald D. Murphey*, II, 349; *Colonial Records*, X, 870; and Drake, *op. cit.*, pp. 52–53).

on more than one occasion.[37] On the question of deism and the doctrine of revelation the two were widely apart. Battle gives this difference as one of the chief reasons why McCorkle did not become the first president of the University.[38] McCorkle was elected Professor of Moral and Political Philosophy and History, but refused to serve, "because Davie was not willing to grant him a salary equal to that of the acting president."[39] They disagreed also on the question of whether the classics or science should predominate in the curriculum, "whether the old collegiate curriculum should give way to the ideas so strongly urged by Franklin in 1749, by Jefferson in 1779, and by Davie in 1795."[40] Davie exerted his efforts in the direction of making science predominate in the curriculum. Joseph Caldwell, a devout and energetic classicist, who became a member of the faculty in 1796, helped the McCorkle group to overcome Davie's opposition, swinging the balance in favor of a classical curriculum, so that by 1804 the University was safely in the classical fold, although Caldwell is said later to have developed a lively interest in the sciences.[41]

One might ask, if the Presbyterians were so strong educationally, why they did not establish and maintain their own denominational college in the first half-century of the state's history. The answer seems to be at least twofold. In the first place, they had their academies scattered over

[37] Record of Trustees, University of North Carolina, *passim.*

[38] K. P. Battle, *History of the University of North Carolina*, I, 60. The Rev. Jethro Rumple, writing in the *Carolina Watchman*, Jan. 6, 1881, said: "In 1795 the Trustees of the University of North Carolina elected Dr. McCorkle Professor of Moral and Political Philosophy and History, with a view to his acting as President. Gen Davie, it seems, objected to the arrangement, and this caused Dr. McCorkle to decline the place. . . . But Dr. McCorkle did not cease to labor for the advancement of the University."

[39] *North Carolina Journal*, Feb. 22, 1796, p. 1.

[40] Drake, *op. cit.*, p. 81.

[41] *Ibid.*, p. 362. Commenting on the influence of preachers on the University, Davie wrote: "Bishop Pettigrew has said it is a very dissipated and debauched place. Some priests have also done us the same good office to the westward. Nothing it seems goes well that these men of God have not had some hand in" (Drake, *op. cit.*, pp. 80–81).

the state.[42] And then, as subsequent paragraphs will tend to show, they seemed to prefer to throw, insofar as practicable, their support to and to depend upon the state institutions, at least so long as they could be a powerful factor in controlling their policies and shaping their destinies. It may help also to remember that the Scotch, like other colonists, sought to transplant their European ideas and customs, educational and otherwise. Even as late as 1861 in Scotland, for example, the minister was still in control of the schoolmaster, who was bound to declare that he would not teach any opinions opposed to the Bible or the Shorter Catechism, or do anything to the prejudice of the Church.[43]

Although we find no reference in the early records of the Presbyterian Church in North Carolina bearing directly on this point, the whole attitude and policy of North Carolina Presbyterians in the early days of the state's history seem quite in line with, if not in obedience to, the urging of the General Assembly of the Presbyterian Church, U. S. A., which, recognizing in 1799 that "a vain and pernicious philosophy had spread its infection from Europe to America," urged Presbyterian ministers to encourage their elders to serve as trustees of schools for the purpose of overseeing the selection of teachers and instruction.[44] Sherrill calls attention to the reality of this attempt at ecclesiastical supervision of schools, "however nicely veiled."[45]

McCorkle, the leader of the Presbyterians, moreover, made numerous journeys into various parts of the state, in search of both funds and students for the University, and

[42] W. H. Foote, *Sketches of North Carolina*, p. 513. Raper also mentions such Presbyterian schools as Sugar Creek, Poplar Tent, Centre, Buffalo, Bethany, Thyatira, Grove, and Wilmington, and adds: "They [Presbyterians] have been more thoroughly devoted to education than any other denomination. It has meant life as well as light to them; it has made them independent and patriotic, strong and noble. They were really our first teachers, and during the latter part of the eighteenth century they were well nigh our only ones" (*Church and Private Schools in North Carolina*, p. 31).

[43] John Stewart, *The Organization of Education at Edinburgh*, p. 5.

[44] *Minutes of the General Assembly Presbyterian Church, U. S. A., 1799*, p. 18.

[45] L. J. Sherrill, *Presbyterian Parochial Schools, 1846–1870*, p. 2.

his country church made a regular contribution to the University.[46] His own Zion-Parnassus Academy furnished six of the first seven graduates of the institution at Chapel Hill.[47]

In 1812 the Reverend James Hall, Presbyterian famous for his Clio's Nursery, the first school in the state to have a "scientific course," made an effort to put more clergymen on the board of trustees of the University of North Carolina.[48] He disavowed any desire to become a trustee himself but thought those in authority were making a grave mistake not to use more ministers as trustees. Although not so many ministers served as trustees as Hall desired, every president and every acting president of the University before the Civil War, and most of them since that time, were members of the Presbyterian Church— an eloquent testimony to the Presbyterian influence over affairs at Chapel Hill and at the same time at least a partial explanation of the jealousies which arose in the course of years.[49] With such a record, therefore, it is little wonder that from the Constitutional Convention down to the present time, with a few rare exceptions, the Presbyterians have shown a marked, almost paternal interest in the University of North Carolina.

By 1811 the Presbyterian Church seems to have begun to doubt the effectiveness of its attempts to secure ecclesiastical supervision of schools. At its General Assembly that year it said that education was "the legitimate business of the Church, rather than the State."[50] Nevertheless, the Presbyterians of North Carolina apparently were not in full agreement with the General Assembly, as shown by their efforts, as late as 1820–24, to found a second state institution,

[46] Shaw, *op. cit.*, p. 5.

[47] *Ibid.*

[48] Letters, U. N. C., 1796–1835 (MSS); E. W. Knight, *Public Education in North Carolina*, p. 40; Shaw, *op. cit.*, p. 5.

[49] Shaw, *op. cit.*, p. 7.

[50] *Minutes General Assembly Presbyterian Church, U. S. A.*, p. 480, quoted from Sherrill, *op. cit.*, p. 2.

which efforts are known as the Western College movement. Whether it was because they succeeded so well in their purposes for the institution at Chapel Hill and wanted another like it in the western part of the state, or whether they disapproved of its policies and product and dared to build a second one more to their liking, the Presbyterians of Mecklenburg, Iredell, and adjoining counties, in 1820, launched a movement for a state institution southwest of the Yadkin River.[51] Although not labeled a Presbyterian enterprise but a state project, this movement rested upon a Presbyterian foundation, as is clearly revealed by the fact that when this movement fell through as a state project, it was soon resumed openly as a Presbyterian undertaking, eventuating in 1837 in the establishment of Davidson College.[52] It seems reasonable, therefore, to infer that the Presbyterian Church in North Carolina hoped, from the beginning, not only to put its imprint effectively and indelibly upon the state's educational policies, but, as some feared, largely to control them.

3. This Western College movement has significance for this study, furthermore, in that it shows, among other things, what some church leaders expected of state institutions. It seems to reveal what these leaders doubtless looked for but apparently failed to find sufficiently at Chapel Hill.

Although the reason for Western College given in the charter was that the more western counties were "distant from Chapel Hill,"[53] other reasons were offered by those agitating for the proposed institution, not the least of which was "the interests of religion and morality."[54] In their

[51] *Western Carolinian*, Oct. 3, 1820, copied in *Raleigh Register*, Oct. 13, 1820, listed twenty-five trustees, most of whom were Presbyterians, nine of the number being ministers.

[52] *Southern Citizen*, Feb. 18, 1837.

[53] Shaw, *op. cit.*, p. 8.

[54] *Western Carolinian*, Nov. 7, 1820. Five reasons were offered: (1) the example of sister states, (2) conveniency, (3) the preservation of resources at home, (4) accommodation of the less wealthy part of society, and (5) the interests of religion and morality.

arguments in behalf of religion and morality the sponsors of this movement argued the case of the church more openly and persistently than ever before. One might safely conclude that with boldness they were trying to make a definite union of religion and morality with civil society.[55]

"Junius" argued that "great talents and learning, rising in conflict with moral excellency, never can be a benefit to society," and that morality is not firmly based on any other bottom but that of religion.[56] Thus, he contended, the interest of both church and state, and the completion of the character and standing of the student, "combine to enhance the importance of the argument now under consideration."

This argument, the writer held, must stand in full force, "except it can be made to appear that the interests of religion and morality are already suitably consulted and supported in our Southern seats of learning."

The University at Chapel Hill was such a seat of learning. Was "Junius" intimating that the interests of morality and religion were being neglected there? Whether this was the case or not, he would let two things determine: first, the paucity of ministers of the Gospel that emanated from it; second, the testimony of those that had had an opportunity of inspecting the state of religion and morals among those that composed it.[57]

Dr. James McRee, Pastor of Center Presbyterian Church in Iredell County, in his address to the convention at Lincolnton,[58] paid particular attention to the *state of the Church*, "the great inequality in the number of Gospel Ministers to

[55] *Ibid.*

[56] *Western Carolinian*, Nov. 7, 1820. In this issue "Junius" wrote also: "In pleading the cause of religion and morality, the church will duly appreciate the weight of the argument. She laments the paucity of competent Ministers of the Gospel, and mourns over her silent Sabbaths. Her eyes are upon the fountains of science, and she devoutly supplicates that they may be preserved pure."

[57] *Ibid.*

[58] The movement, first announced through the *Western Carolinian* on Aug. 22, 1820, by "Vox Populi," was set on foot at a convention at Lincolnton, Sept. 22, 1820 (see *Western Carolinian*, Jan. 23, 1821).

distribute, compared with the number of immortal souls throughout the United States to receive the bread of life."[59] Considering the immediate territory to be served by the proposed institution, McRee estimated a need for three hundred ministers, whereas he found only forty, a deficiency of two hundred and sixty. In the face of these conditions, McRee said: "The Church of Christ lays in her claim. *Now opens* the great object of our Seminary."[60]

Obviously McRee and his associates had in mind a state institution in the western part of the state akin to the College of New Jersey (Princeton), whose services in training ministers of the gospel were highly lauded.[61]

The plan to establish Western College failed, the reasons given being (1) disaffection and disagreement upon the part of its supporters over its proposed location, (2) an endeavor to unite too many discordant interests, (3) the fear that teachers not acceptable to many would have a place in it, and (4) opposition of the friends of the University, who were unwilling to divide what already seemed an inadequate support for one institution.[62] It was impossible to secure the support of other denominations, for they were "unwilling to do much for a college which when founded would almost certainly be manned by Presbyterians," as the one at Chapel Hill was accused of being so manned.[63]

That the religious forces in North Carolina expected a great deal of the University and looked to it to train leaders in both church and state seems clear, also, from other records

[59] *Western Carolinian*, Jan. 23, 1821; Jan. 30, 1821.

[60] *Ibid., passim.*

[61] *Ibid.* McRee summarized the objectives of the proposed institution as follows: a public seminary of learning, to prepare young men, by the knowledge and influence of the Christian religion, with the aid of sound science, to act with honor and advantage in those public departments of life, which the church, the state, and the conditions of mankind, now do, and will in the future, require; founded on the broad and solid basis of Christian and republican principles, to the entire exclusion of all party names and distinctions, whether civil or religious.

[62] Coon, *op. cit.*, p. xlv; Shaw, *op. cit.*, p. 10.

[63] *Ibid.;* Drake, *op. cit.*, p. 156.

of the times. The Reverend Samuel F. McCorkle, who delivered the first public address ever delivered at the University, expected the University to help produce ministers of religion as well as of state.[64] McCorkle's closing words in this address erected a standard at Chapel Hill very high and one by which the University was destined to be tested. "May this hill be for religion, as the ancient hill of Zion; and for literature and the muses may it surpass the ancient Parnassus."[65]

To such a standard it was not difficult for Presbyterians, Moravians, and other churchmen to rally. That the University sought in the early days of its history the esteem and support of the ministers is also apparent.[66] If the pulpit and the press could be brought to support it, the legislature and the people generally would give it money and students. The awarding of honorary degrees was one of the devices used not only to honor but also to curry the favor of influential churchmen, and likewise furnished the opportunity for the recipients to express, to the administration, their hopes and ambitions for the University. For example, the Right Reverend Gotthold Reichel, D.D., bishop in Bethlehem, Pennsylvania, acknowledging the notification of the conferring of the degree of Doctor of Divinity on him by the University of North Carolina, expressed what perhaps was one of the expectations of the churches for the University,

[64] History of the University of North Carolina (MS), p. 69. Speaking at the laying of the cornerstone of the first University building, "Old East," Oct. 12, 1793, two years before the doors were opened for students, Dr. McCorkle uttered memorable words: "It is our duty to acknowledge that sacred Scripture truth, 'Except the Lord do build the house their labor is but in vain that build it.' The happiness of a nation depends on national wealth and national glory and cannot be gained without them. They in like manner depend on liberty and good laws. Liberty and laws call for general knowledge in the people . . . Knowledge is wealth, it is glory, whether among philosophers, ministers of state or religion, or among the great mass of people."

[65] History of the University of North Carolina (MS), p. 71.

[66] Letters of the University of North Carolina, 1796–1835 (MSS).

an expectation that it would prepare ministers of the Gospel.[67]

The University conferred the degree of Doctor of Divinity also upon the Reverend James Hall, of Iredell County, in 1812. Acknowledging the bestowal of the degree upon him by the University, Hall took occasion to charge that political principles had too often stood in the way of talents and integrity at the University and that those having the appointment of trustees had "acted much against the interest of the institution in almost entirely excluding the clergy from the Board."[68]

Obviously, the University had need of the favor and support of the clergy, for it had been so "deserted and frowned upon by the Legislature" that it was "preserved in existence by the talents and exertions alone of its President [Caldwell, who could muster much strength from the churches, especially the Presbyterian]. . . ."[69]

4. Although the influence of McCorkle, Caldwell, and other Presbyterians in the formation of the policies of the University in its early days was pronounced, one must not forget that the influence of Davie, the deist, and of the French and English radicalism was also present. There were times when the latter seemed to be in the ascendency, to the extent that both faculty and students came in for much severe criticism. Paralleling this radicalism, if not consequent upon it, were numerous outbursts of misconduct and breaches of good discipline.[70]

[67] Letters of the University of North Carolina, 1796–1835 (MSS), Bishop Reichel to Major Robert Williams, May, 1812. He said: "My humble and fervent prayers ascend to the throne of Grace for a rich effusion of the divine blessings upon it, and for enabling the University of the State, not only to promote the temporal welfare of the inhabitants by a more general diffusion of useful knowledge through the arts and sciences amongst all the classes of people, but especially to grant grace, that the University may be a blessed instrument in the hand of God, to spread the light of the glorious Gospel of our salvation . . . through every part of the state and that by his Spirit may be raised in this University many faithful witnesses of the evangelical truth. . . ."

[68] Letters of the University of North Carolina, 1796–1835 (MSS).

[69] *Raleigh Star*, March 15, 1810.

[70] Drake, *op. cit.*, pp. 310–321; Battle, *History of University of North Carolina*, I, 60.

In the first place, it seems that, from the standpoint of the churches, the trustees made a series of unfortunate choices of members of the early faculty.[71] Davie, perhaps the most influential member of the first board of trustees, having acquired a pronounced distrust of all preachers,[72] is credited with the responsibility of keeping McCorkle, staunch Presbyterian churchman and educator, from becoming the first president of the University of North Carolina.[73] The trustees gave the position of acting president to another Presbyterian minister, the Reverend David Ker, who had been pastor of the Presbyterian church in Fayetteville and principal of the school there as well,[74] and who obviously was more to Davie's liking, although Drake tells us that, by mixing himself up in the political thought of the time, Ker, too, secured the ill will of Davie and was thus forced to resign in July, 1796.[75] After leaving the University, Ker is said to have "exchanged his Calvinistic tenets for a mild form of infidelity."[76] And one is left to suspect that some of this infidelity may have cropped out while there.[77] Not only was Ker's tenure short and not altogether satisfactory, but that of another member of the first faculty, Samuel A. Holmes, was the occasion of a determined fight, which resulted in his resigning.[78] Charles W. Harris, a

[71] The *North Carolina Journal*, Feb. 22, 1796, announced the following appointments by the trustees: Rev. Samuel McCorkle, D.D., Professor of Moral and Political Philosophy and History; Rev. David Ker, Professor of Languages; Chas. W. Harris, Esq., Professor of Mathematics; Delavaux and Holmes, tutors in the Preparatory School.

[72] Battle, *History of the University of North Carolina*, I, 60.

[73] *Ibid.*

[74] Battle, Sketches of the History of the University of North Carolina, p. 38.

[75] Drake, *op. cit.*, p. 78.

[76] Battle, *op. cit.*, p. 38.

[77] That Davie's attitude toward McCorkle created resentment is shown in a letter in 1789 written by General John Steele, once a member of the National Congress, who said: "I have no sons to educate and my nephew [son of Dr. McCorkle] is relieved of the humiliation of acquiring his education at an institution whose outset was characterized by acts of ingratitude and insults toward his father" (see Battle, *History of the University of North Carolina*, II, 100).

[78] In 1799 there was written, presumably by other members of the faculty, a letter to the board of trustees, objecting to "his [Holmes's] principles and his

Presbyterian layman, who succeeded Ker as acting president, was also charged with skepticism.[79] Nicholas Delavaux, a French Catholic, who served on the first faculty for a short time as teacher in the preparatory school, was not in congenial company with Caldwell and William Richards, fellow teachers, so that James Hogg's high regard for Delevaux' "grammatical accuracy" was not enough to save him to the faculty.[80] He resigned.[81]

---

conduct." It was declared that Holmes's principles are "such as are subversive of all order and regular government in any society—[teaching] That each member of any community is bound to preserve his own particular interest against that of every other. That there is no such thing as virtue, but that it is only a fantastic idea . . . [and that he] called into question every truth of religion." It was charged, also, that he stirred up strife among students and was guilty of "every species of irregularity" (Letters, University of North Carolina, 1796–1835. No signatures appear on the letters appearing in this collection).

[79] Caldwell became president of the University in 1804. A picture of the situation into which young Joseph Caldwell, just from Princeton to assume his position as a member of the faculty at Chapel Hill, is set forth in the following letter written by John Henry Hobart, a tutor at Princeton, Nov. 30, 1796, to Caldwell: "It is to be hoped, however, that the rays of light from your University the sun of Science, will illuminate the darkness of society, and chase away ignorance and vice . . . With all due respect to the Faculty of the University of Carolina . . . they seem to constitute as motley a group as I have lately heard of. Presbyterians and Arians, infidels and Roman Catholics. Bless me what a collection. The *age of Reason* has surely come. Superstitution and bigotry are buried in one common grave. Philosophy and charity begin to bless the earth. Transporting thought. What a glory to the University of Carolina that in her sacred seats they have first appeared.

"I expected something better of Harris. I did not expect that he would become the disciple of infidelity. There is no knowing, however, where mere Philosophy will lead men. Unfortunate indeed is her influence when she exalts the pride of human reason and extinguishes those lights which only can guide her to Truth. I fear for your situation, thus deprived of religious conversation and society and exposed to the insults of the profane or the scoffs of the infidel. Your resolution, however, to stand firm is worthy of your profession . . . Providence seems to have placed you in a situation where you may do much good. It seems as if you were called on to proclaim the glorious truths of the gospel where they have not been known, or known only to be contumed" (Letters, University of North Carolina, 1796–1835, MSS).

[80] Letter of James Hogg to William R. Davie, in *James Sprunt Historical Monograph*, No. 7, p. 35.

[81] Drake, *op. cit.*, p. 79; J. G. deR. Hamilton, "William Randolph Davie: A Memoir," in the *James Sprunt Historical Studies*, VII, 30.

In 1800 Hugh Williamson, a trustee, exercised over conditions in the faculty at Chapel Hill, expressed a desire to see a clergyman, a Yale graduate, chosen as one of the professors at the University of North Carolina to offset the philosophy of the French National Convention.[82]

The McCorkle-Caldwell religious group in the administration at Chapel Hill, trying hard and making some progress in rooting infidelity out of the faculty, had a staunch and sympathetic supporter in Charles Pettigrew, who wrote from Tyrrell, November 10, 1797, a charitable criticism of the teachings of certain professors at the University. He was conscious of the limitations upon one "in the place of the president without his authority." Yet he was tremendously concerned for his two sons, John and Ebenezer Pettigrew. He declared:

> An education without the fear of God may suit those who confine their views to *this world* and to the *present life* only, but to one who expects his children are to survive the ruins of time, in a state of immortal and endless existence . . . such an Education must be very shocking.[83]

There seems to be ample evidence, therefore, to support the belief that among members of the church group was much feeling against the University because of its alleged skepticism and the free thought expressed by its founders and early faculty.

Within the student body, moreover, there were conditions, "undoubtedly bad but grievously exaggerated," which tended to weaken the influence of the University.[84] Drake, who has recently made a thorough-going study of student life of the ante-bellum college and university in North Carolina, gives a detailed account of numerous outbursts of disrespect for members of the faculty, destruction of property, fighting, drinking, immorality, and other vices,

[82] Letters, University of North Carolina, 1797–1835 (MSS).
[83] *Ibid.*
[84] Battle, *History of the University of North Carolina*, I, 136.

and of various measures, including an investigation by a committee appointed by the legislature, in 1809, looking to the correction of these evils.[85]

These conditions brought forth criticism.[86] When one considers the frontier conditions of the times, however, one may well wonder if conditions at Chapel Hill were much worse than they are in most institutions of higher learning today. The churches had not yet tried their hands at running denominational colleges in North Carolina. It is easy, therefore, to see how there would be a great deal of well-meaning criticism.

The University was sensitive to the criticism and sought the good opinion of the churches. It would doubtless be untrue to infer that the bylaws drawn by McCorkle and adopted February 6, 1795, were designed merely to conform to what the churches expected. Yet, it perhaps would not be harsh judgment to state it as an opinion that to win the favor of church people was one of the reasons for requiring all students to attend divine service on the Sabbath, for examining pupils each Sunday afternoon on the general principles of religion and morality, and for enjoining them not to speak disrespectfully of religion or of any religious denomination.[87] In fact, the freshman and sophomore classes were required to study the gospels of St. John and St. Luke in the Greek.[88] The teaching of revealed religion became an important part of the curriculum, "partly due to custom and tradition and partly due to the attacks made by the deistic followers on the theology of the eighteenth century."[89]

One of the most powerful factors which caused the denominations to enter the field of higher education on their own account arose with the growth of the denominations.

[85] Drake, *op. cit.*, pp. 304–321, *passim.*

[86] *Ibid*, p. 156.

[87] Battle, *op. cit.*, I, 56.

[88] Drake, *op. cit.*, p. 239.

[89] *Ibid.*, p. 240.

Recuperating from the ill effects of the Revolutionary War and the deadening influence of the accompanying French rationalism, the churches had, by 1825 or 1830, pulled themselves back together. A great revival swept the state from 1800 to 1811, and small waves of evangelism followed.[90] These brought a deepened religious consciousness and a demand for institutions sound in religious doctrine, in which candidates for the ministry and sons of churchmen could receive an education without danger of compromising their faith.[91]

The Churches Enter the Field of Higher Education

If it be true, as has been shown, that revolt against theology during the Revolutionary period and lack of organization and strength among the denominations, coupled with their reliance upon the University to provide higher education for both church and state, account for the failure of the denominations to establish institutions of higher education in North Carolina during the first half century of the commonwealth, a revolt against skepticism, the organization and increasing educational consciousness of the denominitions, born of an experience of need for trained ministers and a sense of obligation to the boys and girls of the poorer classes, brought forth a series of denominational colleges during the decade of 1830 to 1840 and the years immediately following.

Wake Forest College, one of the first fruits of the Baptist State Convention, dates from 1834. Davidson College, the pride of the Presbyterians of North Carolina, secured its charter in 1838,[92] although its roots run back about fifteen years into the Western College movement. Guilford College, the Quaker institution in Guilford County, began as New Garden Boarding School in 1837, having been

[90] W. K. Boyd, *History of North Carolina*, II, 365.
[91] *Ibid.*
[92] *Davidson College Bulletin*, XXXV, 15.

chartered in 1834. It became a college in 1888.[93] Duke University, affiliated with the Methodist Church, traces its lineage back through Trinity College to Normal College, and back of that to Union Institute, founded by the Reverend Brantley York, in a strong Methodist and Quaker community in Randolph County, in 1838. The Lutherans, at the meeting of their Synod of 1835, appointed a committee to formulate plans for a manual labor school, but next year accepted the overtures of the Synod of South Carolina to make the institution at Lexington, South Carolina, a joint institution for the two synods, which relationship lasted until 1859, when the Synod of North Carolina converted its academy at Mount Pleasant into a college, called North Carolina College.[94] Catawba College, an institution of the Reformed Church, dates from 1851.

The churches were pioneers in the field of higher education for women. They established many colleges in the first half of the nineteenth century.[95] The state did not become interested in the higher education of women until

[93] The method of securing the charter is another indication that the legislature was not regarded as in the mood to hand out charters to churches without careful consideration. The Quakers, aware of the opposition to them on account of their views on the slavery question, secured a charter without indicating the name of the institution. George C. Mendenhall, prominent Quaker in politics at that time, left blank the name, which was inserted after the charter had been secured (see *Guilford Collegian*, Nov., 1889, pp. 64–65).

[94] G. D. Bernheim and George H. Cox, *History of the Evangelical Lutheran Synod and Ministerium of North Carolina*, pp. 158–159.

[95] Salem Female Academy, chartered as such in 1866 and as Salem College in 1907, was opened by the Moravians in 1802 (C. L. Raper, *Church and Private Schools in North Carolina*, p. 86; Chap. 31, Private Laws of 1866; Chap. 3, Private Laws of 1907). Greensboro College, the oldest chartered four-year college for women in the state and the first ever chartered by the Methodist Church, was chartered as Greensboro Female College in 1838 (C. L. Smith, *History of Education in North Carolina*, pp. 120–121). The Baptists formed Chowan College in 1848. Louisburg, a Methodist junior college, dates its beginning from 1802. Several other junior colleges for women had their origin near the middle of the nineteenth century, including St. Mary's, Episcopal, 1842, and Peace, Presbyterian, 1857. Many so-called female colleges, seminaries, or institutes which came into existence from 1835 to 1870 have long since ceased to exist (Raper, *op. cit.*, pp. 104–247). From 1840 to 1860 the number of higher institutions for women increased from one to thirteen (W. K. Boyd, "North Carolina, 1775–1861," *The South in the Building of the Nation*, I, 476).

near the end of the century,[96] so that the higher education of women was not a subject of controversy in this period as was the case with higher education of men.[97]

How may this seemingly sudden outcropping of denominational colleges be accounted for? With what difficulty did they secure from the state a right to exist? And what effect, if any, did they have upon the policies and practices of the institution at Chapel Hill?

The explanation of this denominational college movement has already been suggested.[98] In a word, the denominations established colleges to meet a felt need. They set about to supply a quality or type of education and to give it a religious emphasis and interpretation which, they felt, were not available at the University of North Carolina.[99] As Professor Boyd pointed out, "The prevalence of skepticism in the faculty and student body (at the University in the early years of its history) was as notable as the scarcity of ministers in the board of trustees," even if the trustees did choose the faculty largely from the Presbyterian clergy.[100] The movement for a state institution in the western part of the state brought clearly into view the fact that some of the churches felt that, as the University at Chapel Hill was directing its attention chiefly to the training of politicians and servants of the state,[101] so should there be provided within the bounds of the state a place or places that would specialize in the training of ministers and servants of the church.[102] It seems obvious that the churches acquired a growing conviction that the one institution at

[96] See p. 133.

[97] The State Normal and Industrial Institute, now the Woman's College of the University of North Carolina, began in Greensboro in October, 1892 (Raper, *op. cit.*, p. 213). See pp. 143, 150, 168.

[98] See pp. 18–23.

[99] C. E. Taylor, *How Far Should a State Undertake to Educate?* (pamphlet), p. 41.

[100] Boyd, *History of North Carolina*, II, 363.

[101] Drake, *op. cit.*, p. 362.

[102] *Western Carolinian*, Jan. 23, 1821.

Chapel Hill could not be relied upon as a fit source of a sufficient supply of servants of the church.[103]

It is significant to note that the second proposed state institution was not only to be chartered by the state but, under the plan proposed, was to share with the University of North Carolina in the meager support given by the state to higher education.[104] It is important, also, to keep in mind that it was a church group, chiefly Presbyterian ministers, that sponsored this movement "to prepare young men for public stations in life, and especially for the gospel ministry."[105] It is not clear that anybody except the Presbyterian leaders were ready to commit the state to the responsibility of providing leaders for the church. In fact, as we shall see, when about ten years later the churches applied for their charters, there was strong opposition in the legislature to granting the churches the permission to establish colleges which they themselves would support.[106] One wonders what would have been the history of denominational colleges if this movement to train ministers at state expense had succeeded. But it did not succeed. And in a few years one finds practically all of the leading denominations establishing colleges of their own.

Another reason for the establishment of the denominational colleges was a desire upon the part of some of the churches to place higher education within reach of many deserving young men who, as the church leaders thought, could not afford the cost of going to Chapel Hill.[107] Al-

[103] Boyd, *op. cit.*

[104] The plan was for the revenue devoted to higher education—escheats, sale of public lands, and so forth, to be divided—that coming from that portion of the state east of the Yadkin River to go to the University of North Carolina at Chapel Hill; that west of the river to the western institution. The General Assembly, in 1794, gave the University all unsold confiscated lands, much of which was in Mecklenburg and adjoining counties.

[105] Address of Dr. James McRee, reported in the *Western Carolinian*, Jan. 23, 1821.

[106] G. W. Paschal, "History of Wake Forest College," *Wake Forest Student*, July, 1925, p. 5.

[107] *Tarborough Free Press*, Oct. 25, 1833; Shaw, *op. cit.*, p. 11.

though expenses at the University were not high, travel from the remote counties was quite an item. No railroad connected the east with the west. Economic conditions were unfavorable. The churches undertook to provide institutions, in centers away from Chapel Hill, to be operated on a plan which would enable the student to be largely self-supporting.[108]

And there is some reason to believe that the denominations, with the growth in their membership and influence, experienced also a growth in the conviction that higher education was a function of the church, "not only its legitimate prerogative, but its imperative obligation."[109]

It was not without considerable struggle that the first denominational colleges secured from the legislature permission to operate in the state, and even then they were hedged about by charter restrictions and limitations which proved to at least one of them an embarrassment.

In 1833 two denominations applied for charters to establish educational institutions. The Baptists, who, on March 26, 1830, formed the Baptist State Convention,[110] and who, at the second annual meeting of the convention, appointed a committee to raise two thousand dollars "with a view to

[108] Most of the denominational colleges of this period started out on the manual labor principle (see Paschal, "History of Wake Forest College," *Wake Forest Student*, Nov., 1924, p. 17; *Proceedings, Baptist State Convention, 1832*, p. 7; and C. L. Coon, *North Carolina Schools and Academies*, Introduction, p. xlv).

[109] Drake, *op. cit.*, p. 199. By 1830 many in the Baptist Church in North Carolina had "begun to open their eyes" to the need for a trained ministry and to fight back at those of the denomination who would "inveigh against education". The aggressive wing of the church refused to heed the resolution of the Neuse and Kehukee associations "not to have anything to do by way of fellowship with a person belonging to a missionary, tract, education, or Bible society," or to be frightened by those who held that the convention, in its plans to promote missions and education, was "designed to beget a connection between church and state" (see Paschal, "History of Wake Forest College," *Wake Forest Student*, July, 1925, p. 15; *Proceedings, Baptist State Convention, 1830*, Appendix, p. 65).

[110] *Proceedings, Baptist State Convention, 1830*, indicate the threefold purpose of the Convention to be educating "young men called of God to the ministry," employing missionaries within the limits of the state, and cooperating with the Baptist General Convention of the United States in the promotion of missions in general.

purchasing a plantation for the accommodation of a literary institution on the Manual Labor principle," applied to the legislature, at its session of 1833–34, for permission to establish a "Literary and Manual Labor Institution in the County of Wake."[111] At the same session the Presbytery of Orange asked for a charter for the "Greensboro Academy and Manual Labor School."[112] With these demands from the churches before it, the legislature found itself in the midst of a contest significant for the future educational development of the state.

Even before the bills were introduced in the legislature, opposition to them developed in the state. The *Tarborough Free Press* of October 25, 1833, carried a "Memorial and Remonstrance," on behalf of the citizens of several counties. These citizens argued that "the incorporation of these schools is the first step to a rich church, a proud, pompous, and tithing ministry," and that the legislature had nothing to do with religious matters. They held, furthermore, that "should the Legislature grant such a corporation to any sect, then it will follow that all other sects have a right to claim a corporation at their hands," and maintained that "scholastic divines in all the countries of Europe have been one of the chief supporters of tyrants and upholders of the theories of depots." After insisting that the incorporation of theological schools was not necessary for the support of civil society, these citizens ended their remonstrance, saying: "Is religion of God? Then let God take care of it."[113]

[111] *House Journal, 1833–34*, p. 166.

[112] C. L. Coon, *Public Education in North Carolina: A Documentary History, 1790–1840*, Introduction, I, xl.

[113] *Tarborough Free Press*, Oct. 25, 1833. The memorialists began: "We, the citizens of several counties composing the said Commonwealth of North Carolina, having heard from an unquestionable authority, as well as having seen from documents, that there will be laid before the General Assembly of this State at the session of 1833, two petitions for the incorporation of two Theological Schools in this State—and having taken the same into serious consideration, do conceive if the same petitioned incorporations should be granted by the Legislature of this State—that it will be an abuse of power, and the end of such corporations be a subversion of the rights of both civil and religious liberty—and therefore are bound, as members of a free State, to remonstrate against the incorporation of Theological Schools."

The principal opposition, it seems, came from the anti-missionary Baptists, headed by Elder Joshua Lawrence of the Kehukee Association, and was directed chiefly at the proposed Baptist school. It is said that Lawrence prepared and laid on the seats of the members of the legislature copies of a pamphlet entitled "A North Carolina Whig's Memorial and Remonstrance," signed "Clod Hopper." From the portions of this pamphlet preserved in a review found in the *Baptist Interpreter* of January 4, 1834, and quoted by Professor Paschal in his "History of Wake Forest College," it seems almost identical with the "Memorial and Remonstrance" appearing in the *Tarborough Free Press* of October 25, 1833.[114]

In the legislature the bills proposing the chartering of these denominational institutions were introduced December 4, 1833, and referred to the committee on education. The committee's report, signed by R. H. Alexander, the chairman, recommended that the bills be passed with certain significant amendments.[115] The committee went thoroughly into the question of what, in their judgment, should be the state's attitude toward chartering denominational schools.[116] To the chief argument advanced against chartering these institutions, i.e., that such charters as requested would confer upon a class of individuals in their corporate capacity "privileges, if not incompatible with our Constitution and Bill of Rights, yet inconsistent with the freedom and genius of our institutions," the committee's answer, briefly summarized, was as follows:

1. The bills (providing for the charters) had no object

[114] *Ibid.* This pamphlet warned the legislature against "meddling with religious matters," "trespassing on the Kingdom of God," "supporting and maintaining of a Christian ministry," and contended that "theological schools were more dangerous than the Spanish Inquisition" and "the first step to a rich and a proud and pompous ministry."

[115] Unpublished Legislative Documents, 1833–34, in Coon, *Public Education in North Carolina: A Documentary History*, II, 662.

[116] *Ibid.*, 661–663.

but to found and establish institutions to promote learning and disseminate knowledge.

2. The principles of these bills had heretofore been sanctioned, if not transcended.[117]

3. The state was unable to comply with the forty-first section of the constitution, which, in the opinion of the committee, imperatively required that schools and universities be established by the legislature. To do what alone the state could not do, associations of individuals, whether of the different denominations of Christians or not, should be allowed the privilege of incorporation, "which has been so freely bestowed by the legislature on associations of individuals for inferior objects."

4. Inasmuch as political power is vested in and derived from the people, it becomes the duty of the legislature to make possible the education of the people. The churches, acting for the state and for themselves, would help the state in performing this duty.

5. In doing so, concluded the committee, the legislature would not be impugning another section of the constitution which forbade the establishment of one religious denomination in the state in preference to another.[118]

The Greensborough Academy bill was amended in two particulars: Instead of allowing the Orange Presbytery to fill vacancies in the board of trustees, it was provided that the "remaining and surviving trustees" should fill them.

[117] Reference here was to an act passed in 1796, entitled An act to secure property to religious societies and congregations of every denomination, which act authorized any religious society to select trustees, who were empowered and invested with authority to purchase and hold in trust for such religious society lands, houses, or tenements, and to receive donations for the benefit of such society; and to an act passed in 1809, amendatory of the act of 1796, which gave the trustees the right to sue and be sued, plead and be impleaded. The committee made clear the fact that these acts were manifestly passed to enable the several churches of the state to advance and promote religion, whereas the intent of the bills chartering the colleges was "to diffuse the blessings of an education and a knowledge of the mechanic arts."

[118] Article 34 of the Constitution of 1776: "There shall be no establishment of any one religious church or denomination in this State in preference to any other. . . ."

And a clause was added subjecting the real estate that might be possessed by the corporation to taxation as other real estate, except five hundred acres upon which should be erected the buildings for literary purposes. As amended, this bill was passed.[119] The bill to establish the Baptist institution was amended by adding a clause pertaining to the taxation of real estate, as in the other bill, stipulating that the provisions of the act should continue in force for twenty years "and no longer," and adding such restrictive phrases as "for the purpose of educating youth, and for no other purpose whatever."[120]

The Wake Forest bill was further amended by eliminating the exemption from taxation of five hundred acres of land. As finally amended it passed, but the vote in the Senate was so close that the Speaker cast the deciding vote.[121] A new charter, secured in 1838, changed the name to Wake Forest College, extended the life of the institution for fifty years beyond the original twenty years, granted power to confer degrees, extended the amount of holdings permitted to $200,000, provided that all property, except land in excess of six hundred acres, should be free of taxation, and threw around the institution certain restrictions concerning billiard tables, theatricals, sleight-of-hand performances, and the sale of liquor.[122] Significant and embarrassing restrictions were also included in the Davidson College charter, as is shown in a subsequent paragraph.[123]

In less than ten years after Wake Forest College secured its charter from the state of North Carolina, it was applying to the Literary Board of the state for a loan. Early in 1840 the trustees of Wake Forest applied for a loan of $2,000,

[119] Unpublished Legislative Documents, 1833–34, in Coon, *Public Education in North Carolina: A Documentary History*, II, 661–663.

[120] *Ibid.*; *House Journal, 1833–34*, pp. 177–178, 187, 191–192, 201; *Senate Journal, 1833–34*, pp. 67–68.

[121] *Senate Journal, 1833–34*, pp. 67–68. William D. Moseley, of Lenoir, was Speaker of the House.

[122] Paschal, *op. cit.* (July, 1927), p. 8.

[123] See pp. 33–34.

which was granted on the security of the Reverend Thomas Meredith, president of the trustees, and A. J. Battle and R. T. Sanders.[124] And after about a year, the amount of the loan was increased to $10,000.[125] The Board made the initial loan to the trustees of this Baptist college on its own initiative, but for the larger amount the permission of the legislature was first secured.[126] Nothing having been paid on the note at the expiration of the four-year period for which the note was authorized, it was renewed by the president and directors of the Literary Fund without referring the question to the legislature.[127] When, in 1848, the subject was next brought to the attention of the trustees of Wake Forest, it was found that the financial condition of the college was such that payment of the interest, even, was irksome, and a committee was appointed to ask the legislature to authorize the renewal of the note and to relieve the college from further payment of interest. In reply the legislature offered to remit all interest charges provided the whole of the principal should be paid on or before January, 1851. The college was unable to meet the terms. By 1855, however, the debt had been reduced to $3,000, and, although it is not altogether clear from the records, it is generally understood that the debt had been paid by 1859.[128]

[124] Paschal, *op. cit.* (October, 1925), p. 11.

[125] MS Journal of the Literary Board of North Carolina, II, 185, Jan. 24, 1840; *ibid.*, p. 192, Feb. 20, 1840. The Literary Board, predecessor of the present State Board of Education, at that time was custodian of a fund amounting to over $2,000,000, of which $1,433,757 had come to it as the state's share of a United States Treasury surplus distributed by the Federal Government in 1837 (see *ibid.*, p. 286, March 22, 1841).

[126] The resolution authorizing the loan reads as follows: "That the President and Directors of the Literary Fund of this State loan to the President and Trustees of Wake Forest College, for the term of four years, the sum of ten thousand dollars, upon taking bond with a good and sufficient security for the same, to be approved by the President and Directors of the Literary Fund. The interest of the said loan to be paid annually, and the said bond to be renewed upon each annual payment of the interest, with liberty on the part of said President and Trustees, to pay any portion of said principal sum at an earlier period."

[127] MS Journal of the Literary Board of North Carolina, II, 265, Oct. 3, 1845.

[128] Paschal, "History of Wake Forest College," *Wake Forest Student*, Nov., 1927, pp. 29-32.

Other institutions, also, were aided by loans from the Literary Fund, including $10,000 to Normal College, $7,000 to Greensboro Female College, $3,000 to Chowan Female Institute, $3,000 to Clinton Female Institute, $2,000 to Floral College, and $2,000 to Mount Pleasant Academy.[129] Whether the Literary Board and the legislature regarded these loans purely as business transactions, as Professor Noble says, or whether their interest in aiding the denominational colleges in their struggle for existence prompted them to extend credit to these institutions, it is a fact that but for these loans it is doubtful if some of them would have been able to survive.[130]

With the contest in the legislature of 1833–34 decided in favor of chartering denominational colleges, it was not difficult for the Presbyterians, who had vigorously but unsuccessfully agitated for a second state university from 1820 to 1824, to win the approval of the legislature of 1838 for the establishment of a Presbyterian college, although efforts to secure the charter met with some opposition.[131] The charter, ratified December 28, 1838, restricted the amount of real and personal property belonging to the in-

[129] Boyd, *op. cit.*, p. 249.

[130] M. C. S. Noble, Jr., *A History of the Public Schools of North Carolina*, p. 247.

In discussing the Wake Forest loan, Dr. Paschal registers his conviction that "but for the loan from the Literary Fund of the State the friends of Wake Forest College would have given up in despair. Coming in the time of its sorest need, it was this loan alone which saved the cause of Baptist education in North Carolina and the progress of our denomination from a most serious reversal, from which we should not have recovered even to the present day" (Paschal, *op. cit.*, p. 34).

[131] Letter of E. F. Rockwell to James B. Smith, dated Dec. 22, 1869, in Davidson College Record Book; Raper, *op. cit.*, pp. 150–151.

The friends of education and religion in the western part of the state and adjoining districts of South Carolina, having "long felt and acknowledged the necessity of an Institution of learning under the control of Christian principles, and accessible in its privileges to that large and deserving part of Society who are not able to reap the advantages of expensive Colleges," resolved "with confident reliance upon the blessing of God" to undertake the establishment of an institution responsible only to the church which should establish it, "to be safe and sound as long as the church is sound." The initiative for this institution was taken in 1835 by the Presbytery of Concord, which soon secured the co-operation of the Presbyteries of Morganton and Bethel (see *Southern Citizen*, Feb. 18, 1837).

stitution at any one time to $200,000 and provided that all lands in excess of five hundred acres should be taxed.[132] Although the charter of Davidson College was amended in 1856 and again in 1885, raising the amount of property the institution was permitted to hold, the amendments did not come early enough to save the institution a sizeable portion of the Maxwell Chambers bequest or the state from the consequent blame and criticism for this loss sustained by Davidson College.[133]

Maxwell Chambers, a wealthy businessman of Salisbury, provided in his will that his property should go to his kindred, friends, and Davidson College. The portion left for the college, after his bequests to kindred and friends had been deducted, amounted to over $200,000. Davidson College already had possessions of approximately $50,000. Should she lose, from the Chambers estate, an amount equal to that which she already possessed?[134]

[132] Trustees Record, Davidson College, p. 13. The preamble to the charter reads as follows: "Whereas the Constitution of North Carolina provides that all useful learning shall be encouraged and promoted by the establishment therein of one or more Colleges, and whereas many worthy citizens have, by petition, respectfully manifested their earnest desire for the establishment of a College in the Western part thereof, to educate youth of all classes without any regard to the distinction of religious denominations, and thereby promote the more general diffusion of knowledge and virtue: . . ."

The privileges of Davidson College were thrown open to "persons of all Religious Denominations of good moral character." All students were required to perform manual labor, agricultural and mechanical, three hours each working day. It was to cost the students very little for tuition and board, and it was believed that most of the students might be supplied with their candles and procure their own washing with very little expense. The diminution of expense was not the only advantage claimed for the manual labor department. It also sought a *sound mind in a sound body* and the cultivation of independence and good habits among the students (see *Southern Citizen*, Feb. 18, 1837).

[133] Letter of E. F. Rockwell to James B. Smith, Dec. 22, 1869, in Davidson College Record Book.

The amendment of 1856 was an attempt of the legislature to take care of the situation arising out of the $200,000 property limitation imposed by the original charter. Although Section I of the charter, granted in 1838, permitted the college to acquire, by purchase, devise, or gift, property *without limit*, Section X limited the amount of property that could be held at any one *time* to $200,000 (see Shaw, *op. cit.*, p. 88).

[134] Shaw, *op. cit.*, pp. 86–90.

In 1856, before the legacy had been paid, the legislature amended the charter so as to increase the amount of property Davidson could hold to $500,000. The legislature also attempted to release and convey to the trustees of Davidson College "all right, title, and interest on the part of the State and the University of North Carolina . . . in and to the estate given or attempted to be given in the last will and testament of Maxwell Chambers."[135] Although the legislature did what it could to give the entire bequest to Davidson College, the Supreme Court decided that the excess of the legacy over an amount sufficient to make Davidson's holdings $200,000, immediately upon Chambers' death, vested in his next-of-kin and that the legislature could not divest them.

This bitter experience for the Presbyterians served to bring into focus the policy of the state to restrict the denominational colleges to small amounts of property holdings and to inspire ex-President Morrison, of Davidson, to write, in 1873:

> There are some men living who remember a dark and rainy night when the Committee on Education in the Legislature of 1838 had the present charter so mutilated that the College could not hold over $50,000. By the most strenuous and untiring efforts that was so changed that the College might hold $200,000, and even that change lost us $50,000 of the Chambers' legacy.[136]

The reason the legislature kept the property holdings of denominational institutions so low in the early years of their existence seems to have been a fear that they might become dangerously strong and powerful. At least the limitations seem to have been concessions to whose who professed to entertain such fears and served to remind the churches that the state insisted on the right to regulate these institutions.[137]

[135] *Ibid.*, p. 88.

[136] *Ibid.*, p. 87.

[137] *Tarborough Free Press*, Oct. 25, 1833; *Senate and House Journals, 1833–34, 1837–38.*

The last of the major denominations to establish a college before the Civil War was the Methodist, although this fact does not indicate a lack of interest in higher education on the part of the leaders of this denomination. North Carolina Methodism was identified closely with Virginia Methodism until the organization of the North Carolina Conference in 1837 and shared in the management and support of Randolph-Macon College in Virginia.[138] In 1838 the North Carolina Conference secured a charter for Greensboro Female College, now Greensboro College, the oldest chartered college for women in the state and the first ever chartered by the Methodist Church.[139] Aided by the Quakers, the Methodists also helped to establish Union Institute in Randolph County, in 1838, and thereby unconsciously but, nevertheless, truly laid the foundation for Duke University.[140]

Union Institute was changed to Normal College in 1851,

[138] MS Journal of the North Carolina Conference, Feb. 7, 1838. *Ibid.*, Dec. 11, 1851. In 1840 the Conference adopted a committee's report which declared that "Education is important and recommends itself to every Conference, but especially does it claim our warmest support in this young Conference. The wants of our people call for prompt, vigorous, and untiring action . . . The people and the spirit of the age call for an enlightened ministry. The establishment of Academies . . . we regard as the only means by which the impulse given by our highest institutions can be kept up and the stream of knowledge can be sent abroad to refresh all our people and prepare their sons when converted of God and called to the ministry to be extensively useful in the work . . . How can a Christian education be given to the youth of the Church unless we use our influence to send them to the place where such an education is imparted?" (MS Journal of the North Carolina Conference, Dec. 29, 1840).

[139] Wesleyan College, in Georgia, chartered in 1836 as Georgia Female College, was taken over by the Methodists of Georgia, in 1843. The only other woman's college in the country having a charter older than that of Greensboro College is Mt. Holyoke, chartered in 1837. (C. L. Smith, *History of Education in North Carolina*, pp. 120–121).

[140] Brantley York, a Methodist minister, was the founder and leader around whom Union Institute developed. The institute was a private school in a community of Methodists and Quakers. The word "Union" in the name came from the fact that these two denominations were the principal patrons. With the development of New Garden Boarding School (Guilford College), a Quaker institution, in an adjoining county, the patronage of Union Institute became increasingly Methodist, leading eventually to a strictly Methodist college and to a university.

at which time it became a teacher-training institution, with the patronage of the state.[141] The governor of the state became ex-officio chairman of the board of trustees and as such signed all of the diplomas. The state superintendent of public instruction served as ex-officio secretary of the board of trustees.[142] Although the state made no appropriation to Normal College, the legislature did direct the Literary Board to lend this institution $10,000.[143] Perhaps the most important feature of state patronage was that the state gave to Normal College authority to issue to its students certificates to teach in the public schools.[144] Seeking to utilize this state patronage, Normal College found itself a sort of unwelcome step-child in the family of state institutions. Whether because of institutional jealousy or contempt for the normal courses offered, the State University did not treat Normal College with the respect which its president, the Reverend Braxton Craven, thought was due "an honorable inferior." And President Craven did not hesitate to make both private and public comparisons between the two institutions.[145]

[141] E. C. Brooks, "The First State Normal School Becomes Trinity College," *Trinity Alumni Register*, July, 1915, p. 95.

[142] Calvin H. Wiley reported to the General Assembly of 1854 that "Normal College . . . has been placed partly under the direction of the State, and as Superintendent of Common Schools, I am ex-officio secretary of the Board of Trustees."

[143] Neither had the state made an appropriation to the University of North Carolina up to this time.

[144] Braxton Craven, "Historical Sketch of Trinity College," *Centennial of Methodism in North Carolina*, ed. L. S. Burkhead, p. 181.

[145] In May, 1854, President Craven wrote to President David L. Swain, of the University: "The University, as a whole, treats us ungenteely, and with but little of that courtesy due an honorable inferior . . . We are a state institution equal in every respect to Chapel Hill as to privilege . . . If Chapel Hill has wealth in its interest, we have the mass of people in our favor. We can certainly succeed much better with your favor, but we can certainly live in some way without it. Speak of us respectfully, treat our recommendations honorably, and try them as others do, and if we visit you, treat us as gentlemen, and you will have no more important ally than Normal." President Craven, furthermore, published in his catalogue of 1853–54, in bold type, the statement: "This institution confers the same degrees as the University, and the Governor signs all our diplomas, thus conferring upon our graduates the approval of the State" (E. C. Brooks, "The First State Normal School Becomes Trinity College," in *Trinity Alumni Register*, Vol. I, No. 2, July, 1915, p. 94).

In the same year that Union Institute was changed to Normal College and was placed partly under the care of the state, President Craven proposed to the North Carolina Methodist Conference "to educate without charge young men preparing for the ministry." The conference accepted the proposition, appointed a board of visitors, and asked the bishop to appoint the Reverend A. S. Andrews to a professorship in Normal College.[146] The appointment of the board of visitors and of Andrews to a professorship continued annually until 1858, when the trustees of Normal College gave over the property to the North Carolina Conference.[147] By an act of the legislature of 1859 the college was entirely vested in the conference, and the name of the institution was changed to Trinity College.[148] This transfer meant the cancellation of all state relations in the operation of the college, the surrender of authority to grant certificates to teach in the public schools without further examination, and the giving of a bond to the Literary Board, binding Trinity College in the amount of $10,000 for the loan extended to Normal College.[149]

The encouragement which Normal College and the Methodists interested in it received from the state, although small,

[146] MS Journal of the North Carolina Conference, Dec. 1, 1851.

[147] *Ibid.*, 1852, 1853.

[148] Raper, *op. cit.*, p. 180. The college was offered to the conference in 1856, but the committee to which the matter was referred considered it inexpedient for the conference to accept the offer, for the reason that "the church in the bounds of this Conference" at that time was not "in circumstances to justify this body in taking over the oversight." One of the deterring circumstances was the conference's sense of obligation to patronize Randolph-Macon (see MS Journal of the North Carolina Conference, 1856). That the Methodist conference felt a close relationship with Normal College, even before it became Trinity College, is shown by the educational committee's report of 1854: "This young and flourishing institution, though not under our immediate control, is nevertheless to all practical purposes Methodistical . . . We therefore commend Normal College to the cordial support of all true lovers of sanctified learning" (see MS Journal of the North Carolina Conference, Nov. 6, 1854).

[149] Brooks, "How the First State Normal School Became Trinity College," *Trinity Alumni Register*, Vol. I, Oct., 1915, p. 161.

was sufficient to arouse other denominations to seek state aid for their institutions. The Baptists took the lead. The trustees of Wake Forest College, at their meeting in June, 1852, voted to take measures to secure appropriations from the Literary Fund for the support of Wake Forest. The plan was, if possible, to obtain the co-operation of Davidson College and Normal College, in making request of the legislature for appropriations from the Literary Fund.[150] When the legislature met in 1853, a bill was introduced entitled "A Bill to Provide for the Education of Common School Teachers," the principal provision of which was

> That, upon condition that Wake Forest College, Normal College, and Davidson College, will each educate twenty-seven young men free of charge, said young men to be selected as hereinafter described: the Directors of the Literary Fund are hereby directed to pay to the trustees of each of the said colleges, the sum to which their respective tuition would amount at their ordinary rates.[151]

It was further provided that the Board of Superintendents of Common Schools in each county in the state should select one student for each county, preference, in the selection, to be given to those whose indigent circumstances would prevent them from otherwise obtaining an education. The young men thus selected should be allowed to determine which of the colleges they should attend. In return, the young men should be required to sign a pledge to teach for twelve months in the state.

The measure failed to receive sufficient support in the legislature to make it a law. Opposition was based, at least in part, on the point that Davidson and Wake Forest were sectarian. And this afforded the editor of the *Biblical Recorder* ample opportunity to counter with the charge

[150] Paschal, "History of Wake Forest College," *Wake Forest Student*, Nov., 1927, p. 33.

[151] *Biblical Recorder*, Jan. 14, 1853, p. 6.

that Normal College, too, was sectarian, even more than either of the others.[152]

In the face of the refusal of the state to appropriate money for normal training and of the jealousy of some denominations because of the patronage and alleged preferment which the state was giving to his institution, President Craven came more and more to rely on the Methodist Church for patronage and encouragement, with the result that, as already indicated, Normal College became the property of North Carolina Methodists.[153]

Competition and Controversy Arise

In the midst of the rise of denominational colleges in North Carolina came a change in the presidency of the State University. In 1835, the Reverend Joseph Caldwell, a Presbyterian, who had served as president since 1804, except for the short period 1813–16, and who had been a member of the faculty since 1796, was succeeded by David L. Swain,

[152] *Biblical Recorder*, Jan. 14, 1853, p. 6. "In just the same sense that Davidson and Wake Forest are sectarian, is Normal College sectarian. It is under the control and direction of Methodists, as Davidson is under the control of the Presbyterians, and Wake Forest under the control of the Baptists. We also venture the assertion that at Normal and Randolph-Macon, more effort is made to induce young men to become Methodists and with greater success, than is made at Davidson and Wake Forest, to lead them to become Presbyterians and Baptists. Whatever may be the error of Methodists, want of zeal is not one of their peculiarities." In support of his contention, the Baptist editor cited a number of the *Richmond Christian Advocate* in which it was stated that "The friends of religious education will gladly learn that the Legislature of North Carolina has placed Normal College in a position to equal the best institutions in the country . . . Let Methodism rally its forces, and sustain its own schools with untiring zeal, and the battle is won!"

In further support of his contention that Wake Forest was not sectarian, the editor of the *Biblical Recorder* continued: "Now in all the appeals that have been made in behalf of Wake Forest College, we defy anyone to show us a call made upon us to rally our forces and aid the colleges, for the express purpose of making Baptists. We urge Baptists to send their children to this institution because we know that *there*, no undue influence will be exerted to prejudice their young minds in favor of views of doctrine and practice that we believe erroneous and hurtful. We are satisfied that . . . no efforts will be made to lead them astray. If they become interested in the subject of religion, they will be directed to the Bible, and not to any of the inventions and compilations of man."

[153] See p. 38.

a Presbyterian layman. Up to this time, except for a few months when Professor Harris served as acting president, the leadership of the faculty of the University had been successively in the hands of a minister.[154] When the board of trustees met on December 5, 1835, to select President Caldwell's successor, an Episcopal clergyman was about to be nominated. Judge Cameron, however, expressed the opinion that, although the clergy ought to be represented on the faculty, the president ought always to be a layman.[155] So strongly supported was this sentiment that Swain was elected.[156] And since 1835, except for the short tenure of the Reverend Solomon Pool during the Reconstruction regime, the presidency has always been held by a layman.

In adopting the policy of having laymen rather than clergymen as presidents of the University, the trustees doubtless were influenced by a desire to avoid, insofar as possible, identifying the institution, in the public mind, too closely with one denomination. Perhaps already they had sensed the rising tide of feeling against what many regarded as Presbyterian predominance if not domination; and it may be that they were moving to prevent what soon became an open revolt against too much Presbyterianism at Chapel Hill. There was, also, no doubt, a carry-over of the Davie feeling against all ministers, which found expression in the latter part of Caldwell's administration. Some of the trustees, furthermore, felt that President Caldwell gave too much time to the church.[157] Then, too, perhaps the trus-

[154] All the presidents and acting presidents were Presbyterians. Harris was a Presbyterian layman.

[155] Letter of President Swain, in *Spirit of the Age*, Feb. 15, 1859.

[156] Judge Cameron made the nomination, which was seconded by Judge Gaston, a Catholic.

[157] MS Reports from the Faculty to the Trustees of the University of North Carolina, 1830–1839. This fact was clearly expressed by one of the trustees when Dr. Caldwell petitioned for permission to attend the General Assembly of the Presbyterian Church, to be away twenty-one days near commencement time. The request was reluctantly granted. The petition bears the endorsement of "W.P.," presumably one of the trustees, as follows: "I could wish those clergy having charge of Institutions and young men under their care, would give more time to those *duties* they are paid for performing, less to *Clerical*."

tees may have reasoned that inasmuch as the denominational colleges, whose chief products were to be ministers, were headed by ministers, the state institution, engaged primarily in the training of lawyers and politicians, the future rulers of the state, should be headed by a layman.[158]

While the ministerial mind was thus perhaps somewhat offended and the churches were moving in the direction of establishing institutions of their own, the trustees of the University of North Carolina issued from Raleigh, April 15, 1837, a printed circular which sought to justify the claims of the University for patronage, announced a policy of the University to grant free tuition and room rent to any applicant "of good character, native of the State, unable to pay Tuition Fees," and named as one of the advantages of attending the University, the "formation of lasting friendships and associations . . . among those who are to constitute no small portion of our future rulers, by the patronage of a State institution."[159]

It did not take long for the friends of the denominational colleges to reply to this circular, which doubtless seemed to them an unfair bid for students and an attempt to circumvent the threat of inroads into the state's student population by the denominational institutions. In the *Raleigh Register* of June 19, 1837, came the reply, which, to the friends of the University, seemed a bad-tempered and uncalled-for attack on the University. The charges alleged, among other things, expenditures by the legislature of over $500,000 on the University, terms of admission lower than those at Harvard, Yale, and other institutions, the exclusion of clergymen from the board of trustees, the predominance of Presbyterians in the faculty, and failure to provide properly for religion at Chapel Hill.[160]

One need not assume that the trustees of the University

[158] David L. Swain, their first choice as successor to President Caldwell, had been governor of the state.

[159] MS History of the University of North Carolina (contains copy of circular).

[160] *Raleigh Register*, June 19, 1837.

were unduly excited over the competition of the manual labor colleges of the Baptists and Presbyterians to explain their circular. The trustees had just sold thousands of acres of escheated lands of the Revolutionary soldiers who had died without heirs, located in West Tennessee, netting about $150,000, of which $100,000 was invested in bank stocks. This bank stock yielded 8 per cent dividend, giving the University an income of $12,000 in addition to tuition fees.[161] Why should they not take the suggestion of the churches and extend the privileges of higher education to some who could not afford to pay the usual charges for tuition and room rent?

And one need not allege pettiness on the part of the denominations in order to explain the attack which appeared in the *Raleigh Register*. Were not the members of the churches contributing as citizens and patrons as much as non-church members to the support of the University and also trying to establish institutions of their own? Why then should they calmly acquiesce in a policy which might make it easier to get an education at a "God-less state university" than at an institution of the church? Were there not already a surplus of lawyers and a scarcity of preachers?

The predominance of Presbyterians on the faculty of the University, alleged in the *Raleigh Register* of 1837, continued to be asserted for many years. It was charged, furthermore, that Presbyterians and Episcopalians virtually controlled the affairs of the institution at Chapel Hill. The *Biblical Recorder* and the *North Carolina Christian Advocate*, official publications of the Baptists and Methodists, afforded the channels through which most of the agitation concerning this matter received expression. And the *University Magazine* and other publications were used by the friends of the University to answer the criticisms of the Baptists and Methodists.

The December, 1853, number of the *University Magazine*

[161] Battle, Sketches of the History of the University of North Carolina, pp. 47–48.

carried an emphatic deprecation of a sectarian spirit in institutions of learning, wherever found, a strong denial that such a spirit had ever been manifested in the management of the University, and a claim that the endowment of the University was not the gift of the state but, in a great degree, the result of private munificence.[162]

The Reverend T. H. Pritchard, a graduate of Wake Forest College and the general agent of this Baptist institution, who had been agitating against the Presbyterian influence in the University and charging that the endowment of the University was liberal and the result of grants from the state, and whose attacks helped to provoke the article in the *University Magazine*, used the columns of the *Biblical Recorder* for a reply to the points made by the spokesman of the University and to retract his previous statements concerning the matter of endowment.[163]

On the question of the manner in which the endowment of the University was raised, Pritchard admitted that he had been misinformed by a member of the State Senate

[162] *University Magazine*, Dec., 1853. In decrying sectarianism and the pride of sects, the *University Magazine* editor declared: "Knowledge is knowledge wherever found, truth is eternal, unchangeable, the same in all climates, under all circumstances. . . . Truth is the seed we would sow and nourish, the Universe would be our field of operation. To use a Scripture phrase we would break down the 'wall of partition between truth and error and let the former go forth conquering and to conquer, o'er sea and land till all the world should own its sway.' "

[163] *Biblical Recorder*, March 29, 1854. Referring to the magazine's claim for the universality of knowledge and its reference to Scripture for authority for breaking down the "wall of partition between truth and error," Pritchard replied: "I would ask the chapter and verse of the Scripture. It may possibly be found in the Koran or Zend, it certainly is not in the Bible. Now my dear sirs, all this talk about a world-wide philanthropy, eternal truth, breaking down the walls which sects have thrown up, resisting the influence of truth, etc., may appear to you as very spirited, but it is very far from being strikingly original. On the same theme Hume was as profound, Paine as rational, Voltaire as brilliant, and Bolingbroke certainly eloquent. . . . Mr. Jefferson, disgusted with what he called the absurdities of sects, in founding the University of Virginia, secured the enactment of a regulation, prohibiting a professor of religion from being one of the instructors in that Institution. The old men of the land remember the character of that college so long as that restriction was in force. Suffice it to say that Mr. Madison, when Governor, declared that the University of Virginia gave him more anxiety and trouble than all the affairs of the state."

upon whom he had relied for information, entered a disclaimer against being one of the enemies of the institution at Chapel Hill, pointed to the fact that Virginia appropriated $15,000 annually to the University of Virginia, South Carolina $14,000 a year to her state schools, and Massachusetts large amounts to her institutions, and expressed the opinion that the University of North Carolina, in spite of its neglect by the legislature, had become famous "owing to the public spirit of benefactors and the talents and energies of her officers." His excuse for making a false charge as to the financial support the state had given the University was his ignorance of the facts.[164]

Pritchard held firmly to other points of his charges against the University. No school could be neutral on "this great question of life"; there was not a school in America in which a religious element prevailed, that was not more or less denominational, or sectarian. He took issue with the point of view of those who would have a religious influence "free from contagion of sect" so that the pupils' minds be "warped by no creed of faith or party." Admitting that such was a desideratum, he firmly believed that such a school was also a "venerable chimera." One scarcely ever finds religious men unconnected with some religious denomination. Even if one could secure such instructors, each of them would have his peculiar tenets and in his teaching would reveal the "complexion of his own faith."[165]

[164] The only appropriation by the state for the support of the University before the Civil War was $10,000, in 1791. This amount was originally given as a loan to assist in erecting buildings, which loan was afterwards converted into a gift. For a detailed account of the appropriations for the support of the University, see Blackmar, *History of Federal and State Aid to Higher Education in the United States*, pp. 191–199.

[165] *Biblical Recorder*, March 29, 1854. To support his theory, he pointed to the experience of the outstanding institutions of the country. "Harvard was once a union—'tis yet a State school, and yet for years the Unitarians have controlled it. Brown is the college of Rhode Island, the Baptists claim that. Princeton is the State school of New Jersey, but the Presbyterians hold it by a right peculiarly their own. The same is true of Union, Yale, Amherst, Dartmouth, William and Mary, and in fact of all the schools of the land in a greater or less degree."

Then taking up the case of the University of North Carolina, the agent of Wake Forest declared that the history of that institution established his proposition. He declared that when the University was founded seventy years ago, it was understood to be not a sectarian but a state college in which all the denominations would be represented by instructors. Yet with the *Catalogus Universitatis*, Car. Nor., as his authority, he made the point that of the eighty professors, instructors, and tutors serving the institution from 1794 to 1855, only two, Samuel A. Holmes and Abner W. Clepton, were Baptists.[166] Dr. William Hooper, although turned Baptist while at the University, was an Episcopalian at the time of his appointment to the faculty of the University in 1817, and, of course, did not represent Baptist interests at Chapel Hill.[167]

In further substantiation of his claim that an injustice had been and was being done the Baptists, he gave comparative figures as to the numerical strength of the churches. He declared that the Presbyterian Church in North Carolina numbered between ten and twelve thousand, the Episcopal not more than three thousand, the Methodists forty-one thousand, and the Regular Baptists forty-six thousand, to say nothing of the ten thousand Primitive Baptists, Freewill Baptists, Disciples, and others of the Baptist family. Contrasted with these comparative figures, Pritchard showed that of the thirteen members of the faculty of the University, five were Presbyterians, three Episcopalians, with two others partial to the Episcopal church, two Methodists, and the faith or affiliation of the thirteenth not known. He declared that the Baptists had had no representative in the faculty since 1810.[168] His resentment of what he regarded

[166] Holmes served about two years, and Clepton one year.

[167] *Biblical Recorder*, March 29, 1854.

[168] Concerning the importance of this situation for the Baptist Church, the writer illustrated: "Now let us see the influence thrown about a youth who arrives at the University. Perhaps his parents are Baptists. He is there seeking to quench his thirst for knowledge. He idolizes intellect and reveres learned men,

as a grave injustice to the Baptists was so keen and his zeal for Wake Forest was so strong that again in 1854 Pritchard used the columns of the *Biblical Recorder* to appeal to the pride of his denomination. He said:

Ye forty-six thousand Baptists of North Carolina, have you no denominational pride? You have paid more tax to Chapel Hill than any other denomination in the State—an institution in which from its foundation you have never been represented. Will you still aid an institution where you have been unjustly treated, which has a large investment and near three hundred students, and neglect Wake Forest, the child of your own Convention, and the churches of your principles? Forbid the cause of denominational education and the cause of Christ.[169]

The question of sectarianism in state institutions was still a lively one in 1859. The Methodists, through the *North Carolina Christian Advocate*, called attention to an alleged inequality in the representation of the denominations in the faculty and board of trustees of the University, a situation which had been irritating the Baptists for years. Only one chair in the University was filled by a Methodist, while there were four times as many Methodists in the state as there were Episcopalians and Presbyterians. The editor felt that there was no prospect that Methodists would receive equal representation with these denominations "which virtually control the University" and agreed with the Bap-

---

and very naturally he soon comes to respect that church most which has most men of learning. He looks around him and sees connected with the University the learned Drs. of the Presbyterian and Episcopal churches; the Methodist church too is well represented, but where the Baptist professors? The Baptists have no representative at Chapel Hill, ergo, they have no one worthy of a professorship at the University. He feels that the Baptists are in bad savor there; perhaps hears one of the corps of Editors of the Magazine declare that he 'was not surprised that the Baptists had no professor at Chapel Hill. They had no man of sufficient ability and attainments to grace a chair there.' . . . Under these circumstances the youth in question unless he have firmness unusual, soon dislikes to confess that his parents are Baptists, he becomes ashamed of the faith of his fathers" (*Biblical Recorder*, March 29, 1854).

[169] *Biblical Recorder*, Sept. 23, 1854.

tist point of view that the ecclesiastical connection of the professors exerted its influence upon the pupils.[170]

The election of two professors, the Reverend Andrew D. Hepburn and Dr. William J. Martin, both Virginians and both Presbyterians, in the fall of 1859, tended to confirm the charges of the *Christian Advocate* and served to increase the resentment on the part of some of the denominations of alleged preferment given to Presbyterian applicants for positions at the University.[171] The Methodists had a candidate in the person of the Reverend Charles F. Deems, who had served as adjunct professor of rhetoric and logic at the University from 1842 to 1848, when he resigned to accept an appointment in Randolph-Macon College. So eager were the Methodists to have him at Chapel Hill that the Annual Conference, in its session, December, 1859, passed a resolution urging Dr. Deems "to accept said Professorship, when it is officially tendered to him by the Board of Trustees of that institution, provided he can do so consistently with his sense of duty to himself and to the Church."[172] So confident were they that the place would be offered to Dr. Deems that when it was given to Dr. Hepburn, they doubtless felt they had another good reason for joining with the Baptists in protest.

Having their own college did not cause the denominations to take their eyes off the moral and religious conditions at the University or to be any more charitable or generous toward each other when a possible or suspected advantage of one denomination over the other was impending at Chapel Hill. The attack upon the University made through the columns of the *Raleigh Register* in 1837, alleging failure properly to provide for religion at Chapel Hill, is evidence of this fact. The question of compulsory chapel attendance, arising in 1848, is another case in point.

Whether from genuine interest in the religious welfare of the students or out of a desire to appear as interested in

[170] *North Carolina Christian Advocate*, Feb. 3, 1859.

[171] *Ibid.*

[172] MS Journal of the North Carolina Conference, Dec. 21, 1859.

religion as the denominational colleges, or both, the University of North Carolina had a rule requiring all students to attend the religious services conducted in the University chapel each Sunday morning at eleven o'clock. Although neither the regulation nor the services were ever very popular with the students, both were maintained without much opposition until 1848.[173] Until this time the rule was for Dr. Mitchell, a Presbyterian professor, to officiate one Sunday and Professor Green, Episcopalian, the next.[174]

In 1842 the Episcopalians of Chapel Hill organized a church, and in 1844, under the leadership of Green, inaugurated a movement for a church building, which, when finished in 1848, was the first church edifice in Chapel Hill. As soon as the building was finished, Green asked that students who were members of the Episcopal Church be excused from attending the University chapel on Sunday morning in order that they might attend the Episcopal service in the new building.[175] The other denominations at that time had no buildings in Chapel Hill; and the question, raised by the Episcopal professor, was not settled until after he had moved to Mississippi and become a bishop, and after the Presbyterian, Baptist, and Methodist churches had built their places of worship in the village.[176]

The question of compulsory chapel attendance for every student, Protestant, Catholic, Jew, Baptist, Methodist, Episcopalian, Presbyterian, atheist, or whatnot, brought forth a number of petitions and stirred the faculty and trustees to find a solution.[177] The trustees, meeting on De-

[173] Battle says: "There was no heating of the Chapel in the winter, and in cold weather there was sad shivering in overcoats and cloaks . . . The services lasted about an hour and a half. Although Dr. Mitchell disapproved of forms, his long prayer was always the same . . . Young Deems [C. F. Deems] who occasionally occupied the pulpit, was the pioneer of discoursing on live subjects."

[174] Battle, *History of the University of North Carolina*, I, 558.

[175] *Ibid.*, p. 518.

[176] *Ibid.*

[177] Letter of President D. L. Swain to an unnamed person, written at Raleigh, Dec. 17, 1848, relative to modifying "the ordinance of 1799 in relation to *Divine Worship at the University*" (MS History of the University of North Carolina, pp. 63–64).

cember 11, 1849, considered "sundry petitions from different parts of the State and different Christian denominations on the subject of the modification of the ordinance relating to public worship in the college chapel on the Sabbath."[178] Arriving at no decision at this meeting, the trustees met again on January 4, 1850, when it was decided that communicants who within ten days after entering the University notified the faculty of their wishes, should be allowed to attend the church of their choice. It was specified, however, that the faculty should require attendance somewhere by all as a duty. This plan of 1850 lasted until 1860, when the Episcopalians again raised the issue.

The question of modification of the chapel ordinance was raised this time by the Protestant Episcopal Convention, which, at its meeting in Charlotte in May, 1860, sent a memorial to the trustees concerning the matter. The convention contended that the ordinance was contrary to that section of the constitution of North Carolina and of the United States which guaranteed the right to worship God according to the dictates of one's own conscience. The Episcopalians asked, therefore, that all students, of full age, be allowed to attend public worship on Sunday in the church of their faith or preference and, if under age, where their parents or guardians might desire.[179] The Episcopalians received the support of the *North Carolina Christian Advocate*, Methodist publication, which commented editorially:

> When the citizens of the State send their sons to an institution, which, like the University, professes to be free from denominational affinities, they have a right to expect a practical exemplification of such professions by the extension of religious freedom to the students.[180]

Judge Manly, a Roman Catholic member of the board of trustees, is credited with proposing a plan which was adopted

[178] Battle, *op. cit.*, p. 519.
[179] *Ibid.*, p. 713.
[180] *North Carolina Christian Advocate*, May 29, 1860.

by the trustees and was followed until the University closed its doors in 1868.[181] The plan provided that

The President may grant a dispensation from attending any public worship on the Lord's or other day,

1. Where the parent or guardian resides in Chapel Hill and desires his son or ward to worship with his family;
2. Where the student is a communicant with some denomination having worship in the village different from that of the officiating Chaplain;
3. When the student is a member of a religious denomination or Church, and declares in writing that he has scruples against attending Chapel worship;
4. Where the parent or guardian declares in writing that he has scruples of conscience against his son or ward attending Chapel worship, and indicates what denomination he prefers him to unite with.

The attendance upon Chapel worship elsewhere is compulsory, but if the student has scruples against attending services anywhere he must remain in his room in a quiet and orderly manner.

The board of trustees sought to reinforce these regulations concerning Sunday worship by ordering that "All without exception shall attend morning and evening prayers, except those temporarily excused by the President, or permanently excused by a vote of the Board of Trustees."[182]

The number of Catholics and Jews in North Carolina during the first half of the nineteenth century was small; and like most minorities they were not vocal, so that they hardly became a factor in the educational affairs of the state. With fortitude and silence the few within the state bore whatever displeased them until, by fortuitous circumstances and quiet working, as in the case of Judge Manly's handling of the chapel attendance question to the relief not only

[181] Battle, *op. cit.*, p. 713.

[182] *Ibid.* Looking back upon these efforts of the State University to enforce attendance upon religious services, President Battle said that "This system was pro tanto a union of Church and State, and was attended with the cold-heartedness and formality, evasions and secret hostility, which history shows have been the results of such unions in all ages" (*ibid.*, p. 716).

of the Episcopalians but also of the Catholics, Jews, and others, they secured the remedy desired.

That some of the Protestants, notably the Baptists, were apprehensive lest the Catholics should gain a foothold in the affairs of the University, and that the faculty and trustees of the University were fearful of the consequences which even slight public recognition of the Catholics might bring, are shown by the furore created in 1854 when the senior class chose a Catholic to deliver the baccalaureate sermon at the following commencement.

The story, in brief, is that when the senior class, by majority vote, decided to invite Archbishop John Hughes, Roman Catholic, of New York, sudden fear of what the Protestants would do confounded the faculty.[183] President Swain took the situation in hand. Writing the class a long letter, he insisted that their action was indiscreet—that the appearance of the one they had invited would be painful to about one-fourth of the members of the class and the majority of those who would attend the commencement exercises.[184] The executive committee, approving the president's action, explained, in resolutions, that although they stood firmly against religious intolerance, there were other important considerations the significance of which the committee could better understand than the class. According to President Battle, the problem was happily solved by Archbishop Hughes himself, who declined the invitation.[185]

[183] Battle, *op. cit.*, p. 667.

[184] *Ibid.*, pp. 667–669. President Swain had shown the letter to the faculty and asked their approval of his position, which was given with but two dissenting votes, before sending it to the class. Being a good politician as well as a good executive, President Swain also referred the question to the executive committee, who had given the senior class the privilege of selecting the speaker.

[185] *Ibid.*, p. 669. A writer in the *Louisville Journal*, whose article was reprinted in the *University Magazine*, however, gave a slightly different version, as follows: "Now these members (of the senior class) well knew that there was not the least probability that he would accept the appointment, and that his alternate was virtually elected commencement preacher . . . When they wrote to Archbishop H., informing him of his election, they received answer from his secretary that he was absent from home; and without receiving an answer from the Archbishop himself, they informed the alternate, Rev. Mr. Lowe, of the M. E. Church, of his election, and requested his acceptance" (*University Magazine*, Feb., 1855, pp. 39–41).

The incident served to provoke the charge that the University of North Carolina was about to become a Roman Catholic institution.[186] It was claimed that but for the timely discovery and thwarting of his plans, ex-Bishop Ives would have gained control of the University.[187] To this alleged "puerility and intolerance," "holy horror," "wild consternation," "deep sorrow and refined sarcasm," the answer was that they emanated from "men of weak or ill-regulated minds" and betrayed a spirit of persecution. All the responsibility for the selection of Archbishop Hughes was placed upon the senior class. Neither the trustees, faculty, nor students had a right to object to the choice of the senior class, provided they chose a respectable Christian clergyman. It was declared impossible for the University to come under the control of any sect. The faculty was under the immediate control of a board of trustees chosen by the legislature from every religious denomination, with the exception perhaps of the Romanists.

The Baptist who sounded the alarm concerning the alleged threat of Catholicism had raised the question of what kind of a sermon the archbishop would preach and wondered if he would endeavor to inculcate the admonitions and follies of the Church of Rome or try to prove the supremacy of Saint Peter and his successors, or what, if his sermon should take an educational turn, would he say of the diffusion of education among the masses or of free American institutions. The friend of the University replied by asking the Baptist some questions, doubtless intended to be just as embarrassing. He wanted to know what sort of sermon the Baptist would preach if invited to preach before the next graduating class. He wondered if he would attempt to show that Baptists should not commune with other denominations or

[186] The charges, made by one who signed himself "Chapel Hill," were printed originally in the *Tennessee Baptist* and answered by a correspondent in the *Louisville Journal*. The *University Magazine*, Feb., 1855, pp. 39-41, reprinted the communication from the *Louisville Journal*, with references to the *Tennessee Baptist*.

[187] As evidence it was pointed out that Archbishop Hughes came near being one of the University's commencement speakers.

that baptism by immersion only is well pleasing in the sight of God. He stated that, although Archbishop Hughes certainly would have done so, the Baptist seemed not to have borne in mind the possibility that there are many evangelical doctrines about which all denominations of Christians agree and that, as to education and politics, one might reasonably expect that he would take those grounds on which he attempted to plant Romanism in his celebrated discussion with Breckinridge. He suggested that the Baptist ruminate on these facts and "see if there are not many, many things that Archbishop Hughes would say that should be acceptable to the sons of American Protestants."[188]

That the action of the president, the faculty, and the executive committee of the University was attributable largely to the acuteness of the political situation of the times[189] rather than to a dislike of Catholics as such is shown by the fact that four years later the invitation to Archbishop Hughes was renewed, and he preached a sermon which, it is said, "pleased and instructed a numerous audience, composed almost entirely of Protestants."[190] And there seems to be no record of any outburst on the part of the Baptists or anybody else akin to that which broke out four years earlier.

Concerning the comparative advantages of denomina-

[188] *Ibid.* In a further effort to establish the absurdity of the fears of the Baptist writer and to show that the other denominations had not shown similar fears when commencement preachers were chosen, it was stated: "Had the Methodists raised the hue and cry that the election of Dr. Hawks to this same position by the preceding class was a sure sign that the institution was placed under the control of the Episcopal Church, and for that reason attempted to overthrow it—had the Presbyterians, at the still more recent election of Mr. Lowe, declared that the institution and all connected with it were conniving at the usurpation of the Methodists, and therefore were unworthy of the contenance and patronage of all true Calvinists—they would not have displayed a more unreasonable and persecuting spirit than has this very 'Baptist' in its assault on the University."

[189] Battle seems to think that the invitation was intended as a challenge to the Know Nothing party that was about to assemble in Philadelphia. Curiosity and an effort to tease the faculty are suggested, also, as factors helping to explain the invitation.

[190] Battle, *op. cit.*, p. 669.

tional and state colleges there was a great deal said during this period. One who signed himself "Philomathes" and who took the position that all of the colleges in the state, whether supported by the state or by the denominations, seemed to be necessary, wrote a series of five articles, which were published in the *Biblical Recorder* in 1855.[191] His arguments afforded very little encouragement for the supporters of state institutions and proved to be hardly so impartial as his admission of the necessity of these institutions might lead one to expect. Briefly summarized, his contentions were that by the very necessity of appealing directly to the people for financial and other support, the denominational colleges educated not only the students but their parents; that the expenses at state institutions were such as to prevent many of limited means from enjoying their advantages; that the denominational colleges served the poor boys, who had been and always would be capable of the highest improvement. State colleges, on the contrary, had a tendency to limit their boundaries to the "privileged few," the "sons of great men" who were generally as free with their father's purses as with his reputation, and the sons of rich men, "spoiled and petted children." Professors in state institutions were paid "fat salaries" for one or two hours a day, whereas in denominational colleges the professors were bound to work energetically and thus set an example for self-improvement and inspire the pupils with "a like enthusiasm and love of labor." State institutions emphasized scholarship instead of piety or religion. In cases where pious men were appointed as instructors, the professors were usually from one or two of the minor sects. In favor of state colleges he listed the advantage of a larger amount of means at hand, enabling them to command by larger salaries the best talent of the country to fill their chairs, and making possible large and handsome edifices and extensive and costly apparatus. He listed, also, the

[191] *Biblical Recorder*, July 12, July 19, July 26, Aug. 2 and 9, 1855.

argument that the greatest names in politics, in literature, and in religion were numbered among the alumni of state colleges. He qualified this argument by observing that it had not been a great while since religious denominations first moved forward in endowing colleges independent of state assistance.[192]

A number of writers and speakers alleged immorality, drunkenness, and other vices at Chapel Hill, which allegations brought forth rejoinders from the *University Magazine* and University officials. In 1856 the editor of the *Magazine* said: "We are willing to admit anything that may be held against the students of Chapel Hill, while on the other hand we are ready to defend them, as far as it is in our power, of the false reports against them."[193] And in 1858, President Swain, aroused by what he regarded as misrepresentations, had printed and circulated a circular, in which he concluded that "Upon the whole . . . nothing has occurred during the late term which ought injuriously to affect its [the University's] standing."[194]

In the midst of the attacks upon the University, the Presbyterian Church and its spokesmen stood firmly by the institution which they had helped to establish and in the management of which they had continued to be influential. The Reverend W. H. Foote, Presbyterian historian, in 1846, denied that the University was a Presbyterian institution but affirmed that the building of the University exemplified the genius of Presbyterianism.[195]

[192] *Ibid.*, July 19 and Aug. 9, 1855.

[193] *University Magazine*, March, 1856, p. 138.

[194] MS History of the University of North Carolina, p. 109.

[195] "The University of North Carolina is not a Presbyterian institution, neither does it belong to, nor is it under the peculiar management of any religious denomination. It is the child and property of the state at large, in which all have an interest, and over it the Legislature the ultimate control. As a part of the community that loves the education of youth, the Presbyterian congregations and families have a great and increasing interest in the University, now rising in public estimation" (W. H. Foote, *Sketches of North Carolina*, pp. 527, 549). The fact that the Presbyterian historian felt called upon to deny that the University was a Presbyterian institution may be evidence, however, that he was aware of the current criticism and jealousy on the part of other denominations.

In 1844 the Presbyterian Synod of North Carolina petitioned the legislature to send President Swain, at state expense, to England to collect materials for a history of North Carolina.[196] In 1847 the Synod adopted a report which commended the University in the highest terms: "It has no rivals and cherishes no envy," and expressed the belief that the time might not be far distant when the legislature would be "proudly liberal and munificent towards this first-born, this only daughter of the Republic." It went further and suggested that the legislature adopt the Roman maxim, *Tres Faciunt Collegium*, and establish at Chapel Hill schools of law and medicine, and "with Parental Wisdom, invite all Christian denominations in the State, to plant, near the University, their own Theólogical Seminaries."[197]

And then, as if seeing or foreseeing the criticism of other denominations and feeling the necessity of restating the attitude of the Presbyterian Church toward the University, the Synod of 1847 declared:

> We are not so remote from its origin or its history to forget our birthright. We seek no exclusive privilege,—no preponderating influence. We expect to enjoy the benefits of its ceaseless expansion and maturity, as we do our own Constitution and Laws, in common with our fellow-citizens; and we desire to cherish in our own minds, and in the self-consciousness of all our churches, a corresponding interest.[198]

Instead of appointing a visiting committee to oversee the University, as the Methodists did for Normal College between 1851 and 1859, the Presbyterian Synod, by resolution adopted in 1847, requested "such members of the Synod as may be Professors in the University" to report to the Synod "whatever most concerns morals and true religion, with such suggestions as they may deem most appropriate to their office."[199] And, finally, as though to climax the assertion

[196] *Minutes of the Synod of North Carolina, 1844*, p. 23.
[197] *Ibid., 1847*, p. 27.
[198] *Ibid.*
[199] *Ibid.*

of faith in the benevolence of the institution at Chapel Hill, the Synod declared:

Holding so intimate a connexion as we do with the one institution of all the people, let our prayer evince our sincere desire, that the University of North Carolina rise up, a column of light, shedding down upon our colleges and churches, upon our Courts of justice and Legislature, the choicest influence of learning, genius, and piety.

In the report of the committee on education of the Presbyterian Synod of 1854, doubtless having in mind the charges of Pritchard and the *Biblical Recorder*, there was made a frank acknowledgment of the fact that "No denomination has so full and able a representation in the Faculty [of the University], from its first organization to the present time, as the Presbyterians. . . ." That the committee felt this was not only a very happy but also a very proper circumstance is shown in the remainder of the sentence: ". . . and we may confidently add, that as the Presbyterians were the first to move the establishment of the University, as they have been its firmest friends, and most constant supporters through every possible phase of adversity and prosperity, so they will be the very last to withdraw their countenance, influence, and support from her."[200]

In 1858 the Presbyterian Synod again restated its attitude toward the state institution at Chapel Hill by declaring that

[200] *Minutes of the Synod of North Carolina, 1854*, Appendix. The committee declared that "No denomination in the State contributed more liberally of men and money to found the University than the Presbyterians . . . Our men have been engaged in a noble work in the service of the State; they have contributed their full share in sending forth from the University some of the best scholars of which our country can boast." The report stated, furthermore, that "The University of the State, of which we are justly proud, is one of the best, if not the best State College in the country, with all the patronage of the State and individual munificence it has received, with the council and influence of some of the ablest men of the State as its Trustees." Reference was made, also, to "the combined influence and patronage of all religious denominations"; and claim was made that "The best has been done, for the State and her religious denominations, under the circumstances."

the Presbyterian Church "enters upon no crusade against common schools, colleges, or universities under State patronage. On the contrary she cultivates the utmost harmony of feeling, and develops the greatest possible consistency of action between the Church and State. The one supplements the other."[201]

Reflecting the awareness of the University authorities of the critical attitude of the denominations and the desire to allay the feeling on the part of some of the denominations that the Presbyterians and Episcopalians were too much in the saddle, the trustees in 1838 decided to appoint a regular chaplain, according to the plan of the University of Virginia. The plan was to employ, in rotation, a Methodist, an Episcopalian, a Baptist, and a Presbyterian, each to serve as chaplain for a year. The faculty, students, and the literary societies arranged to pay the salary; and President Swain asked Bishop Morris, in charge of the North Carolina Methodist Conference, to appoint the Reverend E. Wadsworth, husband of a sister of Mrs. Swain. Bishop Morris refused to make the appointment.[202]

That the University, aware of denominational jealousies and the premium placed by the churches on orthodoxy, sought to live in peace with her neighbors and to win their support, is further shown by the fact that all senior commencement speeches had to be submitted to one of the professors for censorship. And it was the job of the censor to exclude all allusions to differences between the denominations, advocacy of higher criticism of the Bible, and any doctrine offensive to average orthodoxy.[203]

[201] *Minutes of the Synod of North Carolina, 1858*, Appendix.

[202] Letter of President Swain published in the *Spirit of the Age*, Feb. 15, 1859; also Battle, *History of the University of North Carolina*, I, 454. Bishop Morris gave as reasons for refusing to make the appointment the fact that, apart from the University, Chapel Hill was too small to support a pastorate to be supplied annually; that to appoint a pastor once in four years for the University community would hardly justify the interruption of the work of an itinerant minister; and that when the next turn to appoint a Methodist chaplain came, there might not be available a preacher suitable to the University authorities.

[203] Battle, *History of the University of North Carolina*, I, 556.

The editorial in the *Christian Advocate*[204] of February 3, 1859, apparently was pointed and weighty enough to prick the official skin of President Swain, already become a bit sore, and to provoke a spirited reply to what he branded as a series of "misconceptions and misrepresentations."[205] In his communication published in the *Spirit of the Age*, President Swain reviewed the history of the organization of the trustees and faculty of the University from the time he was elected in 1835 to 1859, which review is the best available reply to the charges lodged against the administration by the leaders of the Baptist and Methodist churches.

He declared that on December 5, 1835, he, a Presbyterian layman, was elected over the Episcopal clergyman being considered for the presidency, because the trustees decided that the head of the faculty should always be a layman; and that when he entered upon the discharge of his duties in January, 1838, the faculty consisted of Professors Mitchell, Phillips, Harper, and Burgevin, and Tutors McAllister and Owen. Mitchell and Phillips were Presbyterian clergymen, though neither was a member of the Presbyterian Church at the time of his appointment, and Phillips not a clergyman until some years afterwards; Hooper was a Baptist clergyman and Burgevin a Romanist; one of the tutors a Presbyterian, the other a member of a Methodist family. He declared that the religious services at chapel on the Sabbath were conducted by Mitchell and Hooper alternately, until the latter moved to South Carolina early in February, 1838, to accept the presidency of the Furman Theological Institute. He then told of efforts to secure a Methodist, the Reverend E. Wadsworth, to become the first chaplain, inaugurating the plan of rotating the position, annually, between the four leading denominations of the state.[206]

[204] See above, p. 48.

[205] *Spirit of the Age*, Feb. 15, 1859. Also Battle, *op. cit.*, p. 696.

[206] *Ibid.* Bishop Morris having refused to appoint Mr. Wadsworth, President Swain said: "After repeated conferences as to the course to be pursued, and after arriving at the conclusion that further efforts to secure the services of a Methodist or a Baptist clergyman in reasonable time, would be unavailing, the Faculty

Taking up the appointment of a successor to Hooper as professor of ancient languages on September 8, 1838, the board of trustees considered three names, two Episcopalians and one Methodist. Although the president nominated the Methodist, the Methodist refused to serve, having withdrawn his name by letter. The Reverend Charles F. Deems and the Reverend Albert M. Shipp, both Methodists,[207] had received appointments to the faculty in 1842 and 1849, respectively. President Swain added:

> The Trustees have no power to compel gentlemen to accept Professorships, or when they have accepted, to enforce their permanent continuance in office. You will probably be surprised to learn that no instance is known, since the foundation of the Institution, where a Methodist has competed unsuccessfully for either a Professorship or a Tutorship.[208]

On the question of the denominational affiliation of the members of the faculty, President Swain declared that "As at present organized, there are two Episcopal, two Methodist and two Presbyterian clergymen in our corps of instructors. That there is no Baptist clergyman among us, is the fault neither of the Faculty nor the Trustees. One was sought for assiduously to supply the last vacancy which occurred."[209]

Going into the manner in which the board of trustees was constituted, President Swain admitted that the Episcopalians were most numerous but thought that the Methodists, Baptists, and Presbyterians were about equally represented, although he qualified his statement by saying that "With respect to the manner in which the Board of Trustees is

---

determined to recommend the Rev. William M. Green of Hillsborough, for the Chaplaincy. He was appointed Professor of Rhetoric on the 27th February, 1838, and was the first Episcopal clergyman called to fill a Professor's chair in this institution."

[207] Each of these men served as president of Greensboro College, the former from 1850 to 1854, the other from 1847 to 1850.

[208] *Ibid.*

[209] *Ibid.*

constituted, I cannot be expected to speak with as much particularity and precision as in relation to the Faculty."[210]

He stated that the executive committee of seven, living in and near Raleigh, was composed of Episcopalians and Methodists. He did not say how many of each, although he indicated that four were Democrats and three were Whigs.[211]

Notwithstanding all the difficulties through which they had to pass and the antagonisms aroused and jealousies encountered, state and denominational colleges prospered and made progress in the period preceding the Civil War. Governor John W. Ellis apparently did not take all of the squabbles very seriously. Referring to schools and colleges in his inaugural address, in 1859, he declared they had been established in almost every county. He noted "the rich fruit of that free and universal religious toleration which forms a distinguishing feature of our government" and "the harmonious action of all denominations of Christians, in teaching the great truths of practical religion among the people, which is an essential preparation to their expressing properly the functions of self-government."[212] And again in his message to the legislature at the session of 1860–61, Governor Ellis told the lawmakers that "Most of our colleges and high schools have been established by and are now under the control of the several denominations of Christians, which is a fact not to be regretted, since the natural friends of education are to be found among those who are engaged in the advancement of religion and morals."[213]

As has been shown, the criticisms and controversies, from the time of the entry of the churches into the field of higher education in North Carolina to the closing of the University immediately following the Civil War, concerned such questions as free tuition and state expenditures for the support

[210] *Ibid.*

[211] Battle, *op. cit.*, p. 696.

[212] *Raleigh Register*, Jan. 8, 1859.

[213] *Executive and Legislative* (*Public*) *Documents*, *1860–61*, pp. 16–17.

of the University, the alleged exclusion of the clergy from the board of trustees, the predominance of Presbyterians in the faculty, requirements for admission to the University, compulsory chapel attendance, Roman Catholic influence in the University, and the comparative advantages of denominational and state colleges. The attacks on the University did but little immediate damage but forecast a series of skirmishes between friends of the denominational colleges and friends of the University, which carried over into the period following the Civil War.

With the coming of the Civil War went most of the controversies which had engaged the attention of the friends of the educational institutions. At least they were submerged temporarily while the attention and energies of leaders of both camps were absorbed for four years in fighting a different sort of warfare from that which they had been fighting.

II

The Closing of the University and the Struggle to Re-establish It

ALTHOUGH against terrific odds, due primarily to the war, the depreciation of Confederate and state treasury notes and bonds, and the general demoralization of affairs following the war, President Swain kept the doors of the University open through the commencement of 1868 and, backed by the old trustees and determined to resist the approaching Reconstruction regime to the last ditch, made plans for reopening the University in the fall.[1] In July, 1868, however, the old trustees were removed; and the new ones, predominantly if not exclusively Republican, chosen under the Reconstruction constitution, declared all the chairs vacant.[2] The new board elected new professors, with the Reverend Solomon Pool, D.D., a Methodist preacher, who had served as instructor or an assistant from 1854 to 1860, as president. Only thirty-five students were enrolled in 1869–70, compared with 76 in 1865, 107 in 1866, and 86 in 1867, and the attendance for the next two or three years was so unsatisfactory that the trustees in 1872 ordered the University to be indefinitely suspended.[3]

The closing of the University is attributable to several causes, chiefly economic, political, and social. The religious factor was relatively insignificant, although, as will be shown, the weight of sectarian opposition made itself felt at the time when these other factors conspired to put this ancient institution temporarily out of business. The economic depression following the war made the institution at

[1] Battle, Sketches of the History of the University of North Carolina, pp. 50–51

[2] *Ibid.*, p. 51.

[3] *Ibid.*, pp. 50–55, *passim.*

Chapel Hill almost penniless. The legislature was not disposed to aid in any way.[4] The empty treasury left the president and professors dependent upon tuition fees and loans for their salaries.[5] And politics helped to keep the number of students very small.[6] Democratic alumni and friends found it too great a strain on their loyalty, at a time when party spirit was bitter, to send students to an institution controlled by Republicans.[7] Then, too, the Negro question was about to become embarrassing. There was talk of providing, at Raleigh, a branch of the University for Negroes on a parity with the branch for whites at Chapel Hill, although there was not at this period a proposal to admit Negroes into the institution at Chapel Hill.[8]

The religious factor involved in the closing of the University, although relatively insignificant, is interesting. Both party and religious affiliations were considered in selecting the new faculty in 1868; at least, some of the applicants thought so.[9] And the fact that there was a Methodist, instead of a Presbyterian, in the president's chair probably helped to divorce the Presbyterian support from the institution at Chapel Hill.[10] Whether on account of religion or politics, or both, one finds the *North Carolina Presbyterian*, erstwhile strong supporter of the University, saying that there were not a few of the new board of trustees who were "total strangers to the wants of North

[4] Battle, *History of the University of North Carolina*, II, 14, 16–17, 27, 44.

[5] *Ibid.*, pp. 18, 27–28.

[6] *Ibid.*, pp. 22–23, 24.

[7] Governor Holden, a Republican, controlled and virtually appointed the board of trustees, and naturally named Republicans. The president and professors were all Republicans (*ibid.*, pp. 4, 11, 22).

[8] *Ibid.*, pp. 8, 14. The same board of trustees, it was proposed, was to have control of the branch (at Raleigh) for Negroes and the branch for whites (at Chapel Hill).

[9] *Ibid.*, p. 12.

[10] Until the election of President Pool, the presidency had been held continuously by a Presbyterian. Politics doubtless also influenced the Presbyterians; it is impossible to say with assurance how much.

Carolina," "careless of those wants if known," and "bent only on mischief to our people."[11]

Whether the *North Carolina Presbyterian* reflected accurately the opinion of North Carolina Presbyterians, one cannot be altogether certain. If one may presume that it did, then one finds a most abrupt change in their attitude toward state education in 1869 from that maintained almost uniformly from the time of the opening of the University in 1795 to its temporary closing in the days immediately following the Civil War. In 1863, for example, the *North Carolina Presbyterian*, observing that the number of students at "our State University" to be only seventy-three, offered public prayer that God might "speedily restore peace to our country, and thereby give prosperity to the noble institutions of learning throughout the State."[12] And even while its doors were still open, at least nominally, the old guard hardly conceded that it was alive. The *North Carolina Presbyterian*, for example, on July 22, 1868, expressed the regret of the people of the state that "the exercises of the University are suspended for the present," and, as if delivering a sort of funeral eulogy, declared that "the career of the University has been a noble one. No institution in this country presents a more brilliant array of statesmen, jurists and divines among its graduates." And the *Presbyterian* then forthwith proceeded to urge the denominational colleges to "lengthen their cords and strengthen their stakes." With the old board of trustees, which Baptists and Methodists had complained of as being predominantly Presbyterian and Episcopalian, supplanted by the Reconstruction regime, one finds the mouthpiece of the Presbyterians, in 1869, saying the whole subject of popular education should undergo a thorough discussion in the light of experience and observation: "Shall it be *by the State*, or shall it be *by voluntary effort* on the part of the people?"[13]

[11] *North Carolina Presbyterian*, July 22, 1868.
[12] *Ibid.*, May 30, 1863.
[13] *Ibid.*, Oct. 13, 1869.

If one may judge from the report of the State Superintendent of Public Instruction of 1869, he, too, with the possibility of the discontinuance of the University staring him in the face, was beginning to take interest in the denominational colleges. Referring to them, he said: "As a matter of propriety, all *chartered* institutions should hold themselves ready to respond to the State's inquiries for information." He included in his annual report references to the receipt of reports from the University, Davidson, Trinity, and other institutions, but not from Wake Forest.[14]

The attitude and activities of the denominations during the Reconstruction period was decidedly against the continuance of the University. From time to time objections were raised on the grounds: (1) that state education leads to infidelity, (2) that state education tends to official corruption, (3) that the University was not a necessity, (4) that the University was sectarian in its management, (5) that the University created prejudice against the denominational colleges, and (6) that its low academic standards were unworthy of a university.

Alleging that state education leads to infidelity, the *North Carolina Presbyterian* admitted that at the establishment of such (state) schools provision might be made that seemed in direct conflict with any intention to promote irreligion or infidelity. But in a country like ours circumstances which could not be controlled removed all this in a little while. It showed how

To avoid all appearance of sectarianism, under the carping and caviling of fault-finders, *all religion is excluded from these State*

[14] *Annual Report, State Superintendent of Public Instruction, 1869*, p. 7. This report indicated only twenty-eight enrolled in the University.

An interesting proposal, made by President Pool in 1870, was to bring the colleges of the state under the State University in such a plan as would allow them to retain their chartered rights and to receive such aid as colleges of the University as might be agreed upon. It was proposed, furthermore, that the property of the University should be leased, presumably to a combination of the colleges. The scheme fell through, however; the denominational colleges preferred to stay out of entangling alliances (Battle, *op. cit.*, p. 26).

institutions. Or, if not entirely eliminated, what remains is so diluted as to be powerless for good . . . . Where good seed is not diligently sown and cultivated, noxious weeds are sure to spring up and produce a harvest of evil.[15]

The editor was basing his remarks upon observation and experiences. He pointed to the example of New England, where the people "almost worshipped" this state system of education.[16] He held up the experience of the Northern and Northwestern states, also, as horrible examples of the consequences of state education.[17]

The *Raleigh Christian Advocate* likewise alleged that "for the last twenty-five years of its existence the University was a source of positive evil."[18] Little care was given to the moral and religious culture of the students. Stressing intellectual superiority, the University excited its students to an admiration of "worldly greatness without any particular reference to the higher and grander interests of the soul," with the result that many of them went to a "moral grave."[19] The Baptist paper declared that the moral influence exerted at Chapel Hill was deprecated even by its most enthusiastic admirers.[20] A healthy piety was held to be an indispensable element in institutions of learning.

The Presbyterian editor, moreover, held that state education tends to official corruption and consequently to a general demoralization of the people.[21] He declared that corrupt partisans in religion and in politics controlled the expenditure of the school fund so as to advance their own interests.[22] He alleged that members of the University

[15] *North Carolina Presbyterian*, Oct. 13, 1869.

[16] *Ibid.* "That land has been a hot-bed of *isms* of every conceivable shape and color for years past, while it is an admitted fact that evangelical religion has comparatively little power over the masses of the people."

[17] *Ibid.*

[18] *Raleigh Christian Advocate*, Aug. 23, 1871.

[19] *Ibid.*

[20] *Biblical Recorder*, July 30, 1873.

[21] *Ibid.* The *Raleigh Christian Advocate*, June 28, 1871, also referred to the evils incident to the "ins and outs" of political chance.

[22] *Ibid.* He declared: "A Charge of this kind has been made against the officials of our own State, both in the matter of the University and in the more recent selection of textbooks for the common schools."

faculty were selected, not because of their fitness for the position, but because of their political views and feelings, in order to serve party purposes. Private and denominational schools were the only hope for education of children and young people.[23]

That the University was not a necessity was argued by the *Raleigh Christian Advocate*.[24] The state was already being served by Wake Forest, Trinity, Davidson, and a Lutheran college, and also had access to out-of-state institutions. To operate the University, $300,000 would have to be raised by taxation for endowment, indebtedness, and repairs—which amount could be saved by relying on the colleges, which lived without public taxation.[25]

As to the sectarian management of the University, one who signed himself "Philo" held that the two churches (Baptist and Methodist) strongest numerically and ahead of the others in wealth and influence had not had, until recently, any controlling voice in its management.[26] Others shared this same feeling.[27]

From the Baptist camp, moreover, came the charge that arrogating to itself an aristocracy in education, the University fostered prejudices against the denominational colleges, accusing them of being narrow and sectarian. The result was that when the University ceased to exist, North Carolina students were induced to go to other states for their education.[28]

The Baptist editor charged that, whereas the University should have stood on a plane above the denominational colleges and drawn its students from them for graduate

[23] *Ibid.*

[24] *Raleigh Christian Advocate*, June 28, 1871.

[25] *Ibid.*

[26] *Ibid.*, Aug. 23, 1871.

[27] *Ibid.*, Sept. 13, 1871.

[28] *Biblical Recorder*, July 30, 1873.

In 1874 there were only about 350 students in Wake Forest, Davidson, and Trinity combined as compared with approximately 2,000 in the colleges of Virginia (*Biblical Recorder*, Jan. 7, 1874). The number of young men in all the colleges of the state, including the University, in 1881 was between 600 and 700 (Battle, *op. cit.*, p. 229).

work, its scholarship standards were no higher than those of the colleges.[29] The Methodist editor held that the denominational colleges equalled or excelled the University in scholarship and far excelled it in usefulness. Many of those holding diplomas from the University would not be able to compete with members of the junior class in other colleges.[30] Such low standards, it was held, were unworthy of a university and unfair to the denominational colleges.

The denominational leaders opposed a proposal of "Justice" to turn the University over to the alumni. To do so, they held, would be equivalent to running it as it had been run for seventy years; the majority educated there were either Presbyterians or Episcopalians, or under their influence.[31] Previously, the *Raleigh Christian Advocate* had proposed to "sell the property, pay its debts," and divide the balance, if any, among the denominational colleges. Similar distribution was suggested for the $300,000 of tax money regarded as necessary to put the University on its feet.[32] To turn the institution over to the alumni would mean that the Methodists and Baptists would lose their proportional part of what the University would bring at public sale.[33]

It seems clear, furthermore, that, while the University was in a state of coma, the leaders of the denominational colleges were not slow to see their opportunity. In fact, one finds even the organ of the Presbyterian Synod urging the friends of the various denominational colleges "to bring these institutions forward and show to be worthy of the confidence of the people of the state."[34] It was argued

[29] *Ibid.*

[30] *Raleigh Christian Advocate*, Aug. 23, 1871.

[31] *Raleigh Christian Advocate*, Oct. 4, 1871. It was argued that "all denominations and all parties are and have been equally opposed to the University as at present [1871] organized, and the Methodists and Baptists have been opposed to the *way* it has been organized for the last 70 years."

[32] *Ibid.*, June 28, 1871.

[33] *Ibid.*, Oct. 4, 1871.

[34] *North Carolina Presbyterian*, July 22, 1858.

that the University had already subserved the objects for which it was instituted and had died a natural death.[35] Why not close it out and divide the proceeds for the benefit of the denominational colleges, which were prepared to accomplish every desirable object for which the University was founded?[36] The denominations not only opposed the reopening of the University but sought to win support for their own institutions.[37] With the closing of the University, some of them saw a "new era" dawning upon denominational colleges, and rejoiced that the patrons of education were beginning to realize that denominational education could be as thorough and extensive as that acquired under state patronage.[38]

Friends of the University, desirous of seeing the institution revived, fought back. One argued that forty-three times the $300,000 necessary for the recovery of the University was spent in the state annually for intoxicating liquors and that thousands who did not patronize the university were benefited by it. To this argument the reply was made that Americans were benefited remotely by the colleges of Europe, but Americans were not being taxed to

[35] *Raleigh Christian Advocate*, June 28, 1871.

[36] *Ibid.*, Aug. 23, 1871.

[37] For example, at a Baptist educational convention in Warrenton in the fall of 1873, the Baptists adopted a plan for raising an endowment for Wake Forest College, and the committee in charge of the endowment campaign appealed to the Baptists of the state to do their part by the college and thus show themselves "enlightened and liberal friends." "We must take care of ourselves first. We must show that we are worthy Stewards of the Lord Jesus by providing for his Churches until He comes again; and when we have done this, or rather, as we do it, we shall assist all others in pouring light into the dark places of the State." The committee declared, furthermore, that "The light of the University has gone out. It may be a quarter of a century before that light shall again burn brilliantly and steadily." Emphasizing the need for strengthening Wake Forest, the committee declared that whereas Virginia had approximately two thousand students in her colleges, North Carolina, in her three colleges—Wake Forest, Davidson, and Trinity—had not more than three hundred and fifty (*Biblical Recorder*, Jan. 7, 1874).

[38] *Biblical Recorder*, July 30, 1873.

support them, and that consent would be given to any means of reviving the University without increasing taxes.[39]

The Reverend A. D. Betts, an alumnus of the University and a prominent Methodist preacher, did not agree at all with the contentions of those who would condemn the record of the University and consign it to eternal sleep. He testified. He talked out of experience. Of the two hundred and eight students at Chapel Hill in 1854, twelve had become ministers, three of them members of the North Carolina Methodist Conference. He was converted there. He recalled the Sunday morning prayer meetings in the Old Chapel. He heard two or three sermons on Sunday and generally two or more during the week. Every student was required to recite a Bible lesson on Sunday. The professors had a private Bible class. And participating in the Chapel Hill prayer meetings were such men as those educating the youth at Cary, Mebanesville (now Mebane), Louisburg, and other places.[40]

One of the most helpful steps toward reopening the University was the return of the election of the board of trustees to the legislature. In 1871 friends of the University procured the passage of an ordinance taking the election of trustees from the Republican State Board of Education, which ordinance became a part of the constitution in 1873.[41]

[39] *Raleigh Christian Advocate*, Sept. 13, 1871. Ex-Governor William A. Graham, writing to Mrs. Cornelia Phillips Spencer, Sept. 29, 1870, stated the opinion that, considering the experience of the last two years, there was no hope of the *revival* of the University under the management of the then present board of trustees. He revealed a strong desire for its revival, even at the expense of the common schools, if necessary, believing in "the system of education downwards" because he thought more good might be accomplished with limited means by endowing the University and sustaining it, than by expending a like amount in common schools, if both were not possible. His reference to "education downwards" forecast an issue which was to figure prominently in the arguments twenty to thirty years later, when the leaders of the denominational colleges argued for state support of common schools in preference to state support of higher education (see Hope Summerell Chamberlain, *Old Days in Chapel Hill*, pp. 185–186).

[40] *Ibid.*, Oct. 18, 1871.

[41] Battle, *op. cit.*, p. 50.

Thus the control of the University reverted to its friends. Some of the former trustees, ousted by the constitution of 1868, were returned to office; and public confidence was thereby greatly restored.[42]

The Presbyterians were among the first to return to the support of the proposed new university. Although in 1869 their denominational paper was arguing against state education and advising the denominational colleges to entrench themselves in the educational life of the state, the *North Carolina Presbyterian*, four years later, was softening in its attitude toward its old friend, the University, whose enemies seemed to take a bit too seriously the Presbyterian paper's advice of 1869. Referring to proposals to revive the institution at Chapel Hill, the *Presbyterian* declared that "those who believe in the power of prayer will send up many a petition that such measures may be adopted and may be successfully carried into operation, as will light again the flame that once burned brightly on the hills of Orange,—measures that will prove to be for the advancement of God's glory, the good of His church, the safety, honor, and welfare of our people."[43]

To aid the movement to restore the University, the State Board of Education called a meeting of the friends of education in Raleigh, July 9, 1873. This meeting, attended by about one hundred delegates, representing twenty counties and every shade of religious and political faith, including lawyers, doctors, preachers, teachers, editors, printers, merchants, and farmers, gave the greater part of over two days to discussions.[44] The convention unanimously adopted a resolution "That the revival of the University at the earliest practical moment, is essential to education in North Carolina."[45]

[42] *Ibid.*, pp. 2, 50–51.

[43] *North Carolina Presbyterian*, May 14, 1873. On the same editorial page, referring to the educational meeting to be held two months later, it was stated sarcastically: "It will be so refreshing about the middle of July to have another grand fizzle on the laughable subject of Education in North Carolina."

[44] *Biblical Recorder*, July 23, 1873.

[45] *Report State Superintendent of Public Instruction, 1873*, p. 44.

The proposed bases of the reopening of the institution at Chapel Hill, discussed and apparently agreed upon at the educational convention, are significant. Ex-Judge William H. Battle, declaring that the University was *articulo mortis* and that the convention was called upon to save it from death, advocated the establishment of the University upon a lofty and stable foundation, with terms of admission and the requirements for taking degrees "so high as to place it above all the other schools and colleges, so that it may not be their rival, but rather their honored head." He would place it on the same level with Harvard, Yale, and the University of Virginia. He would make it the head of the state's educational system and insisted that to make the head sound would be to make the whole body sound.[46] President W. M. Wingate of Wake Forest and Dr. T. H. Pritchard, for the Baptists, and President Braxton Craven and the Reverend A. W. Mangum, for the Methodists, spoke in favor of resurrecting the University as a university proper but not as a rival of Wake Forest, Davidson, and Trinity.[47] They insisted, furthermore, that the Baptists and Methodists should have a fair representation in the board of trustees and the faculty.[48] It was agreed that "the early revival of the University and its establishment in a position of dignity and usefulness" was impossible "unless upon a basis entirely impartial in denominational and political controversy."[49]

[46] *Ibid.*, pp. 43-44. Ex-Judge Battle was an Episcopalian who taught at the University from 1845 to 1868 and from 1877 to 1879.

[47] Discussing further the proposal to make the University an institution which should afford to graduates of colleges an opportunity for further study and for preparation for some of the professions, the *Biblical Recorder* admitted that there were serious but not insurmountable difficulties in the way, including about $125,000 to pay off the indebtedness and an annual appropriation of $20,000. The Baptist paper contended, however, that the money required would be a paying investment, estimating that $130,000 were being taken from North Carolina annually by students attending institutions out of the state, that "a pious and learned Faculty would infuse new vigor into the intellectual life of the state," and that the influence of the University upon the general educational interest of the state was worthy of consideration (*Biblical Recorder*, Jan. 14, 1874).

[48] *Biblical Recorder*, July 23, 1873.

[49] *Report State Superintendent of Public Instruction*, *1873*, p. 47.

In 1875 the new board of trustees provided for the reopening of the University.[50] On May 4 they organized and adopted a scheme of reorganization providing for six colleges.[51] At an adjourned meeting in June a faculty of seven was decided upon, including the Reverend Charles Phillips, D.D., LL.D. (Presbyterian), professor of mathematics; J. DeBerniere Hooper, A.M. (Episcopalian), professor of Greek and French; the Reverend Adolphus W. Mangum, A.M. (Methodist), professor of moral philosophy and English literature; Alexander Fletcher Redd (Baptist), professor of physics and chemistry; Ralph H. Graves, B.Sc., C. and M.E., professor of engineering; John Kimberly, A.M., professor of agriculture; and George Tayloe Winston, adjunct professor of Latin and German. Dr. Phillips, who with Dr. Hooper, had previously been a member of the University faculty, served as chairman of the faculty until Dr. Kemp Plummer Battle became president in 1876.[52] Money contributed by alumni and the $7,500 interest on the land grant enabled the University to open its doors in September, 1875.[53] The attendance the first year after the reopening reached 69, the second 112, and the third 160.

Although Dr. Pritchard and his followers were disappointed in that Battle and not Vance was made president of the University, the Methodists were very happy over the election of one of their number, the Reverend A. W. Man-

[50] Battle, Sketches of the History of the University of North Carolina, p. 55.

[51] A "college" meant merely a department with one professor composing it. The fact that the terms of the land grant required the maintenance of a college of agriculture doubtless influenced the decision to use this term. Then, too, it suggested expansion into a real university.

[52] *Ibid.*, p. 56. Dr. T. H. Pritchard, who had been active in educational matters since 1855, showed interest in the question of who should be president of the University. Over a year before the members of the faculty were elected and over two years before Dr. Battle became president, Dr. Pritchard suggested to the trustees that they elect ex-Governor Zebulon B. Vance, and that the first duty assigned the president be that of raising from the alumni and friends of the University a permanent endowment of not less than $250,000 (*Biblical Recorder*, Feb. 18, 1874).

[53] The legislature of 1875 gave a bond of the state for the entire principal of the Land Scrip Fund of $125,000, lost in various transactions following the war (Battle, *History of the University of North Carolina*, II, 64–71).

gum, to the chair of moral philosophy and English literature. By formal resolution, the North Carolina Annual Conference, in December, 1875, expressed its appreciation of the action of the trustees of the University and requested the presiding bishop to appoint Mangum to the position to which the trustees had elected him.[54] And Professor Mangum, apparently recognizing one of his opportunities, if not duties, to be that of winning Methodist support for the University, as well as taking care of Methodist interests in it, lost no time in appealing for the co-operation of Methodists. Writing from Raleigh, July 21, 1875, he declared that although the Methodist Church had an interest in the University which it could not afford to neglect and that representation in the faculty was necessary for the denomination's interest, there was to be no *sectarianism* in management or instruction, that precautions were to be taken to shield the young men from the vices of the day, and that the University was to be the *friend* and *ally* of Trinity, Davidson, and Wake Forest. "We propose to work with them for the country and for God."[55]

The denominations, nevertheless, mistrusted the University. Even the Methodists, with Professor Mangum proclaiming the University to be non-sectarian, a shield against the vices of the day, and a friend and ally of the denominational colleges, went on strengthening their stakes. In their conference of 1876 they declared: "We must have full control of the Institutions whose students are separated from their homes. . . . We need not confide it to others

[54] *Minutes of the North Carolina Conference, 1875*, p. 19.

[55] *Raleigh Christian Advocate*, July 28, 1875. Professor Mangum had back of him the statement of Dr. Phillips, the chairman of the faculty, who, on the very opening day of the University, answering the sarcastic remark that the University had "neither politics nor religion," declared that in the broad sense of the word it was false, the University teaching the principles of true statesmanship and Christianity. But in the sense that the professors would rigidly abstain from attempting to influence students for or against any political party or religious denomination, the charge was true. He promised that all parties and sects would be treated with perfect impartiality (Battle, *History of the University of North Carolina*, II, 96).

and must not."[56] A great deal was made of the fact that college students were separated from their homes, "separated from their natural guardians, removed from childhood's church, social restraints and the home altar, distant from the father's authority and mother's sleepless care; thrown largely upon their own resources of restraint and self-direction; and subjected to the caprices, passions, and temptations of congregated youth."[57] Hence, the Methodists insisted that Methodist students, if they would speak her dialect, must "drink from her own sweet fountains."[58]

This strong statement by the Methodist Conference no doubt was inspired by the strenuous efforts being made by the friends of the University to rally support to the institution at Chapel Hill. In July, for example, one who called himself "Robert" aroused the ire of the denominational leaders by alleging narrow sectarianism in the colleges of the denominations. President Craven of Trinity, in reply to "Robert," said that no one proposed sectarian schools in North Carolina, denied that Trinity, Davidson, and Wake Forest were sectarian, insisted that "the denominationalism of the state will not quietly tolerate anonymous *non sequiters* and misstatements," and retorted that such statements were probably intended to buildup an educational influence

[56] *Minutes of the North Carolina Conference, 1876*, p. 25. The report of the committee on education adopted at the 1876 conference, after stating that Methodist children, "not one sex alone, but both; not only for the ministry and the professions, but for all purposes," must be educated, declared the Methodist church must do the teaching, determine the scholarship, execute the discipline, and supervise the religious instruction and moral requirements of the students, and insisted that Methodists can and must control the education of their sons and daughters. Emphasizing her sense of peculiar mission, the Methodist conference explained: "Whatever excellencies other denominations, anti-denominations, and the so-called neutral world may have in scholarship, culture, and thoroughly furnished Institutions, none of them can in all respects make the men and women we need for the work which the Great Head of the church has committed to our charge. What they can do in all classes and degrees of learning, so can we; what they will do in some things we do not want done; what they cannot do in many particulars, we do successfully."

[57] *Ibid.*, p. 25.

[58] *Ibid.*, p. 24.

in the state that would substitute "a formal morality for a religion."[59]

Presbyterians, under the leadership of Henry H. Banks, agent of Davidson College, were being rallied in support of their own institution. Although one does not find the *North Carolina Presbyterian* speaking editorially on the subject in 1876, its columns were used by the agent of Davidson College to call attention to "the precariousness and rottenness of all institutions dependent on the patronage of the State" and to declare that the hope of the future weal of *Church and State alike* was in the sustaining and fostering of the church college.[60] It seems clear that at this particular time, when an Episcopalian instead of a Presbyterian was at the head of the University, efforts were being made to lead the Presbyterians to feel but little identity with the institution with which they were so prominently identified earlier in its history.

Denominational leaders were not slow to check the reopened institution at Chapel Hill by the standards and conditions virtually agreed upon when its reopening was under consideration and to criticize it severely at the points where it failed, in their judgment, to meet the specifications.[61] Within twelve months after the reopening there arose a bitter controversy, led by Dr. L. S. Burkhead, president of the board of trustees of Trinity College, involving, chiefly, (1) questions of educational standards and (2) alleged discrimination against the larger denominations.[62]

[59] *Raleigh Christian Advocate*, July 19, 1876. Eight months after the Methodist Conference had declared so emphatically in favor of denominational colleges as opposed to state institutions, the *Raleigh Christian Advocate* stated, editorially, that "The University was in good hands and in a fair way to recover its lost prestige and prosperity and that President Battle deserved the gratitude of the people of the state for the unselfish devotion and great energy he had manifested in 'resuscitating the college' " (*Raleigh Christian Advocate*, July 25, 1877).

[60] *North Carolina Presbyterian*, Feb. 25, 1876.

[61] See above, p. 74.

[62] Dr. Burkhead alleged, also, that the department of agriculture and the state geologist had been attached to the University with great harm to them (*Raleigh Christian Advocate*, July 25, 1877). Dr. Burkhead drew into the contro-

It was claimed that, notwithstanding the pre-opening talk about placing the University on a level with Harvard, Yale, and the University of Virginia, the institution at Chapel Hill was a university only in name.[63] Dr. Burkhead alleged that the requirements for admission were as high at the colleges as at the University, the courses of instruction at the colleges equal to and sometimes better than at the University, the examinations equal if not superior at the church colleges, the professors equal in every sense, and speaking and other exercises, "except dancing," at least equal to those at the University.[64] Dr. Columbus Durham, a prominent Baptist, and an avowed friend of the University, sought to bring the University matter to the attention of the Baptist State Convention.[65] He wanted to enlist the support of the Baptists in efforts to make the institution at Chapel Hill a university in reality.[66] The editor of the *Biblical Recorder* agreed with Burkhead and

---

versy, as supporters, C. C. Dodson, Rev. Columbus Durham, prominent Baptist, the *Raleigh Christian Advocate*, and the *Biblical Recorder*. Defending the University, W. L. Steele, a Methodist trustee of the University, took the lead, and was ably supported by Rev. William Closs, a Methodist presiding elder; Rev. A. D. Betts, Methodist alumnus of the University who became a trustee in 1879; Rev. A. W. Mangum, the Methodist member of the University faculty; and Rev. R. L. Abernethy, a Methodist preacher. Through Professor Redd, a strong Baptist lay preacher and at one time associate editor of the *Biblical Recorder*, who taught chemistry at the University from 1875 to 1880, the Baptists objected to the regulation of the board of trustees requiring all students to attend morning and evening prayers. He could not see why it was not as much a violation of the principle of religious freedom to enforce attendance upon prayers as to require chapel attendance; and the board, in 1860, had modified its compulsory chapel attendance regulation. Enforced attendance upon prayers was certainly against the tenets of his church. His arguments were effective in that for a short time the faculty put attendance upon prayers on a voluntary basis. The numbers dwindled, however, so much that the marking of absences was soon resumed (Battle, *op. cit.*, pp. 178–179; chap. i, p. 51).

[63] *Raleigh Christian Advocate*, Aug. 22, 1877.

[64] *Ibid.*, Sept. 26, 1877; Nov. 28, 1877. Dr. Durham thought the state should have a university delivered from the necessity of competing with colleges for patronage, not one which could underbid them and, in time, cripple if not break down all similar institutions.

[65] *Minutes Baptist State Convention, 1880*, p. 31.

[66] *Biblical Recorder*, Jan. 19, 1881.

Durham that it was "an ordinary college, in competition with other colleges of the state," and contended it could not remain so and draw on the state treasury for support.[67] Until within a few years the institution at Chapel Hill had the ordinary college curriculum. If it had the right to be called a university, why could not the other institutions also be called universities?[68] The editor ridiculed the idea that at Chapel Hill there were six colleges. In the old curriculum days the various studies were assigned to different professors as in all colleges at that time. A change, however, had been made at Chapel Hill; the studies were distributed into so-called colleges, without any extension of courses, advance in scholarship standards, or increase in the corps of instructors.[69] It did not appear that they conferred degrees. In what sense the colleges, without presidents, principals, or deans, were independent it was hard to see He insisted two pertinent questions still remained unanswered: (1) In what respect did the University so differ from the colleges that it claimed the name of university, and (2) What was the peculiar work of the institution at Chapel Hill which the colleges could not do, and vice versa?[70]

[67] *Ibid.*, Dec. 1, 1880. When Professor A. W. Mangum resorted to the dictionary to prove that it was already a university, the Baptist editor insisted that the professor's dictionary definitions did not satisfy. He wanted to know if there was any difference between a college and a university.

[68] *Biblical Recorder*, Jan. 5, 1881.

[69] President Battle (*op. cit.*, p. 86) said that the chairs were called colleges, i.e., Charles Phillips, Professor of the College of Mathematics. In the six colleges established at Chapel Hill, said the Baptist editor, the University stood alone in the country and in the world. "Certainly nowhere else can we find six colleges manned by less than a dozen professors."

[70] He invited Professor Mangum to use the columns of the *Biblical Recorder* for his answers (*Biblical Recorder*, Jan. 5, 1881). Professor Mangum, in a brief note to the editor, however, declined the privilege of discussing the questions in the *Recorder* (Jan. 12, 1881). He preferred not to become involved in a controversy, although of the correctness of his views and statements, in all material points, and of his ability to vindicate them he was clear and confident beyond all doubt. The comment of the editor on Professor Mangum's refusal to answer the questions and his reasons therefor was that he thought the professor prudent in declining, but for reasons different from those given. He insisted that there need be nothing harmful or unpleasant in discussions upon such subjects, and the

Dr. Durham, moreover, held that the state institution was a university "in the same sense that the average crossroads politician is a statesman—only in the estimation of those of like calibre."[71]

Neither the Baptists nor the Methodists felt that they had a fair representation either on the board of trustees or faculty of the reopened University. Dr. Burkhead alleged, furthermore, that those in control had little or no use for Methodism.[72] The election of Professor Frederick W. Simonds, of New York, in 1877, to the position of professor of natural history, in preference to a Methodist applicant, was the immediate cause of the allegation. Professor Mangum, it was alleged, had told the Methodist Conference that the board of trustees and the president of the University desired to have another Methodist professor in the faculty, and that if the Methodists did not make a fair showing at Chapel Hill, they had no one to blame but themselves. Whereupon a number of Methodists presented the claims of one of their number, only to be told, they reported, that there were not sufficient funds to fill the vacant professorship desired by them for their capable candidate. Whereupon Dr. Burkhead questioned the fairness of "Episcopal control" of the University when there were only 4,500 Episcopalians as compared with 100,000 Methodists in the state.[73] Although accused of making charges against the character of the whole board and individual members of the board, Dr. Burkhead declared he did not attack the character of the gentlemen of the board individually or collectively. The question of whether the Methodist can-

---

Recorder's position was misunderstood if it was supposed that it cherished ill will towards "Chapel Hill." It did not dispute the claim that respectable collegiate work "in some branches" was done there but maintained that the institution made unwarrantable and absurd pretensions by professing to do the work of a university (*ibid.*, Jan. 19, 1881).

[71] *Ibid.*

[72] *Raleigh Christian Advocate*, Aug. 29, 1877.

[73] *Ibid.;* also *ibid.*, Sept. 26, 1877.

didate's application was rejected simply because he was a Methodist was, he thought, a pertinent one.[74]

Dr. Burkhead's reasons why Methodists and Baptists should be properly represented in the faculty and board of trustees were summarized as follows:

1. They are taxed[75] to support an institution which can underbid, and in time, cripple, if not utterly break down all "similar institutions."
2. They are taxed, not simply to build up a rival institution where Episcopalians have undue influence and control; but indirectly at least to destroy their own institution.
3. If the State proposes to make or continue the institution at Chapel Hill a mere college competing with other institutions of similar character, and by taxing the whole State to break down all the denominational colleges—then Methodists have greater reason to demand equal rights in the management of Chapel Hill.[76]

The editor of the *Advocate* endorsed the position taken by Dr. Burkhead.[77] He held that the Methodists of North Carolina were entitled to all the rights and benefits in the University claimed by Episcopalians and others.[78]

C. C. Dodson thought the criticisms of the University were proper. The explanation that there was not a qualified person in the state for the chair of natural history reflected not only on the Methodists but upon the University, which, Dodson contended, should have prepared its students so that one of them could have filled the position.[79]

Dr. Durham went beyond any point previously made by other critics in his particularity concerning the extent and

[74] *Ibid.*, Sept. 26, 1877; also Nov. 28, 1877.

[75] See p. 87, *et seq.*

[76] *Ibid.*, Nov. 28, 1877.

[77] *Ibid.*, Sept. 26, 1877.

[78] *Ibid.*, Sept. 12, 1877. He declared, "We will not sit with folded arms and say *well done!* until we, as a church, have a just and proper representation in the board of trustees and faculty of the University." He thought North Carolina Methodism would sustain him in his views.

[79] *Ibid.*, Sept. 19, 1877.

evil consequences of the Episcopal influence at Chapel Hill. Like most of the other critics, he professed a firm friendship for "a University." He characterized the institution at Chapel Hill as North Carolina's "poor kin."[80] It was "woefully wanting in grip" as evidenced by the small number of students in the prosperous condition of the people. The fact that the legislature had not been induced, in the face of large expenditures in other ways, and perhaps could not be induced, to give a yearly appropriation of ten thousand dollars, was another proof that the institution did not "grapple the people."[81]

Its strong sectarian bias was, to Dr. Durham, the reason. Having no kind word for the Episcopal brethren, he did not hold them responsible for the conditions of the institution. But stating "a few facts plainly," he said that with perhaps nine-tenths of the people of the state, the Episcopal church and the Episcopalians, as such, were "most unpopular." The people believed that whatever of denominational influence the University had ever exerted had been toward that church.[82] Chapel Hill seemed to them an Episcopal college.[83]

And the more Dr. Durham and the people investigated, he said, the more they were impressed with this idea. Of the board of trustees, a majority of the active members were Episcopalians. Of the eight "additional trustees" required by law to be "from points conveniently accessible to the seat of government and the University," five were Episcopalians. Of the executive committee, four were of the Episcopal church (a majority every time). The president was an Episcopalian, and in the faculty *the church* was "in full force." All of this Episcopal predominance existed, it was claimed, in a state which had thirty-seven counties (out of less than a hundred) in which there was not even an Epis-

[80] *Biblical Recorder*, Jan. 19, 1881.

[81] *Ibid.*

[82] Dr. Durham perhaps had overlooked the time when it was the Presbyterian, instead of the Episcopal Church, which was favored at Chapel Hill.

[83] *Biblical Recorder*, Jan. 19, 1881.

copal church and in a state of whose citizens only about 6,000 were Episcopalians, and 400,000 were of other denominations. He was not prepared to believe that it was purely accidental. He thought that the Methodists, "an intelligent, active, popular, influential, progressive, wide-awake, educating people," numbering about 150,000, might furnish more than one member of the faculty if "this religiously unpopular and unprogressive 6,000 Episcopalians" had three. And he could not quite understand how it was that the Baptists, numbering at least 204,000 in the state, were "hardly known at all" among the trustees and executive committee, and had only one member of the faculty.[84] To his way of thinking, there could be no special reason why a man should control what ought to be the great heart of the state's educational interest simply because he belonged to one of the "smallest, most unpopular and most non-progressive" religious denominations in the state. He suggested that it would be the part of wisdom for those desiring the institution to run successfully the race set before it, to free it from this weight.[85]

The main arguments and grievances against the University, as developed through a long series of discussions, are summarized in the following seven points:

1. The state should have a university—delivered from the necessity of competing with colleges for patronage, where young men may pursue higher branches of learning.
2. Such an institution cannot be established and made the pride of the state, as long as rights of Methodists, Baptists, and others are ignored or overlooked.
3. In the University of North Carolina the Episcopalians have an undue and controlling influence in Faculty, Executive Committee, and Board of Trustees.
4. This is not fair or just to the larger denominations.
5. As the Methodists and Baptists are the two largest denominations in the state and pay more taxes to support the University

[84] *Ibid.*
[85] *Ibid.*

than any other two denominations, they should *of right* be properly represented in the Faculty and Board of Trustees.
6. There is no probability of them securing proper representation on the Faculty as long as the Board of Trustees remains organized as at present.
7. The only mode of redress is through the legislature by way of primary caucuses.[86]

The University did not lack for friends to uphold its side of the controversy.[87] They defended the right of the state institution to be called a university and denied any unfairness to Methodists or Baptists in their failure to be represented more strongly on the board of trustees and the faculty.

Professor Mangum seemed to be the University's chief spokesman in defense of its educational standards. Although when Dr. Burkhead made his complaint, Mangum only came back with a plea for brotherly recognition, encouragement, and spiritual co-operation on the part of Methodists toward the institution at Chapel Hill,[88] he pulled the dictionary on the Baptists when they raised the issue.[89] He quoted Worcester.[90] He argued that the University carried its instruction beyond the college curriculum "in proportion to the means at command and to the degree that the present educational interests of North Carolina justify." His answer to those who, having formed their ideal from the models of the great schools of Germany, would restrict the University to postgraduate studies, was that the managers of the University would gladly and promptly make the change suggested, provided the denom-

[86] This summary was prepared by Burkhead (see *Raleigh Christian Advocate*, Oct. 17, 1877).

[87] See footnote 62, for a list.

[88] *Raleigh Christian Advocate*, Aug. 29, 1877.

[89] *News and Observer*, Dec. 15, 1880.

[90] "A school or seminary of learning of the highest class, in which various branches of literature and science, including sometimes theology, law and medicine, are taught, and in which degrees are conferred on individuals who are found on examination to possess certain qualifications, or who have complied with certain prescribed conditions."

inations would (1) provide colleges to cover the ground as effectually, in every sense, as the gymnasia of Germany did their work, (2) provide for the tremendous expense involved, and (3) show that the interest of the state would be thereby best subserved. He held that the University ought to be conducted with respect to things as they are and not as anyone wished them to be or imagined that, in an educational Utopia, they might be.[91] W. L. Steele declared that although the desirability of restricting the University to graduate work had not been established, it was no doubt regarded as desirable by many professing friends of the institution.[92]

Professor Mangum, trying to pour oil on troubled waters, explained that Professor Simonds was from Cornell University and an accomplished teacher. An expert was required, and none could be found in the Methodist or any other church in North Carolina.[93] He had written to Nashville and Baltimore to learn if such a person could be procured in the Methodist Church. No expert came before the trustees from the South.[94] W. L. Steele also entered the controversy to defend the action of the board of trustees in electing Professor Simonds. He stated that the candidate proposed by the Methodists was not qualified for the position. The trustees did not give preference to any denomination. They wished success to all the colleges of the state. He denied that the Episcopalians had an undue and controlling influence in the faculty, executive committee, and trustees of the University, unfair and unjust to the larger denominations.[95] He admitted the preponderance of Episcopalians on the board of trustees but denied that they had been chosen because they were Episcopalians. The preponderance

[91] *News and Observer*, Dec. 15, 1880

[92] *Raleigh Christian Advocate*, Nov. 21, 1877.

[93] Steele contended that the proper principle was selection without regard to religious views, but admitted such views had to be taken into account, "to silence envious tongues" (*Raleigh Christian Advocate*, Nov. 21, 1877).

[94] *Ibid.*, Aug. 22, 1877; Sept. 12, 1877.

[95] *Ibid.*, Nov. 21, 1877.

of Episcopal students at the University was due to the fact that the Episcopal Church had no college in the state under its special care.[96] He called attention, also, to the fact that the state had done but little in establishing and maintaining the institution at Chapel Hill, which had subsisted mainly on tuition fees and the charity of graduates and friends.[97] Concerning the denominational complexion of the board of trustees, Professor Mangum declared that the legislature, composed of more Methodists and Baptists than Presbyterians and Episcopalians, elected the trustees. He reminded Methodists that others were more interested in the University than they; Methodists did not seek what they wanted in the right way.[98]

The Reverend R. L. Abernethy believed no attempt should be made to make the University sectarian. Dogmatic theology should be confined to the church schools. Professors should be men of piety and universal learning and should demand a high standard of ethics of their students as well as exercise a rigid but parental control of those under their care. "Each and every applicant for admission should be required to subscribe to his faith in the Holy Trinity," for the reason that people should not be required to pay taxes to increase infidelity in the land. The board of trustees and faculty should be allowed to manage the affairs of the institution; if any church people were not pleased with the University, let them patronize their own church institutions.[99]

Presiding Elder Closs took issue with Burkhead. He alleged the impropriety of making the church paper a medium of attack on the University.[100] He also interpreted Burkhead's contention for a fair representation in the trustees and faculty for the denominations as meaning that the Methodists, Baptists, Presbyterians, and Episcopalians

[96] *Ibid.*, Oct. 10, 1877.
[97] *Ibid.*
[98] *Ibid.*, Sept. 12, 1877.
[99] *Raleigh Christian Advocate*, Oct. 10, 1877.
[100] *Ibid.*, Sept. 12, 1877.

should be represented according to their numerical strength in the state. Then what would become of the rights of the smaller denominations and those belonging to no denomination? He called attention to the difficulty in defining the meaning of the four denominations, there being several kinds of Methodists, Baptists, and so forth. He contended, furthermore, that representation of Methodists, according to their numerical strength, carried with it the obligation to patronize the University according to numerical strength. He held, also, that no denomination of Christians was taxed to support the University, that Methodists were taxed as citizens of the state, that the University was not denominational, and that no denomination as such had a right to representation.[101]

Burkhead claimed that Closs misrepresented his position. Others than the four leading denominations should be represented. The Methodist and Baptist denominations were taxed. It was not right for 4,500 Episcopalians to have control of the institution, when there were 220,000 Methodists and Baptists. And representation in the management of an institution did not carry with it the obligation to patronize that institution.[102] If so, said he, would that obligate those represented in the management of the penitentiary to furnish their full quota of convicts?

It was the avowed policy of President Battle to work quietly and tactfully in dealing with his critics and those who opposed the policies of the University. He knew he had a delicate task to perform. Explaining his method, he said: "It was of utmost importance that... no acrimonious words should be used nor angry controversy engaged in. My plan was to confine myself to a simple explanation correcting errors in good temper, on the assumption that the adversary was under an honest mistake and would be pleased to know the truth."[103] Then, too, he doubtless found it

[101] *Ibid.*, Jan. 23, 1878.
[102] *Ibid.*, Feb. 13, 1878.
[103] Battle, *op. cit.*, p. 103.

diplomatic, if not always effective, to leave to his Methodist trustees, his Methodist faculty member, and the Methodist presiding elder the task of dealing with the president of the board of trustees of the Methodist college and with others of like opinion concerning conditions at Chapel Hill.

Another means doubtlessly employed to promote friendly relations between the denominations and the University was to use as many ministers as possible as often as possible, on the various public programs, as in the case of the University Day program of 1879, when ministers of at least four denominations were used.[104]

Whether designed as such or not, the summer sessions for public school teachers, inaugurated in 1877, afforded a means also of helping to popularize the University.[105] Not only did they bring teachers who received a free service and returned to their home communities to make friends for the University, but they gave the University a chance to use as speakers and teachers in the summer sessions outstanding leaders of the denominations. For example, in 1878 and 1880, the president of Wake Forest was on the summer school program, and occasionally representatives of other denominational colleges were similarly honored.[106] Public addresses, furthermore, directed the thinking of the summer school students concerning such topics as "Public and Private Education" and "Relations of Teacher to Church and State."[107] President A. D. Hepburn of Davidson congratulated President Battle on being "called by God's good providence" to inaugurate this normal school " . . . to popularize culture" and "to show that the University was for all the citizens of the state."[108]

[104] *Ibid.*, pp. 190–191.

[105] Battle, Sketches of the History of the University of North Carolina, p. 61.

[106] Battle, *History of the University of North Carolina*, II, 159, 162–163, 165, 200. F. S. Blair, a prominent Quaker, chosen to take charge of a section of the normal school at the University in 1879, reported to the Yearly Meeting of Friends that he "had a good opportunity to see" and thought he "saw very prominently the decided advantage of trained teachers over the untrained" (*Minutes of the North Carolina Yearly Meeting of Friends, 1879*, p. 18).

[107] Battle, *op. cit.*, pp. 144, 188.

[108] *Ibid.*, pp. 164–165.

Official notice was taken, moreover, of the Sunday afternoon lectures given at the summer sessions. In his report of 1881, President Battle stated that "lectures were given by President Battle on sacred subjects, viz.: On the Shipwreck of St. Paul, and on Herod's Temple; by Professor Atkinson and Professor Shepherd, on the New Testament Revision; and by Prof. W. B. Phillips on the Deluge."[109] Appraising the effectiveness of the summer session of 1881 and using language which the denominational mind of the times could easily understand, President Battle declared: "The souls of the teachers were made stronger by attendance on the great educational camp meeting."[110]

In the midst of the discussions of the relative merits of state and denominational institutions, the Methodist professor at Chapel Hill did his best to convince those interested that the University was making encouraging improvement in its religious atmosphere. He sent at least two articles to the *Raleigh Christian Advocate* in 1878, one in April and another in November, telling of such improvement since the first year of its revival. He mentioned the Young Men's Christian Association with its regular Sunday afternoon meetings conducted almost entirely by students and characterized by earnestness and devotion, and the daily prayer services, announced every evening by the ringing of the bell just before time for studies. Several of the students were teaching in neighboring country Sunday schools, some had formed Bible classes in the village churches, and a number attended divine services in the church of their choice. He spoke, also, of the chapel services being well attended and of the beautiful singing in the morning service at chapel Sunday morning. At least two students were preparing for the Presbyterian ministry, one for the Lutheran, one for the Episcopal, one for the German Reformed, and there were quite a number, including some

[109] *Annual Report of State Superintendent of Public Instruction, 1881–1882*, p. 68.
[110] *Ibid.*, p. 69.

Methodists, who were working "like young men ripening for the noblest of all callings."[111]

In his November letter from Chapel Hill, Professor Mangum told of the special services of the Y. M. C. A.'s week of prayer, to which "the Faculty and village ministers were invited." The leader of the opening service, who had become a Christian since he entered the University, made "a truly appropriate, sensible, and touching exhortation." Another student spoke touchingly of the "hopes and prayers of fond hearts in distant homes" and exhorted his companions so to act that "those loved ones may not be disappointed in the sons they so fondly cherish." The number of those belonging to the association was "encouragingly large." Again Professor Mangum called attention to the fact that the students held not only Sabbath services but also a short prayer-meeting every day at six o'clock when "the University bell rings and calls them to their spacious hall for the worship of the great Father." He declared that the morale of the students was "exceedingly good." He greatly rejoiced over the indications that the University was to be "a genuine blessing to society." He reported over thirty Methodist students in the University.[112]

[111] *Raleigh Christian Advocate*, April 3, 1878.
[112] *Ibid.*, Nov. 20, 1878.

III

The Struggle to Place the University on a Sound Financial and Educational Basis

THE struggle between the friends of the denominational colleges and those of the University took on real magnitude when, in 1881, efforts were made to secure an annual appropriation from the legislature for the support of the University.

Not until this time had any serious effort been put forth for such an appropriation. Suggestions of appropriations had been made, by the Presbyterian Synod in 1847, by Dr. T. H. Pritchard, a Baptist, in 1859, by Governor W. W. Holden in 1866, and by the *Biblical Recorder* in 1874.[1] The Synod had suggested that the legislature be "proudly munificent." Dr. Pritchard had pointed to what other states were doing for their institutions, and the Baptist paper estimated the need of an appropriation to carry through the suggestion that the institution at Chapel Hill be made a "real University." Governor Holden proposed to the legislature that an appropriation of "a few thousand dollars" be annually made, for four years, to the University, and suggested that, if necessary, this be done on condition that a certain number of pupils be eduated free of tuition.[2]

On February 11, 1867, to make good the income from the $125,000 of federal land scrip money lost in the post-war crash, the legislature assumed responsibility for paying the interest on this amount to the University, representing $7,500 a year, on condition that the University grant to each county in the state the privilege of sending a student free of charge for tuition and room rent. Not all the coun-

[1] See chap. i, pp. 57 and 45, and chap. ii, p. 74, footnote 47.

[2] *Public Document No. 7*, Jan. 18, 1866, p. 33 (attached to the *Annual Report of Calvin H. Wiley, State Superintendent of Schools*).

ties availed themselves of this privilege, only sixteen sending students under this plan in 1877–78. But President Battle promised to call the attention of the county commissioners to the matter in the hope that they might be induced to have representatives at the opening of the session in August, 1878.[3] In 1881, eighty-nine of the one hundred and sixty-six students paid no tuition.[4]

Governor Thomas J. Jarvis, at the session of 1881, recommended, besides the $7,500 appropriated in 1867 to take care of the interest on the land scrip fund, an additional annual appropriation of $7,500, on condition that the number of county students be increased to two to each county.[5] The trustees and faculty were endeavoring to educate so many young men unable to pay any tuition fees that the institution was laboring under financial embarrassment. The state constitution placed the responsibility of the maintenance and management of the University on the General Assembly, one of whose responsibilities, according to the governor, was to extend the benefits of the University, as far as practicable, to the youth of the state free of charge for tuition. Little had been done to carry into effect the mandate of the fundamental law, except to make good the loss of the federal money, which the state was forced to do or repay the whole amount to the United States.[6] The free tuition provision had seriously diminished the number of paying students. In addition, the University had been in the habit of receiving all indigent young men of good character free of charge for tuition. Governor Jarvis wanted the number not curtailed but increased.[7]

The governor might have added, also, as President Battle

[3] *Report of Hon. Kemp P. Battle, President of the University of North Carolina (to Governor Vance) on the State of the University and the Normal School* (pamphlet), Jan. 15, 1878.

[4] *Executive and Legislative Documents, 1881 (Governor's Message)*, p. 7.

[5] *Ibid.*, pp. 7–8.

[6] The land scrip fund, amounting to $125,000, was invested chiefly in special tax bonds by a former board of trustees of the University, and lost.

[7] *Executive and Legislative Documents, 1881*, pp. 7–8.

did later, that the sons of clergymen and students intending to become clergymen were given free tuition, and that other young men, with the assent of their parents, compared themselves to the county students and argued that they were entitled to the same privileges, to their own advantage and to the hurt of the University treasury.[8]

Already, as has been shown, some of the denominations, especially the Baptists and Methodists, were criticizing the state's institution for higher learning.[9] With such a state of public mind, one would hardly regard this as an auspicious time for asking the state legislature to levy a new tax. But the financial condition of the University was desperate. Something had to be done. Tuition fees from the few were inadequate to support an institution for the many. To the alumni, in and out of the legislature, the University turned for help.

At the meeting of the Alumni Association in June, 1880, at the instance of President Battle, plans were laid for the fight for an appropriation in the legislature of 1881. On January 26, 1881, while the legislature was in session, a meeting of alumni was held in Raleigh, in the hall of the lower house of the legislature, with addresses by President Paul C. Cameron of the Association and President Battle of the University. The Association adjourned from the legislative halls to a hotel banquet hall, where various members of the legislature and others were guests of the alumni.[10]

No less than fifteen prominent men responded to toasts, including Speaker of the House Charles M. Cooke, who promised that the legislature would help the University extend its usefulness; Representative John Manning, who spoke of the "steady stream of generous, intelligent, well bred gentlemen" produced by the University, of the good work of the summer normal school, the friendship of the University for the common schools, and its faithfulness in

[8] Battle, *op. cit.*, p. 214.
[9] See above, pp. 76–88.
[10] Battle, *op. cit.*, pp. 205–213.

carrying out the provisions of the land grant act; the Reverend Thomas E. Skinner, D.D., who, for the clergy, admonished the University not to underrate the denominational colleges as sectarian and the denominational colleges not to antagonize the University, "the mother of high education in North Carolina"; Representative J. G. Morrison, responding to the toast to "Our Sister Institutions—Davidson, Wake Forest, and Trinity," who spoke for Davidson and pledged a helping hand; Senator H. R. Scott, for Wake Forest, who thought there was no conflict between the University and the colleges of the state and declared, "On behalf of my Alma Mater permit me to say she is in sympathy with every ally enterprise in the state"; Representative D. B. Nicholson, for Trinity, who declared education to be the hope of the Old North State and the University and the colleges to be the "fountains from which flow, and from which must continue to flow, the crystal streams of knowledge and culture from which the manhood of our grand old Commonwealth may quaff the waters of refinement, of honor and distinction"; and Representative J. S. Bradshaw, for the press, who promised the alumni that the press would prove "the strongest ally, the warmest advocate, and the truest friend" of the University.[11]

The trustees sought to do their part in behalf of the proposed appropriation for the University. They gave to the public, through resolutions circulated by the daily press, a statement in which they represented the University as an integral part of the educational system of the state and themselves as seeking to advance the "sacred cause of education" in common schools, denominational colleges, and the University, regardless of class, locality, sect, creed, denomination, or party. They also held up its work in behalf of poor boys and teacher training.[12]

[11] *Ibid.* Also *Proceedings: Annual Meeting of the Alumni Association Held in the Capitol, Raleigh, N. C., Jan. 26, 1881* (pamphlet).

[12] The resolutions, offered by Calvin H. Wiley, former state superintendent of common schools, and adopted by the trustees January 29, declared: "That . . . the University is and ought to be conducted as a part and parcel of the general educa-

The case for the University, in elaborate detail, was set before the legislature in a brief carefully prepared by President Battle and Professor G. T. Winston.[13] This brief covered the high spots in the origin and history of the institution, a summary of its work, and an inventory of its holdings, and sought to answer some of the major criticisms of the University and objections to the proposed appropriation.

It was the people's university. They had imposed its maintenance upon the legislature at six different epochs, including the constitutional conventions of 1776, 1835, 1861, 1865, 1868, and 1875; the people had overwhelmingly voted their ratification of the constitutional provisions for the University in 1873 and 1876. And all the legislature had done was to pay the interest on the land scrip fund.

The University had given instruction to 270 county students and beneficiaries since 1875. It had furnished teachers for public and private schools. Instruction was largely practical, including surveying, bookkeeping, chemistry, mechanics, botany, rights and duties of citizenship, business law, and so forth. The number of students had risen to two hundred since 1875, with 50 per cent more from North Carolina than the University had up to 1850. The state owned a great deal of University property. The University was essential to the common school system. It saved annually from $75,000 to $100,000 to the state by educating

---

tion system of the State, and that between the University and other public schools of the State there can be and there ought to be no conflict of interest, and in the discharge of the duties imposed upon us as Trustees by the Legislature, we seek not the good of any particular class or locality, but the good of the whole people of North Carolina, without regard to sect, or creed, or denomination, or party, and that in every way in its power this Board will exert itself to the utmost to promote and advance the sacred cause of education wherever it may be done, whether in the common schools, in denominational colleges, or in the University.

"That in carrying out their views this Board in the future as in the past, so far as its means will permit, will welcome to the University and in every way aid poor young men who have not the means of acquiring otherwise a liberal education, and will . . . offer every possible facility for the successful conduct of the Normal School" (*Morning Star*, Jan. 30, 1881).

[13] Battle, *op. cit.*, pp. 227–230, 486, 487.

North Carolina boys at home.[14] No other institution could do the work of the University. The fact that Trinity, Wake Forest, and Davidson did good work was no reason why the University, started fifty years before either of these, ought to desert its old work and get out of their way. To do so would cut the University off from its connection with the great mass of poor young men in the state struggling to acquire a liberal education.[15] No institution in the state, other than the University, could do the beneficiary work that the University had done and desired to do.[16] What the University needed was a little more money. Already it was doing more for the $7,500 than any similar institution in the United States that had as little money. Virginia was appropriating $40,000 annually to her university and $65,000 a year to four other state-aided institutions. South Carolina was putting a little more than Virginia into four institutions in that state. Figures concerning numerous other states were shown.[17] Money contributed by individuals to revive the University and intended to pay professors' salaries had been applied to improving the property of the state. And the history of the institution entitled the University to the support of the state.[18]

Concerning the objections which had been raised, the

[14] It was argued that before the war the University served 185 from other states, who brought into North Carolina at least $100,000 a year. The University, therefore, gained and saved, together, about $200,000 annually to the state.

[15] Said the University spokesmen, through the brief: "The University is not intended alone for the benefit of graduates of other institutions and the rich, but for the poor and needy as well. . . . It is and ought to be emphatically a State institution, doing the State's work, and the real question at issue is not whether young men shall go to Chapel Hill or to other institutions, but whether they shall go to Chapel Hill and there acquire a liberal education, or remain at home without one" (Battle, *op. cit.*, p. 227).

[16] And then: "But let us not quarrel about this, for Heaven knows that in the field of education there is work enough for all; that there are, and will always be, boys enough in North Carolina seeking higher education to fill all of our institutions of learning" (*ibid.*).

[17] *Ibid.*, pp. 228, 486–487.

[18] *Ibid.*, pp. 223–228.

spokesmen of the University sought to answer four, as follows:

(1) To the objection that the University took so many beneficiaries, the answer was, "Guilty and proud of it." The constitution required it. The principle was right. Very few county students were able to pay. And ninety-nine out of one hundred were certainly needy, of whom some would become strong and valuable men.[19]

(2) To the objection that by taking beneficiaries the University hurt the denominational colleges, the answer was that the opening of the University had helped the colleges. Wake Forest had twice as many students in 1881 as it had before the University opened. The other institutions also had increased their enrolment. There were 2,500 or 3,000 boys in the state who should go to college, whereas only 600 or 700 were there. The denominational colleges wanted paying students, whereas the constitution required the University to take poor boys.[20]

(3) Answering the contention that the University should raise its standards so high as to be out of the way of the colleges, the proponents of the appropriation asked how it could be done and what institutions in America were doing it. They held that there would not be ten students if the University restricted itself to graduate work only. It was hard to induce students to stay in college long enough to graduate; it was fanciful to expect many of them to go higher. Already the standard of admission at Chapel Hill was as high as at Princeton, the University of Virginia, and other institutions of the same rank.[21]

(4) To the charge that the University did not meet the requirements of the Land Grant Act, the answer was that by theoretical teaching of the branches of learning relating to agriculture and the mechanical arts the University was carrying out the requirements.[22] The cultivation of fields

[19] *Ibid.*, p. 229.

[20] *Ibid.*

[21] *Ibid.*

[22] *Ibid.*, pp. 122, 230.

and orchards and the rearing of cattle and experimentation concerning such subjects could not be undertaken without special funds.[23]

A number of newspapers took up the fight for the appropriation, including the Raleigh *News and Observer* and the Wilmington *Morning Star*. The *News and Observer* charged the friends of the denominational colleges with attempting to control the state and to unite the church and state contrary to the principles of civil and religious liberty.[24] This paper also sarcastically pointed out that there were other interests in North Carolina besides those of the denominational colleges. It declared that the University was neither established nor revived for its own sake nor to make money, and did its work without regard to creed, sect, or denomination, or political affiliation.[25] The *Morning Star* thought there was room for all the institutions, both state and denominational. Referring to what it regarded as an attempt on the part of the *Biblical Recorder* to disparage the University, the *Star* declared that "He is no friend of North Carolina who would rejoice in the destruction of the University, and he is a vandal who would lay his unsanctified hands upon its hallowed walls and level them to the ground." The Wilmington paper thought that if already the University was not equal to Berlin or Heidelberg, to Oxford or Cambridge, to Harvard or Johns Hopkins, then the legislators should do all they could to make it so.[26] The *Morning Star* argued, furthermore, that the state would not listen to intense fanaticism and that it was a grand mistake to

[23] The *Morning Star*, replying to the critics of President Battle's report on the Land Grant Act, quoted from the report to the effect that the act required that the classics should be taught but did not prescribe the teaching of agriculture or the teaching of mechanics, or the keeping of an experimental farm. It did not prescribe any manual labor in farm or shop. It explicitly commanded "the teaching of such branches of learning as are related to agriculture and mechanic arts" not "agriculture and mechanic arts" but the branches relating to those subjects (*ibid.*, Feb. 15, 1881).

[24] *Biblical Recorder*, Feb. 23, 1881.

[25] *Carolina Watchman*, Feb. 24, 1881, quoting the *News and Observer*.

[26] *Morning Star*, Jan. 27, 1881.

suppose that a cultivated man necessarily preferred a denominational college merely because he was a Presbyterian, or Methodist, or Baptist, or Lutheran, or Christian, or whatnot. This paper was of the opinion that there were sectarians who would rejoice if the University should close. The true friends of the University, among whom were some men of the various churches, however, felt that it was important to have a college that was undenominational.[27] The Wilmington paper regretted to see that a war was about to be made upon "the chief literary ornament and glory of North Carolina," by the friends of the denominational colleges. It was so like North Carolina, standing at the foot of the class of states in education, "quarreling among ourselves when we ought to be united and resolved in our purposes to 'spell up.'"[28] The legislature should take care of the University. Provision should not be made for additional scholarships, but there should be an appropriation of $20,000 annually to make the institution what all of its friends desired it to be. The *Star* quoted from a private letter from the Reverend J. D. Hufham, D.D., favoring "all reasonable appropriations needful for it," even "unlimited appropriations with universal tuition," provided it be made a university indeed, and thought the most intelligent Presbyterians, Methodists, and Baptists would sustain such action.[29]

One might think that, with such support as that pledged in the alumni meeting,[30] the University could get almost anything from the legislature it might ask. But the friends of the denominational colleges had other spokesmen than those selected by President Battle or the University alumni to respond to the toasts. The faculty of Wake Forest College, becoming alarmed at the possibility of an appropriation, called a conference of the friends of the college,

[27] *Ibid.*, Feb. 3, 1881.
[28] *Ibid.*, Feb. 15, 1881.
[29] *Ibid.*, Feb. 23, 1881.
[30] See above, pp. 94-95.

in Raleigh, February 9, 1881. Before the meeting was held, the Methodists and Presbyterians interested in Trinity and Davidson had joined in the movement to consider the expediency of attempting to defeat the proposed measure.[31] The concrete product of the meeting was a memorial in behalf of the denominational colleges of the state, through which they protested against the proposed measure as "inexpedient, unfair and unjust" and served notice on the legislature and friends of the University that, on principle, they would resist its passage by every legitimate means within their power.[32]

Pointing out that the proposal would, if passed, give Chapel Hill $15,000 per annum and make available free tuition to 188 students, the memorialists opposed the appropriation, not because of ill-will towards the state institution but from considerations of right and in order to protect their own interests. They gave four reasons. They opposed the measure:

First, *because they deemed it unwise that so large a part of the public money should be appropriated for higher education when the special and peculiar want of the state at that juncture was common school education.*[33]

Second, *because it proposed to educate the youth of the state at a very expensive rate of tuition.* Each of the eighty-nine

[31] *Biblical Recorder*, Feb. 23, 1881. Although President Pritchard of Wake Forest wrote to President Bickle of the North Carolina College (Lutheran) at Mt. Pleasant concerning the matter, it appears that the Lutherans did not participate in the gathering.

[32] "A Memorial in Behalf of the Denominational Colleges of the State," printed in full in the *Biblical Recorder*, Feb. 16, 1881; also in the *Carolina Watchman*, Feb. 17, 1881. It was signed by T. H. Pritchard, J. D. Hufham, and L. L. Polk, on behalf of the Baptists, Braxton Craven and F. L. Reid, Methodists, and L. M. McKinnon and John L. Brown, Presbyterians. Pritchard, Craven, and McKinnon were presidents of Wake Forest, Trinity, and Davidson, respectively.

[33] They explained: "When only one-third of the children of the State are at school; when the State is so poor that it provides only money enough to keep the public schools in operation 10¼ weeks in the year, and the appropriation for the education of each child for a whole year is only 81 cents, it seems unreasonable that the State should pay $80 a year for the tuition of each student it may send to Chapel Hill" (*ibid.*).

students at Chapel Hill last term cost the state at the rate of $84.27 per annum, a higher rate than any college in the state charged for its students. They argued that the state was not called upon to give beneficiary education at Chapel Hill at so great a cost, that by this plan many enjoyed this charity who were not worthy objects of charity, and that the number of poor young men who would be aided would not be materially increased. They said that if the tendency of the free tuition principle should result in North Carolina as it had resulted in Virginia and all state students be free, then the state would have a benefaction enforced by involuntary taxation enuring to the benefit of the well-to-do and even to the richest families of the state.[34]

Third, *because they believed it would be detrimental to education throughout the state.* Chapel Hill was but one of several colleges imparting the same grade of instruction. It was not fair for the state institution to enjoy the benefit of special legislation to the injury of the other colleges, especially when it had no larger patronage than one of them and contributed but a small part of the educating force of the state in comparison with what all the other colleges were doing. The injury, furthermore, reached to the academies and high schools, inasmuch as the state institution at Chapel Hill admitted students of "almost any degree of preparation."

Fourth, the memorialists submitted *that the denominational colleges were entitled to the respect and protection of the state.* Indeed, they contended, these colleges possessed "a value and vitality, as factors in the great work of education, which do not belong to the State school at Chapel Hill." When for years the state school was in "a state of

[34] They held, furthermore, that no worthy youth had ever asked help from either of the denominational colleges in North Carolina in vain, and that one hundred and sixty-five young men were being educated, either wholly or in part, by Wake Forest, Trinity, and Davidson. They feared the proposed measure would detract from the patronage of these institutions and deprive them of the power to help these poor promising young men and thus not advance the cause of education (*ibid.*).

suspended animation," these denominational institutions, "revived and sustained by the noble sacrifices of their friend," were dispensing, far and near, the blessings of "sanctified learning."[35]

Reflecting an appreciation of the deliberation and determination with which these denominational leaders entered into the contest, and forecasting the prolonged nature of the struggle, the editor of the *Biblical Recorder*, February 16, 1881, said that the action of the friends and representatives of the colleges was not either spasmodic or hasty and therefore not to be repented of in the near future.[36] Previously the editor of the Baptist paper had quoted from the minutes of the Baptist State Convention in 1877. At that convention, the Reverend J. D. Hufham, D.D., chosen for the task, had set forth the Baptist position, which, briefly stated, was that (1) the state needed the University; (2) Baptists grieved when the institution went down soon after the Civil War; (3) it was a Baptist who first called through the public press for its revival; and (4) in return, they demanded that the institution at Chapel Hill be made a university. They would not be content to have it merely a college, a rival of the denominational colleges; they would have no "electioneering" on the part of University officials, whether trustees or faculty, to draw away students from denominational colleges.[37] The editor asked that the board of trustees

[35] They held that there was great significance in the alleged fact that "Chapel Hill, with its magnificent outfit of buildings, apparatus, etc.; its long line of illustrious Alumni; the overshadowing influence of State prestige and an endowment amounting to $125,000 was unable to sustain itself while the denominational colleges were in an effective and even prosperous condition" (*ibid.*).

[36] The Baptist editor declared: "They have carefully considered the whole question in all its bearings, both for the present and for the future, and have deliberately reached the conclusions given in the memorial. On this basis they have made up their minds to stand and contend for their rights, not only before the General Assembly, but before the people of North Carolina. The contest is inevitable; and it may last for years. They are prepared for the issue. The fate of the colleges and the fate of higher education in the State depends upon this issue. The result is doubtful."

[37] *Biblical Recorder*, Feb. 2, 1881.

raise the standard of scholarship above that of the other colleges and require a competitive examination "on a course equal to that of the advanced classes in our colleges." Then no one, he said, could object to the appropriations.

Miscellaneous objections to the annual appropriation came from various sources. "A Baptist" wrote his church paper that he did not feel willing to be taxed to support the University. Already it was receiving $7,500 of the state's money every year, to which it was no more entitled than the denominational colleges; it was but little if any more of an agricultural college than they. He and other Baptists were opposed to one of the established institutions at Chapel Hill—"that Ball Room." There was a political relation of this matter which he warned politicians carefully to consider.[38] Some argued that the University's claim to furnishing teachers for the common schools was but poorly grounded in fact. One said that not one in twenty teachers in North Carolina ever saw the University, unless during a visit to the summer normal school.[39] A Methodist felt about as positively as the Baptist about the dance question; he complained that dances were held at Chapel Hill in defiance of the majority of the state.[40]

President Pritchard, as spokesman for the memorialists, answered the charge of an effort to unite church and state and a deliberate attempt to control legislation by a combination of sectarian denominations.[41] He insisted that they had given a respectful and manly expression of reasons for opposing the recommendation of the governor. They had a right to do so as citizens and taxpayers and as friends of the denominational colleges, whose interests they regarded as imperilled, and as representatives of Christian churches—a

[38] *Biblical Recorder*, Jan. 12, 1881. The Baptists already had their college; they had never had a fair and just recognition either in the board of trustees or the faculty.

[39] *Ibid.*, Jan. 26, 1881.

[40] *Raleigh Christian Advocate*, March 16, 1881.

[41] *Biblical Recorder*, Feb. 23, 1881. The charge was made by the *News and Observer* (see above, p. 99).

right given by the Constitution of the United States and the Bill of Rights of North Carolina and guaranteed by the charters creating the colleges. He thought it amusing to hear "the Episcopal editor of the *News and Observer* [S. A. Ashe] charging the Methodists, Presbyterians, and Baptists, especially the Baptists, with an attempt to unite the church and state, and with violating the principles of civil and religious liberty." He retorted: "The sun shines too high in the heavens for anybody to be scared by that ghost!" He explained that they did not oppose the appropriation already made to Chapel Hill, with one free indigent student from each county, but did oppose the increased appropriation, with the 188 free scholarships. It was painful to take a position of apparent hostility to the state college. Their motives had been misunderstood, and bad feeling and even indignation had been excited on that account. They did not want to injure the state institution—merely aimed to protect themselves.[42]

Having read the memorial of the denominational colleges, the editor of the *Carolina Watchman* brought forth a proposal which may have been in the minds of the memorialists but which was not specifically expressed. He proposed that the legislature give the county students the privilege of selecting for themselves any college in the state. He favored an appropriation of $7,500 or $15,000, as the legislators thought best, for paying the tuition of two students from each county.[43] There is no indication that the *Watchman's* proposal received support, except doubtless from the denominational leaders, who did not press this proposal until 1885.

The contest was hard fought, and the result was a compromise. J. D. Hufham, acting for the denominational

[42] *Ibid.*

[43] *Carolina Watchman*, Feb. 17, 1881. "If the Legislature desires to do a liberal thing on this subject, we think the way is open to them. . . . It is obvious that it would be more satisfactory to those who have to pay the taxes than the present proscription of colleges in all respects the equal, not to say the superior, of Chapel Hill."

college group, proposed that if the friends of the University would withdraw the additional county student feature and reduce the amount asked from $7,500 to $5,000 annually, he would cease his opposition and advise others to do likewise. The proposal was accepted, and the bill, as amended, was passed.[44]

President Pritchard of Wake Forest and others seemed happy over the solution. They understood that there would be no increase of free tuition and that only really poor young men would be considered as eligible for the privilege. Their chief protest had been against increased free tuition, and that point they had gained.[45]

The friends of the University seemed equally happy. Their attitude was expressed by President Battle, who quoted Colonel William L. Saunders, secretary of state, an ardent supporter of the appropriation measure, as saying, when the passage of the bill was reported to him, "That settles the question—more will follow.[46]

The appropriation of $5,000 was to continue annually for four years. In 1885 an effort was made to increase the amount.[47] In the meantime, friends of the University gauged their step with regard to the "more to follow," and the friends of the denominational colleges intensified their pleas for patronage of their colleges and focused a critical eye upon Chapel Hill.

The friends of the University gave repeated notice of the fine moral tone and positive religious emphasis at the state institution. For example, the committee of investigation appointed by the board of trustees, in 1882, reported to the board and to the press, not only about the accounts of the treasurer and the mode of management of the institution, but declared the moral tone pervading the institution was "worthy of all praise" and assured parents that they might

[44] *Ibid.*, p. 217; *House Journal, 1881*, pp. 296, 479; *Senate Journal, 1881*, pp. 350, 375, 420.

[45] *Biblical Recorder*, Feb. 23, 1881.

[46] *House Journal, 1885*, p. 260; *Senate Journal, 1885*, p. 371.

[47] See below, pp. 109–121.

feel, with entire confidence, that their sons would be "as free from temptations to do wrong as they would be at any similar establishment either within or without the borders of the state."[48]

In 1884 the University visiting committee included in its report a paragraph on morality and religion, in which attention was called to the healthy moral and religious atmosphere of the institution, to the fine work of the Young Men's Christian Association and of the village churches, to the absence of such things as "deviling the faculty" and "paping," or cheating on recitation or examination.[49] Reference was also made to the efforts of the faculty to extend to the youth of the state the benefits of the University free of tuition. Forty counties were represented by students receiving free tuition. The faculty had dispensed charities with a liberal hand, allowing time for the payment of tuition, and, in some extraordinary cases, remitting the fees altogether.[50] Since 1875 about two hundred had been granted free tuition, in addition to the county students.[51]

[48] Report of the Committee of Investigation to the Board of Trustees of the University of North Carolina, June 1, 1882, in the *Raleigh Christian Advocate*, June 21, 1882. The committee also not only spoke of the religious services in the University chapel and in the several churches of the village but stated that there was a distinct recognition of the Christian religion, that "its doctrines are regularly taught in one of the schools of the University, as not only essential to the life which is to come, but as a means of preserving the liberties of the people, and otherwise advancing their temporal welfare." The committee claimed that "This, with other advantages of the institution," rendered it worthy of patronage of this and other states of the union.

See above, pp. 95–99, for reports concerning 1881.

[49] Battle, *op. cit.*, pp. 276–277.

[50] Nearly a year before the attempt was made to secure an increased annual appropriation from the state treasury for the support of the University, the *Raleigh Register* was proclaiming that at the University education was within the reach of every aspiring young man. "Such is the state of economy, so favorable are the terms offered, so welcome is everyone—whether he does or does not bring money in his hand—that none should despair of obtaining a diploma from our highest State institution" (*Raleigh Register*, March 19, 1884). Here the friends of the University, playing up to the legislature, were also playing into the hands of the denominational colleges, one of whose chief objections was to free tuition at the University.

[51] *Ibid.*, p. 272. In referring to this committee, President Battle, who no doubt

Governor Jarvis, in his message to the legislature of 1883, moreover, wanted to see the legislature endow a chair to be known as the "Chair of Moral Science and Christian Evidences."[52] Although all the professors were, in his opinion, Christian gentlemen and taught in and out of the recitation room by precept and example the doctrine of the Christian religion, he thought there should be a special chair devoted to the subject "to meet the demands created by these times for special instruction."[53] To this end he asked that an appropriation of two thousand dollars be made and that the trustees be required to select the instructor. There was no appropriation made as recommended by the governor. The recommendation, however, no doubt, served the purpose of showing the financial need of the University and a willingness to give religion a place in the curriculum.

Alexander McIver wrote of "the large religious element" which he saw in the commencement exercises of 1885. Bishop A. W. Wilson preached on the religious element in education. Congressman Reid had religious teaching in his address, and several of the young graduates spoke on the same subject.[54]

---

had a hand in selecting it, made clear the point that, inasmuch as one of the accusations against the University in 1884 was that it was under Episcopal influence, no Episcopalian was put on the committee, of which there were seven members—the chairman and two others being Methodists, two Presbyterians, another of Presbyterian lineage, and one a Baptist, the president of the board of trustees of Wake Forest College.

[52] *Executive and Legislative Documents, No. 1, 1883*, p. 27.

[53] He would combat the fearful tendency among the advanced thinkers of the age to ignore, if not to hold in contempt, the claims of the Christian religion. He wanted to see the state declare in unmistakable manner that "at her University no system of philosophy is to be listened to for one moment that does not teach that God is the Creator of all things, and the ruler of all things and as such entitled to the service of all men," and that "the Bible is the great book for the study of mankind." Although the trustees were not asking for more help, he knew they desired such a chair but did not have funds sufficient to provide it. The faculty had undertaken to endow by private subscription such a chair but failed because it was difficult to induce people to give to a state institution.

[54] Letter of Alexander McIver to Mrs. Cornelia Phillips Spencer, June 5, 1885, in the *Spencer Papers*.

The denominational leaders kept alive their differences with the friends of state education. And through the church press and otherwise they pointed out the need for fostering denominational colleges. President Craven of Trinity branded national and state educational efforts, "sustained by office, political favor, and money" as hostile to Methodist colleges, in theory, method of support, moral interpretation, and religious emphasis.[55] Some of the Baptists brought up again the contention that Baptists were being ignored in all public matters and renewed the complaint that the University was virtually the property of the Episcopalians, who were getting out of it virtually the benefits of a denominational college without having to pay for them.[56] Others agitated against making higher education free unless to young women.[57] Dancing at the University gave the denominations another point of attack upon the institution at Chapel Hill. Some insisted that the situation called up the question of whether the University would give up dancing or force the good people to give up the University.[58]

The Reverend B. M. Smith, D.D., speaking before the Presbyterian Synod of North Carolina in 1882, pointed out that the state had no religion and that the churches had to have denominational colleges to train candidates for the ministry; secular colleges furnished very few.[59] At Davidson a committee went to work to find ways and means of offering free tuition to all pupils in order to meet the competition of the state institution.[60]

Governor Jarvis, in his message to the legislature of 1885,

[55] *Raleigh Christian Advocate*, July 19, 1882.

[56] *Biblical Recorder*, Sept. 3, 1884.

[57] *North Carolina Christian Advocate*, July 31, 1883.

[58] *Raleigh Christian Advocate*, Feb. 14, 1883. The trustees and alumni were criticized for making possible, in 1883, a dance on Washington's Birthday in addition to the one usually given at commencement. President Battle was quoted as emphasizing, in connection with a proposal of the alumni to build a gymnasium which could be used as a ballroom, the importance of having a place for dancing.

[59] *North Carolina Presbyterian*, Oct. 11, 1882.

[60] *Ibid.*, Sept. 12, 1883.

spoke to the subject of the relationship between the denominational colleges and the University[61] and concluded with a recommendation that additional appropriations be made. He wanted to see the doors of the University opened to the poor young men of the state and, therefore, urged the legislature to make an additional annual appropriation of $10,000.[62] He advised, also, another appropriation of $10,000 to pay a debt to a friend who had made a loan to enable the University to complete a building, and suggested that a debt of $4,522 which the University owed the state for convict labor be cancelled. The total appropriations recommended in the message, therefore, amounted to $37,022.[63]

Having thus received encouragement from the governor and thinking that the people approved the five thousand dollar annuity appropriated in 1881, President Battle, members of the faculty, and the trustees decided to ask that the additional annual appropriation be $15,000, an amount $5,000 in excess of Governor Jarvis' recommendation, and for $12,000 with which to pay a debt on a building.[64] Lee S. Overman, a graduate of Trinity College, who later became a United States Senator, introduced the bill,

[61] *Executive and Legislative Documents, Session of 1885, Document No. 1*, pp. 10–11. He held that the work of education, the greatest interest of the state, must be begun in the common schools and ended in the University. Private enterprise had done much; the denominations had built up schools and colleges that were monuments to their wisdom and generosity. But the work of educating the masses was too vast for the combined energy of individual enterprise and denominational effort. The University should be made in fact the head of the state common school system and should be sufficiently equipped to furnish teachers and specialists wherever needed. Its doors should be open to all intelligent, meritorious young men even if they should be unable to pay tuition. The denominational colleges were not able to offer free tuition. The governor felt more deeply on the free tuition controversy than might be considered proper to write in his message to the lawmakers.

[62] *Executive and Legislative Documents, 1885, Document No. 1*, pp. 10–11. This amount, with the $5,000 appropriated in 1881 and the $7,500 appropriated in 1875, would make the annual appropriation from the state's treasury $22,500 a year.

[63] *Ibid.;* also *Biblical Recorder*, Jan. 14, 1885.

[64] Battle, *op. cit.*, p. 304.

based upon the wishes of President Battle.[65] Its principal provisions were the $15,000 annuity, $12,000 for the debt, repeal of the code requiring county students to teach in the public schools, release of those who had made a promise to teach from the obligation, two students from each county to receive free tuition instead of one, a commission to study the question of industrial education, and annual reports to the governor and the legislature.[66]

The governor's message and the Overman bill stirred deeply the denominational leaders. Already apprehensive concerning the fate of their own institutions in competition with the state institution at Chapel Hill, and incensed at the alleged injustice done the church colleges, representatives of the colleges seemed to regard the proposals to increase the state appropriation and to increase the number of free county students as adding insult to injury. They, therefore, resisted the proposals by throwing against them all the old arguments used in the fight of 1881,[67] and to each new argument for using tax money for higher education made vigorous denial. Apparently the denominations, through their criticism of the low admission standards at the University, had aroused the preparatory schools; at any rate, some of them, in 1885, fought with the denominational colleges against the askings of the University.[68]

The principal objections, which stand out among the many voiced by the denominational leaders in the fight

[65] *House Journal, 1885*, p. 260; *Senate Journal, 1885*, p. 371.

[66] *Ibid.;* also *Raleigh Register*, Feb. 11, 1885.

[67] The memorial of the denominational colleges, proposed in 1881, was used again in 1885 (*Biblical Recorder*, Feb. 5, 1885).

[68] The proposal previously made that the University raise its standards so as to be equal to the best colleges and universities of the country was renewed in 1885. The charge was reiterated that the University was not only taking students from the denominational colleges but away from the preparatory schools, private and denominational. James H. Horner, representing the preparatory schools, argued that free tuition at the University was breaking down, or tending to do so, the preparatory schools, "the nurseries of the University and our denominational colleges." Classical education was being made cheaper at the University than at the preparatory schools (Raleigh *News and Observer*, Feb. 3, 1885, and *Morning Star*, Feb. 5, 1885).

of 1885, were to (1) the free tuition proposal of the Overman bill and to (2) the implications of the governor's message that the University was the head of the common school system.[69] Objection was renewed also to (3) the alleged unfairness to the stronger denominations, which maintained their own institutions, to tax them to support an institution for the smaller denominations which had no college.[70]

As long as the University remained in competition with the denominational colleges, it was argued, it should not offer free tuition, for the reasons that those who went to the University as a rule were able to pay tuition, including most of those who received scholarships, and that free tuition tended to cripple the colleges, a thing which the state could not afford to do.[71] The tuition bill was only a small matter in comparison with board bills and other expenses. The plan proposed would simply take from the other colleges and high schools the young men who were

[69] See above, p. 110, footnote 61, and p. 111.

[70] See above, p. 109.

[71] *Raleigh Christian Advocate*, Jan. 14, 1885. It was argued that many of the boys who received free tuition at the University were not the sons of poor farmers and mechanics, but the sons of men abundantly able to pay tuition, room rent, and traveling expenses, as well as board, laundry, and the rest (*Biblical Recorder*, Jan. 28, 1885). Some of the free students protested against the statement, and the *University Magazine* declared that only a small percentage of the students at Chapel Hill were rich men's sons (see *Morning Star*, Feb. 7, 1885, and the *University Magazine*, Feb., 1885, pp. 219–220). Replying to the free students' protests, Dr. C. T. Bailey, editor of the *Biblical Recorder*, challenged the friends of the University to say that all, or even a majority of the free students then at Chapel Hill or who had been there during the past three years, had complied with the law governing free tuition. He asked also for a list of the free students then at Chapel Hill and the counties they represented, and added: "Does the committee know that some counties have two if not more free students in attendance when the law allows but one? Do none of our friends know, or did they ever hear of young men who were preparing to enter some of the other colleges being written to and invited to come to Chapel Hill without tuition? If no one at Chapel Hill has heard these things, we have. If they do not know that the law has been abused, we do" (*Morning Star*, Feb. 7, 1885). The demand for information concerning county students reached the legislature. Senator Cyrus Thompson of Onslow introduced a resolution requiring President Battle to furnish the information. A substitute for the resolution was offered by Senator Gudge of Buncombe and was passed (*Senate Journal, 1885*, pp. 438, 440–441).

able to pay board and tuition without putting education in reach of a single young man in the state. A resolution was introduced in the senate to abolish free scholarships at the University altogether, but it failed of passage.[72] The spokesmen of the denominations were willing that all expenses not met by the receipts from tuition be paid by the state. The right of the legislature to destroy the denominational colleges by donating large sums to the establishment of a mammoth free college was denied.[73] Denominational colleges were obliged to charge tuition. Governor Alfred M. Scales, in his inaugural address, had referred to some of the demoninational colleges being endowed and thought all would be sustained by their respective denominations.[74] The reply was that only two were even partially endowed and not one of them could live one term without large aid from tuition fees.[75] The denominations could not hold students at such a disadvantage.

To the statement of the governor that the denominational colleges could not open their doors to the poor young men of the state,[76] the editor of the Presbyterian paper said that, if so, it was because the state had not appropriated $5,000 a year to each of them as it had done to the institution at Chapel Hill. He claimed that Davidson College educated a large number of young men free of tuition and had publicly declared that no poor young man should be denied instruction because he was unable to pay his tuition.[77]

The Baptists furnished the leadership of the fight against the claim that the University was the head of the common school system. When Governor Scales, the Raleigh

[72] *Ibid.*, Feb. 25, 1885; *Morning Star*, Feb. 23, 1885; *Senate Journal, 1885*, p. 421.

[73] *Biblical Recorder*, Jan. 28, 1885; Feb. 11, 1885. *Morning Star*, Feb. 6, 1885.

[74] *Executive and Legislative Documents, Session 1885, Document No. 2*, pp. 8–11.

[75] *Biblical Recorder*, Feb. 11, 1885.

[76] See above, p. 110, footnote 61.

[77] *North Carolina Presbyterian*, Feb. 11, 1885. The denominational colleges were an acknowledged necessity for the Baptists, Methodists, and Presbyterians, who did not look to the University for their ministers.

Chronicle, and other friends of the proposed increased appropriation argued that the University formed a most important part of the common school system and therefore deserved special attention at the hands of the legislature,[78] the *Biblical Recorder* replied that, according to the constitution, the common school system and the University were separate and distinct the one from the other. Article IX, Section 2, provided for the common schools without the slightest reference to the University.[79] Only those between the ages of six and twenty-one years were included in the common school system. If the governor could make the University one of the common schools, then he would have to admit to its instruction children from six to twenty-one years of age, all free of tuition. Funds designated for the support of the common schools could be appropriated for "free public schools and for no other purpose whatsoever."[80]

It was contended, furthermore, that the Code of North Carolina, Volume 2, 1883, fully sustained this position of separation. The sections dealing with public schools said nothing whatever about the University, and the sections referring to the University made no reference to the common

[78] *Morning Star*, Jan. 23, 1885.

[79] Constitution of 1875, Article IX, Section 2, reads as follows: "The General Assembly, at its first session under this Constitution, shall provide by taxation and otherwise for a general and uniform system of public schools where intuition shall be free of charge to all children of the State between the ages of six and twenty-one years. And the children of the colored race shall be taught in separate public schools; but there shall be no discrimination in favor of, or to the prejudice of either race."

[80] *Biblical Recorder*, Feb. 11, 1885. Constitution of 1875, Article IX, Section 4: "The proceeds of all lands that have been or hereafter may be granted by the United States to this State and not otherwise appropriated by this State or the United States; also all money, stocks, bonds, and other property, now belonging to any State fund for purposes of education; also the net proceeds of all sales of swamp lands belonging to the State and all grants, gifts and devises, that have been or hereafter may be made to the State, and not otherwise appropriated by the State, or by the term of the grant, gift or devise, shall be paid into the State treasury; and together with so much of the ordinary revenue of the State as may be by law set apart of that purpose, shall be faithfully appropriated for establishing and maintaining in this State a system of free public schools, and for no other purpose whatsoever."

schools. There was, therefore, a clear bill of divorcement between the two. As further evidence it was pointed out that the public schools were under the management of a state board of education, a superintendent of public instruction, a county superintendent, and school committeemen; whereas the University was controlled by a separate and distinct board of trustees elected by the legislature.[81]

The contention was further made that the University was not only not "a most important part of the public school system," as claimed by spokesmen of the University, but was not any part of it. It had been, by virtue of Article IX, Section 5, of the Constitution of 1868.[82] But this was changed by the legislature of 1871–72, approved by a vote of the people in the general election of 1872, and ratified by the legislature of 1873.[83] The Convention of 1875, "to cut loose from the poor and contemptible free school system and to dodge the provisions of the Civil Rights legislation," designedly separated the University from the common school system. But now since the common school system had become respectable and since the Supreme Court had emasculated the Civil Rights Bill, the friends of the University, it was charged, were seemingly very anxious to remarry the University and the common schools.[84] President

[81] *Biblical Recorder*, Feb. 11, 1885. He was careful to make the idea of separation clear, for he feared the legislature might give the University not only all the money asked for but make it "a glorious, grand free school," no matter what might become of all other school interests.

[82] Constitution of 1868, Article IX, Section 5: "The University of North Carolina, with its lands, emoluments and franchises, is under the control of the State, and shall be held to an inseparable connection with the free public school system of the State."

[83] Laws of 1871–72, chap. 53; Laws of 1872–73, chap. 86.

[84] *Biblical Recorder*, Jan. 14, 1885. The Constitution of 1875 effectually divorced the University from the free public school system of the State, it was argued, and there was no marriage certificate on record to show that it was ever remarried. (Constitution of 1875, Article IX, Section 6: "The General Assembly shall have power to provide for the election of Trustees of the University of North Carolina, in whom, when chosen, shall be vested all the privileges, rights, franchises and endowments thereof in anywise granted to or conferred upon the Trustees of

C. E. Taylor of Wake Forest College reminded the friends of the University of the danger of being compelled to open the University to Negroes, if it was held to be a part of the common school system, or to give them advantages elsewhere equal in all respects to those afforded at Chapel Hill.[85] He argued that the same principle of law, which had just recently opened the first cabin of the Baltimore steamers to Negroes, would prove an embarrassment to the state institution.[86]

The denominations did not take kindly a suggestion of Professor Mangum that the state should support a college "for the sons of other denominations who have no college, and for those who cannot conscientiously attend" denominational colleges. They answered that the Presbyterians, Methodists, Baptists, Methodist Protestants, Christians, Roman Catholics, Lutherans, and Quakers had colleges, established at great sacrifice, leaving only the Episcopalians and Anti-Mission Baptists with no institution of their own. For which of these, it was asked, were the people of the state being asked to spend $30,000 a year? "They must be a peculiar people, a very important and peculiar people to make such a demand. If this is all the use there is for the University,

---

said University; and the General Assembly may make such provisions, laws, and regulations, from time to time as may be necessary and expedient for the maintenance and management of the University.") It gave the legislature the right to provide for the maintenance of the University, but attention of the legislature was called to the point that the Constitution left it to the judgment of the legislature to determine whether or not it should do so. (Constitution of 1875, Article IX, section 7: "The General Assembly shall provide that the benefits of the University, as far as practicable be extended to the youth of the State free of expense for tuition; also that all property which has heretofore accrued to the state or shall hereafter accrue, from escheats, undivided dividends or distributive shares of deceased persons, shall be appropriated to the use of the University.") The question of practicability and expediency was to be considered (*Biblical Recorder* Feb. 11, 1885).

[85] He doubtless intended, also, to suggest that even in North Carolina, during the Reconstruction period, such a "danger" had confronted the state (see above, p. 65).

[86] *Morning Star*, Feb. 24, 1885, quoting a communication from President Taylor in the Raleigh *News and Observer*.

the sooner it is disbanded the better."[87] The Baptist, Methodist, and Presbyterian people, furthermore, paid a large proportion of the taxes.[88] This argument, and others used in 1881, were renewed in the contest of 1885.[89]

[87] *Biblical Recorder*, Jan. 7, 1885.

[88] *North Carolina Presbyterian*, Feb. 11, 1885.

[89] Friends of the denominational colleges again, as in 1881, charged that the University was not keeping faith with the United States Government in the matter of the land scrip fund. It was held that the purpose of the land grant fund and, therefore, of the $7,500 turned over to the University each year by the state treasurer, was to maintain an agricultural school. "If showing the students once a session three or four old plows and explaining to them the difference between a 'harrow' and a 'turning plow,' or the difference between a 'bulltongue' and a 'scraper' constitutes a department of agriculture, then the University at Chapel Hill is properly using this $7,500" (*Biblical Recorder*, Jan. 14, 1885).

The reply of the University, given in 1881, was restated in President Battle's report to the trustees of the University in 1887 (see Battle, *op. cit.*, p. 381).

The question of using the University buildings for dances, raised by some of the preachers, created a considerable flurry in 1885. Some of the trustees agreed with the preachers; and it was decided that instead of using the library as a dance hall, a gymnasium should be built by a gymnasium association on a lot adjacent but not belonging to the University (*University Magazine*, Feb., 1885, p. 220). With money subscribed by alumni the building was built and used for dances at commencement time. At other times it was rented by the University and used as a gymnasium, the University paying a rental to finish the building and keep it in repair. The Rev. R. B. John, a Methodist alumnus of the University, criticized the move as out of harmony with popular sentiment. He shared with "W.T.J." the feeling that the faculty included men incompetent to man a university; he spoke of people who hoot at the mention of the church and declared it hard for a village pastor to lead in prayer, feeling that a member of the faculty present regarded him as "a pitiable simpleton, or a stubborn fool" for believing in prayer (*Raleigh Christian Advocate*, May 27, 1885, and *Biblical Recorder*, May 13, 1885).

W. L. Steele, one of the prominent trustees, attempted to answer the Rev. Mr. John by pointing to the fact that the gymnasium was not erected by the trustees but by private individuals and by declaring the trustees and faculty were Christian gentlemen (*Raleigh Christian Advocate*, June 15 and June 24, 1885). The depth of feeling aroused by the question of dancing is perhaps best shown by an incident related by President Battle. Referring to the wealthy trustee who had declined to "surrender to the circuit riders" and therefore to aid in building the gymnasium off the campus, he said that this trustee, who occasionally talked in his sleep, once while asleep, pending the dance controversy, was heard to burst forth, "D——d if they shall drive me out of the Campus" (Battle, *op. cit.*, pp. 314–315). Balls held regularly in the gymnasium brought forth occasional criticisms from Church leaders (*Raleigh Christian Advocate*, April 24, 1889).

A number of counterproposals were made by the denominational leaders. The suggestion made in 1881 by the *Carolina Watchman*[90] that deserving students be allowed to attend, at state expense, whatever institution they might prefer, was renewed by the Methodist and Baptist papers.[91] Seeking, as they claimed, to separate the idea of helping young men from that of helping the University, the editors proposed to let the $37,500 or an equally liberal amount be spent in paying the tuition of a certain number of young men from each county. Then upon the certificate of the faculty of the University, or of any of the chartered male colleges of the state, that they have given any number of young men tuition gratis, specifying the number, let the governor issue his warrant upon the state treasurer for the payment of the tuition charge of such young men to the institution. It was argued that this was the plan of the United States Government in educating the Indians. The Wilmington *Morning Star* thought the proposition worthy of the attention of enlightened legislators. There ought to be an endowment for the University, but it should be on "the line of building up and not tearing down" other institutions.[92] When the governor held that under the constitution the state could not help the denominational colleges, Editor Bailey replied that perhaps the governor was mis-

[90] Feb. 16, 1881.

[91] *Raleigh Christian Advocate*, Jan. 28, 1885; *Biblical Recorder*, Jan. 28, 1885.

[92] Feb. 5, 1885. This paper contended that there ought not to be any state school to tax unjustly the people against their interests and inclinations when such a tax would be applied to build up an institution that could succeed only by crushing the denominational institutions. To do so would mean that in ten years Davidson, Trinity, and Wake Forest would become mere preparatory schools or be given over to the bats and owls (*Morning Star*, Jan. 20, 1885).

"If it is deemed proper to give up for all time the true idea of an University, and to bend all energies in making Chapel Hill the great head centre for training teachers and the cultivation of the common school system, then we think the legislature might make an appropriation." But if Chapel Hill was to be a mere rival of the five or six denominational colleges and by state aid help break them down, then there would be a loud cry from one end of the state to the other (*ibid.*, Jan. 10, 1885).

taken. The denominations, under Article 1, Section 27, of the Constitution, had the right to have schools and the state was obligated to guard and maintain them. He explained that the churches did not expect any pecuniary aid from the state. "But," said he, "if this clause of the Constitution should be as literally interpreted as another to which reference has been made where 'poor' is put for the 'youth of the State', we might get it." The state had no right to draw off the patronage from all academies and colleges to their destruction. He went back to Article IX, Section 1, of the Constitution[93] and interpreted this to mean "not one central free school sustained by the state," but "schools" and the "means to education." He thought that from these two sections of the Constitution the governor ought to see his duty to do something for the other colleges of the state.[94]

Perhaps as an effort to reduce the free tuition matter to an absurdity, Editor Bailey offered the suggestion that inasmuch as the state was safely Democratic and the state treasury full, due to the selling of a railroad which had been paid for by taxing the people, the sum of $100,000 be added to the governor's proposal. This would enable the state to "board and clothe all the young men whose fathers and mothers belong to the denominations which have no denominational colleges."[95] Senator W. C. Troy,

[93] "Religion, morality, and knowledge being necessary to good government and the happiness of mankind, schools and the means of education shall forever be encouraged."

[94] *Biblical Recorder*, Feb. 11, 1885.

[95] *Ibid.*, Jan. 14, 1885. He thought this would be an admirable way to train those who could not, as Dr. Mangum said, conscientiously go to a denominational college. And then he added: "To be sure they are not a very pious class, but they have very squeamish consciences, and ought to be educated at the State's expense, even if it bankrupt the State. Then what a grand University we would have! A thousand, or it may be ten thousand, splendid young gentlemen, with exceeding light and cultivated heels and most delicate consciences, in a college so arranged that each one, in a year or two years at most, could become just what he wished to be—a teacher, a farmer, a mechanic, a scientist, a lawyer, or a gentleman of leisure!" (*ibid.*).

of Cumberland, whether seriously or otherwise, talked in terms of free transportation, room rent, and tuition at the University to five hundred students.[96] The *Biblical Recorder* referred to Troy's bill, as if he had prepared one for the purpose of providing so generously for those who would get their education at Chapel Hill, but one does not find in the Senate Journal of 1885 any reference to such a bill. President Battle evidently took seriously Troy's gesture; he said that so far from abolishing the free student feature, Troy thought the number of free students should be doubled or trebled.[97] But when the matter came to a test in the legislature, Troy voted against the bill to appropriate even $15,000 annually.[98]

Having heard already from the church colleges and anticipating still further opposition, the leaders of the University prepared to fight for the state institution.[99] The trustees appointed a committee to present the claims of the institution upon the legislature.[100] The committee prepared a memorial.[101] They told the legislature that it was the duty of the trustees, under the constitution of the state, to present to the legislature the fullest information as to the necessities and conditions of the institution, that there was a crisis in the affairs of the University, whose income was not equal to its expenses, and that unless help came from the state, the University would have to go backward on a course that would end finally in death. They

[96] *Biblical Recorder*, Feb. 11, 1885.

[97] Battle, *op. cit.*, p. 307.

[98] *Senate Journal, 1885*, p. 422.

[99] *Raleigh Register*, Feb. 11, 1885; Battle, *op. cit.*, p. 304.

[100] Raleigh *News and Observer*, Feb. 6, 1885. The committee was composed of President Battle, an Episcopalian, the Rev. N. H. D. Wilson, a Methodist, and Charles M. Cooke, a Baptist. Julian S. Carr, a prominent Methodist layman, however, served on the committee in the place of the Rev. Mr. Wilson (*Raleigh Register*, Feb. 11, 1885).

[101] *Senate Journal, 1885*, pp. 224–262. The House transmitted a communication from the governor, with the memorial of the committee of the trustees of the University, and the House recommended that the memorial be printed. The Senate concurred in the proposal to print.

stated, furthermore, that the institution had to have additional professors and improved laboratory and library facilities and itemized professorships and improvements aggregating $17,100 annually. They made it quite clear, also, that the matter of free tuition was not involved.[102] It was neither the purpose nor the desire of the University to come in collision with other institutions. And the trustees proposed to render an account every year showing plainly how the money appropriated by the state had been spent.[103]

Overman was aided in the leadership of the fight in the legislature by a number of prominent Presbyterians, including Augustus Leazar, a graduate of Davidson College, Colonel Thomas M. Holt, an alumnus and a trustee of Davidson College, who later became lieutenant governor and governor of the state, and John D. Stanford, a Davidson alumnus who became a Presbyterian minister.[104] A number of amendments were offered, some proposing to reduce the amount of increase to $7,500, some to $5,000 annually.[105] The amount of $15,000, as set forth in the bill, however, was voted, with the understanding that $2,000 formerly given to the University for its summer school, should be placed at the disposal of the Board of Education for the support of other normal schools.[106] The total amount given to the University, including the $5,000 given in 1881 and the $7,500 made available in 1875 to restore the income from the land scrip fund, now was $27,500.[107]

[102] Before the bill had gone very far, the proposed increase from one to two county students from each county was eliminated, thus freeing the measure of one of its most objectionable features, from the standpoint of the denominational colleges, and leaving the situation, so far as free tuition was concerned, where it was before.

[103] Raleigh *News and Observer*, Feb. 6, 1885; *Raleigh Register*, Feb. 11, 1885; Wilmington *Morning Star*, Feb. 13, 1885; also Feb. 19, 1885.

[104] Battle, *op. cit.*, p. 305.

[105] *House Journal, 1885*, p. 402; *Senate Journal, 1885*, p. 421.

[106] *House Journal, 1885*, p. 419; *Senate Journal, 1885*, p. 422; Battle, *op. cit.*, p. 307.

[107] *Morning Star*, Feb. 23, 1885.

The legislature of 1885 continued, with only slight modifications,[108] the plan whereby one student from each county might receive free tuition at the University. The denominational leaders, however, obtained no little satisfaction, no doubt, from the fact that in 1881 and in 1885, when efforts were made to double the number of free students, they withstood these attempts and held the number to the minimum. They also felt that they had won the contention that the institution at Chapel Hill should not be a free school and that the people had determined that it should be a university in fact.[109] Some of the church papers, which had fought so ardently against the increased appropriations, advised that inasmuch as the bill had become a law it should be submitted to by all good citizens, and expressed the wish that the University's sphere of influence might be greatly enlarged.[110] There were those among the denominational groups, however, who did not take the situation quite so gracefully. Some continued to express misgivings for the fate of the denominational colleges and to write articles seeking to show that the institution at Chapel Hill was neither a university nor representative of the people of the state.[111]

[108] *Morning Star*, March 6, 1885; Battle, *op. cit.*, p. 307. A competitive examination, after due notice publicly given, was required, and the obligation on county students to teach in the public schools of the state was repealed.

[109] *Biblical Recorder*, March 11, 1885.

[110] *Ibid.*, March 4, 1885; *Raleigh Christian Advocate*, June 10, 1885.

[111] *Biblical Recorder*, March 18, 1885; March 25, 1885; April 1, 1885; April 22, 1885; May 13, 1885.

"W.T.J.," in the last of a series of three articles, charged the University with receiving students whose bad morals had driven them from other colleges and with permitting students entering upright in their lives to go away from the institution "ruined in morals, in manners, and in character." He alleged, furthermore, that "Chapel Hill" had been run too much in the interest of a denomination which had no college of its own but had managed "by tricky, political legislation" to obtain money for the education of its sons "from the rest of us." He took a fling at the legislature which had included among the twenty-one new trustees chosen for the University "a Baptist or two, a Methodist or two, and a Presbyterian or two"; he regarded this action as a 'bone to Towser,' "who knows it is not sound, though he may eat it." He suggested, in conclusion, that the University ought to change its name to "The State Episcopal School at Chapel Hill."

The *Morning Star*, referring to the selection of new trustees, said that "with

One of the significant outcomes of the contest of 1885 was progress toward placing the University on a sound educational basis. Increased appropriations without permission to increase the number of students receiving free tuition enabled the trustees to increase the faculty from nine to fifteen members.[112] And this gain to higher educational standards was increased in 1887 when in response, in part at least, to criticisms from the denominational groups, the legislature withdrew the $7,500 appropriated in 1875 to make good the income from the land scrip fund and repealed the county student law.[113]

Before 1887 it was the practice of the University to admit certain students without examination. The law required the county students to be admitted into the branches relating to agriculture and the mechanic arts without taking the examination which the University required of those admitted into the classical curriculum. Some of the county students who were teachers desired to learn some elementary Latin and Greek, and the faculty assigned undergraduate students to instruct them. This had led to the criticism that the University had established a preparatory department, and was therefore injuring the preparatory schools.[114]

---

the usual modesty that characterizes legislators they only took seven from among themselves. The selections were made adroitly and take in most of the denominations." Lee S. Overman, Julian S. Carr, J. H. Horner, T. H. Pritchard, and Richard H. Battle were among those elected.

[112] Although Battle (*op. cit.*, p. 335) declares the denominational affiliation of those elected in 1885 was not known and, therefore, not considered by the trustees, it is interesting to note that two of the new members were Baptists, one a Methodist, two Presbyterians, and one a Congregationalist.

[113] *House Journal, 1887*, p. 276; *State Chronicle*, March 10, 1887. Governor Daniel L. Russell thought it quite proper to help deserving young men. A limited number of free students did not add appreciably to the expense of maintaining the University, and this state aid did not subtract materially from the efficiency of the public schools. The money saved by withdrawing the scholarships would extend the public schools only a little over a day each year. He thought complaints from the denominational colleges should be heard with the deference due to their authors, who should be made to feel that the state rejoiced in their growing prosperity and power. But the University is a part of the state and as such must be preserved (*Executive and Legislative Documents, 1887, Document A*, pp. 14–15).

[114] *Raleigh Register*, Feb. 11, 1885.

The transfer of the land scrip fund to Raleigh cost the University $7,500 a year, but it removed the possibility of the criticism, by the denominational leaders, the farmers' organizations, or anyone else, that the University was defrauding the farmers and mechanics. It also made it possible for the University to maintain a uniform standard of admission; it was no longer necessary to lower the standard to a point where the boys from the remote country places might enter. With relief from the necessity of teaching agriculture and the mechanic arts, the institution at Chapel Hill began, as President Battle said, "to develop the institution along the lines of the most approved universities. . . without being embarrassed by the constant demand to build stables and workshops, buy prize cattle and modern machinery."[115]

By 1888 the University was beginning to feel itself upon a rather solid financial and educational footing. Twenty thousand dollars annually was regularly forthcoming from the state treasury to supplement the income from other sources.[116] It was beginning to feel, also, that it was taking on the ways of a university. With the addition of instructors in 1885 came the offering of postgraduate courses leading to the degrees of Master of Arts, Master of Philosophy, and Doctor of Philosophy, additions to the various museums and laboratories, the combining of the libraries of the University and the two literary societies totaling over twenty thousand volumes, and other improvements, which enabled President Battle to advertise, in 1885 and 1887, the University's claim to a place in the front rank of educational institutions.[117]

[115] Battle, *History of the University of North Carolina*, II, 377–378.

[116] Eighty-six years after the institution at Chapel Hill was chartered, it had never received an annual appropriation of any amount from the legislature. It took ninety-two years to get the first annual appropriation—$5,000. On its hundredth birthday it was receiving $20,000 a year.

[117] Battle, *op. cit.*, pp. 337–338; 379–382. The graduate courses were offered to graduates of any institution without tuition charge, a fact which was doubtless intended, among other things, to curry the favor of the denominational colleges of the state (*ibid.*, p. 337).

The period from 1886 to 1892 was one of comparative, though far from absolute, freedom from the friction which had kept the leaders of church and state arrayed against each other before this time. The outstanding example of sectarian jealousy arose from an alleged discrimination against one of the denominations when the faculty was increased in 1885. Although the trustees had sought to avoid criticisms such as those hurled at them on former occasions when additions were made to the faculty, their caution had availed but little.[118] This time it was the Christian denomination that felt left out, and said so. It had offered a candidate, Professor Kernodle, who was one among 107 applicants for the position of assistant professor of pure mathematics; and President Battle had recommended and the trustees had elected James Lee Love, a Presbyterian, a graduate of the University and a relative of one prominently identified with the institution. The Christians felt that favoritism had brought an injustice to them and their candidate.[119] President Battle replied to the editor of the *Christian Observer*, declaring that there was no real foundation to the accusation that he had treated the Christians with injustice.[120]

[118] The trustees advertised the creation of new chairs and invited persons interested in securing positions to file their credentials. The applicants ran into the hundreds, making necessary the employment of a man to classify them and to make an abstract of the qualifications and testimonials (Battle, *op. cit.*, pp. 333, 335).

[119] *Ibid.*, pp. 336–337.

[120] Addresses and Papers of Kemp P. Battle, containing an undated clipping from the *Christian Observer;* also undated clipping from the *Caucasian.*

Commenting on the election of Professor Eben Alexander, a graduate of Yale, professor of Greek, the *State Chronicle* (edited by a Presbyterian whose wife was an Episcopalian) took occasion to chide those denominational groups for their alleged deep concern about the denominational complexion of the University faculty. The editor prophesied that "What church does he belong to?" would be the first question asked by three-fourths of the readers of his paper. He added: "The Methodists, who have fewer professors than any other denomination, expected that a member of their church would be elected to this chair. And relying on the former precedents they had a right to expect this, and two distinguished Armenian scholars had filed their applications, either of whom would have brought a reputation with him to the University. But unhappily—for the Methodist

The Presbyterians, as usual, took the lead in efforts to restore friendly relationships between denominational and state institutions. The *North Carolina Presbyterian* had remained silent for a long time and looked on while numerous Baptists and Methodists and some Christians criticized the University, perhaps sharing with them some of their resentment of the Episcopalian influence at Chapel Hill and no doubt thankful that it was the Episcopalians rather than the Presbyterians who were receiving the darts which, before the reopening, were hurled at the Presbyterians. In 1888 the editor urged: "Stop it! Not the University but the false, persistent and interminable charge of sectarian jealousy and hatred of the same."[121] Reviewing the profound interest of Presbyterians in the University's welfare from its foundation, the large number of presidents and professors furnished by the Presbyterian church, and the large number of Presbyterian students who had received their education at Chapel Hill, the Presbyterian Synod of 1888, moreover, declared that what was true as to the interest felt by Presbyterians in the University in the past was no less true in 1888.[122]

---

brethren, some days ago one of these gentlemen was elected to a professorship at Vanderbilt University and the salary of the other one was raised and both withdrew their applications. The Methodists therefore are estopped from making any complaints. The Baptists are satisfied with the election because they secured two professors last year. We hope that the Jews, Greeks, and Mesopotamians will raise no cry about having too many Calvinists in the faculty and that we will not have a repetition of the newspaper war that the last election brought about" (*State Chronicle*, July 1, 1886).

[121] *North Carolina Presbyterian*, June 20, 1888. Like Dr. Battle, he restricted this charge of sectarian jealousy and hatred of the University to the churches which had denominational colleges—the Baptists, Methodists, and Presbyterians, in particular. Dr. Battle excepted also the Quakers and Guilford College, the Reformed Church and Catawba College, the Christians and Elon College, the Lutherans and Mount Pleasant College—small denominations which did not enter vigorously into the fight alongside the friends of Wake Forest, Trinity, and Davidson (Battle, *op. cit.*, p. 308).

[122] *Minutes of the Synod of North Carolina, 1888*, p. 244; *North Carolina Presbyterian*, Nov. 28, 1888.

A large proportion of the professors were distinguished Presbyterians, and of the one hundred and seventy-five students enrolled in 1888, more than one-fourth

Forces were at work among the Methodists and Baptists, also, to improve the relationships and to restore a spirit of co-operation between the denominational institutions and the University. Speaking at the laying of a corner-stone at Trinity College in Durham in 1890, former Governor Jarvis, a Methodist layman, declared, "We are bringing Trinity nearer our State University, geographically speaking,[123] and I urge that we bring it nearer to that honored institution in sympathy and in earnest co-operation in the advancement of the general educational work of the State."[124] Denying the allegation of the *Charlotte Chronicle* that every religious denomination in the state more or less antagonized public education, moreover, the *Raleigh Christian Advocate* called attention to the large percentage of students at Chapel Hill who were Methodists and added that quite a number of the trustees and some of the warmest friends of the institution were Methodists.[125] The *Biblical Recorder*, for the Baptists, put in a similar disclaimer. It admitted that Baptists had vigorously opposed the county student law, because it was then being grossly abused, and took the credit for securing the change of the law and the transfer of the $7,500 from the University to the Agricultural and Mechanical College at Raleigh. The *Recorder* dismissed the matter by alleging that a few "feeble-minded people howled" about this and disclaiming responsibility for the "raving of such people."[126]

State Superintendent of Public Instruction S. M. Finger took advantage of the temporary calm after the storm of

---

were of Presbyterian families. There were half as many Presbyterians at Chapel Hill as at Davidson College.

[123] Trinity was being moved from Randolph County to Durham.

[124] *State Chronicle*, Nov. 13, 1890. Reminding his audience there was an abundance of room for both, he begged that there be no bickerings between them. "I appeal to the friends of these two institutions and to those of all other institutions of learning in the State to see to it that no jealousies shall rise up among any of them."

[125] *Ibid.*, May 26, 1891.

[126] *Biblical Recorder*, May 27, 1891.

1881 and 1885, moreover, to help bring about a friendly feeling between the denominational and the state institutions. He declared in favor of the liberal support of the public schools, including the University, and the careful fostering of the private denominational colleges.[127]

President Battle, always in favor of any innovation or enterprise that might win the favor of the churches, furthermore, joined with his faculty in 1888 in inaugurating the custom of choosing a preacher once a month to deliver a sermon in Gerrard Hall on Sunday evening, the University paying the expenses of the preacher. Care was taken to invite influential preachers from the leading denominations, in order not only to provide a succession of instructive discourses, but also to win the favor of these leaders. President Battle himself declared that the plan was successful; there had been a marked diminution of hostility to the University as a result of this policy.[128]

Another method used by the University of honoring influential preachers, and hoping to win their favor or to make it more secure, was to award honorary degrees. In 1876 the degree of Doctor of Divinity was conferred upon two ministers; in 1877, upon three; 1878, two; 1879, one 1880, four; 1881, two; 1882, three; 1883, one; 1884, three; 1887, two; 1888, one. The degree of Doctor of Laws was conferred upon one minister in 1877, two in 1881, two in 1883, one in 1887, and one in 1888. The presidents of Trinity, Wake Forest, and Davidson, moreover, were given honorary degrees in 1889, President John F. Crowell of Trinity and President Charles E. Taylor of Wake Forest receiving the degree of Doctor of Letters, and President W. J. Martin of Davidson, the degree of Doctor of Laws. Professor W. B. Royall of Wake Forest also was given the

[127] *Annual Report of State Superintendent of Public Instruction, 1887–1888*, pp. xxxviii, xxxix. He did not think, however, that there was a religious denomination in the state which was not able to endow, liberally, an institution of learning; he was glad that most of them were moving in that direction.

[128] Battle, *op. cit.*, p. 365.

degree of Doctor of Laws. Of all the seventy-nine doctorates either given or earned at the University of North Carolina between 1876 and 1889, thirty-six were given to ministers and presidents and professors in denominational colleges, mostly ministers.[129] Even the Raleigh *Chronicle*, staunch supporter of the University, commenting on "the business of conferring honorary degrees," admitted that those awarded by the University were "judiciously placed."[130]

It should be noted here that, although until 1887 each county could send one student to Chapel Hill free of charge for tuition, the legislature of 1887 eliminated the one-to-the-county provision. It made it possible for free tuition to be given to four classes of young men: (1) sons of ministers, (2) candidates for the ministry, (3) cripples and deformed boys, and (4) young men intending to teach. It also reduced the tuition rate and authorized the faculty to take unsecured notes from poor young men for their tuition.[131] The substitutes for the county student law were, as the *State Chronicle* prophesied, the next thing to making the University free to all.[132] How this new situation affected the relationships between the University and the denominational colleges, however, is treated in detail in the next chapter. Sufficient is it here to point out that so intent were the denominational colleges upon the elimination of the free tuition arrangement at the University that, having carried their point, they doubtless failed to scrutinize very carefully the substitute provisions. A little experience was necessary to show how the new arrangement would work out.

In the midst of the struggle to put the University of North Carolina upon a sound financial and educational

[129] Battle, *op. cit.*, pp. 114, 133, 156, 175, 196, 238, 256, 266, 286, 332, 363, 388, 397, 439.

[130] *Morning Star*, Feb. 18, 1885, quoting the *Chronicle*.

[131] *State Chronicle*, March 10, 1887.

[132] *Ibid.*

basis, while the denominational leaders were hurling verbal brickbats at the administration at Chapel Hill and receiving honorary degrees in return, there was a progressive tendency toward the secularization of the control of the University. Three of the four presidents and acting presidents serving the University before 1835, and a large percentage of the professors were ministers. In 1835 the board of trustees adopted the policy of giving the presidency to laymen only. Not since 1835 has a minister served the institution at Chapel Hill as president, except during the short period of the Reconstruction regime,[133] although some of the professors have been ministers. Gradually the number of ministers in the faculty decreased. When in 1890 the Reverend A. W. Mangum, professor of moral and mental philosophy, died, in the midst of much discussion as to his successor, Josephus Daniels, editor of the *State Chronicle*, close to the administration at Chapel Hill, stated, editorially, that it was not only not necessary to elect a preacher but a preacher ought not to be selected unless a man of great ability and promise.[134] And Walter Hines Page, speaking at the inauguration of Dr. George Tayloe Winston, who succeeded President Battle in 1891, advised President Winston to "renounce forever all servitude to ecclesiasticism and partyism," to remember that the "day of compromise is done," and to have nothing whatever to do with "every narrow ecclesiastical prejudice that shall demand tribute."[135]

Another indication of the extent to which secularization had gone at Chapel Hill at the close of President Battle's administration in 1891 is the fact that, whereas up to that time a number of ministers has served on the board of trustees, including eleven in the period of Dr. Battle's presidency, not one minister was added to the board after 1889. Two, the Reverend W. S. Black and the Reverend J. H. Cordon, were made trustees in 1889, the latter's term

[133] The Reverend Solomon Pool was then president.

[134] *State Chronicle*, June 3, 1890.

[135] Battle, *op. cit.*, p. 466.

expiring in 1893. The Reverend Mr. Black and the Reverend T. H. Pritchard, who became a trustee in 1885, served until 1897, when they were succeeded by laymen. In 1897 and for a number of years thereafter all the members of the board of trustees of the University of North Carolina were laymen.[136] Of the one hundred members of the board at the present time, only two or three are ministers.[137]

[136] *Idid.*, pp. 786–793, containing a list of the trustees since the reopening.
[137] *University of North Carolina Record*, March 5, 1937, pp. 5–7.

IV

The Crisis in the Conflicts in Higher Education

THE last decade of the nineteenth century experienced the fiercest contest ever waged between the forces of church and state in education in North Carolina. At the time the churches first sought charters to establish denominational colleges and in the decades following, as has been shown, there arose issues which, modified with the changing conditions of the passing decades, have recurred to perplex educational leaders in the state. Most of the issues which arose rooted back in a group of related questions, centering chiefly about moral and religious influences at Chapel Hill, financial support, and rivalry for students. The contest of the nineties was based upon residuary issues; many of the old issues and arguments were continued or revived. With increased financial support to the University, supplied principally by public taxation, went greatly intensified and almost frantic opposition on the part of some of the denominations and denominational institutions, which found difficulty in maintaining themselves, in an era of depression, against what they regarded as unfair competition. And although, as has been pointed out, following the fierce and prolonged battle in the legislature of 1885, there was a temporary suspension of hostilities between the opposing forces, with no major engagements on the sector of higher education during the latter eighties and early nineties, there is abundant evidence that the period of the truce was also a period of rapid reinforcement and careful preparation for another major offensive which broke out in the legislature of 1893.

By 1892 had begun again the rumblings of discontent. Smouldering feelings began to express themselves. Old unsettled, or only temporarily adjusted, problems rose again. There were reasons. The state, which before 1890 was competing with the churches in two institutions, the University and the Agricultural and Mechanical College, chartered a third in 1891, the State Normal and Industrial Institute, bringing competition to the women's colleges and adding them to the side of the opposition.[1] Then, too, an economic depression had begun to be felt. Short crops, low prices, and the consequent financial stress, not to say distress, were weighing heavily upon the denominational institutions. Whereas in 1891 some of the denominational colleges were reporting a larger number of students than ever before, and were telling their constituency it had become necessary, in order to accommodate the increasing number of students knocking at their doors for admission, to "press steadily forward in the establishment of new chairs, [and] the improvement of the increase of endowment," in 1892 they were crestfallen.[2] The Baptists, for example, with 233 students enrolled at Wake Forest in 1890–91, were talking of getting ready for 500 students. But the trustees reported to the Baptist State Convention in the winter of 1892 only 185 students enrolled, with the number not likely to go over 200.[3] Yet the State University was enjoying an increased patronage.[4] The denominational leaders did not charge the depression with the full responsibility, or even the major part of the responsibility, for the decrease in students at their institutions. Sharp competition by the State University, competition "more serious at present than in former years," was mainly responsible, or so they thought.[5] The church institutions, moreover, did not

[1] *House Journal, 1891*, pp. 135, 159, 167, 802; *Senate Journal, 1891*, pp. 133, 140, 148, 151, 156, 157, 164, 166, 173, 248, 277, 353, 413.

[2] *Minutes Baptist State Convention, 1891*, p. 45.

[3] *Ibid., 1892*, pp. 44–45.

[4] *Biblical Recorder*, Jan. 18, 1893.

[5] *Minutes Baptist State Convention, 1892*, pp. 44–45. The state's gift of $240 tuition for four years was drawing young men from the church colleges and making it harder to get them to pay tuition at these colleges.

"The recent increase in patronage at the State University is believed to be, in some degree, at the expense of patronage lost by other institutions" (Charles

get the relief expected from the repeal of the county student law in 1887.[6] The idea prevailed, at least among certain denominational leaders, that the laws of 1887 were abused. President Taylor, of Wake Forest, for example, complained that, according to prevailing ideas, fees were remitted at Chapel Hill, and some felt that the unsecured notes accepted were not collected and were, therefore, a device for issuing an unlimited number of free scholarships.[7]

Methodists were deploring "the growing number of State institutions of learning, which with their cheap rates and hundreds of scholarships" were appealing strongly for the patronage of Methodist people.[8] The Methodists, too, one sees, were feeling the effect of competition, and they were attempting to do something about it.

Before the end of 1893, therefore, some of the denominations, notably the Baptists and Methodists, were becoming desperate. They had become extremely fearful of a state

---

E. Taylor's letter to W. H. Kitchen, Jan. 11, 1895, published in *Biblical Recorder*, Jan. 18, and in *Raleigh Christian Advocate*, Jan. 25).

[6] *State Chronicle*, Feb. 12, 1893. The trustees of Wake Forest, referring to the large number of free scholarships provided at the University, admitted that some of them were provided not by taxation but by donation, and to them they did not object "when properly used." Baptists and friends of Wake Forest, nevertheless, were admonished to face squarely the consequences of such competition, to be "wide awake and eagle-eyed" that they might meet most wisely and overcome most successfully all influences that might diminish or endanger the patronage of Wake Forest, and to project and execute such plans as would enlarge the usefulness of their ancient and beloved institution (*Minutes Baptist State Convention, 1892*, pp. 44-45).

[7] Raleigh *News and Observer*, Feb. 23, 1893.

[8] Dr. John Franklin Crowell had just been made president of Trinity College, and had set about to arouse the Methodist constituency to a high pitch of enthusiasm for their chief institution and to build up a system of high schools or preparatory schools as feeders for Trinity. State-wide Methodist educational conventions were held, in Durham in 1891 and in Charlotte in 1892, for the purpose of the unification of Methodist education in North Carolina, and a number of mass meetings were held in several presiding elders' districts to point out the advantages of an education, to counteract the tendency among Methodist families to send their children to institutions of other denominations or to non-sectarian institutions, and to raise money for endowment (*Raleigh Christian Advocate*, Jan. 18, Jan. 27, Feb. 24, April 13, April 20, and July 13, 1892; *Minutes Western North Carolina Conference, 1892*, p. 41).

monopoly in higher education. To some of their leaders it appeared that they would at least be limited to the training of ministerial students if they did not actually suffer the extinction of their colleges.[9] Presbyterians shared in this fear to some extent. At any rate, President J. B. Shearer, of Davidson College, shared it sufficiently to become quite actively allied with President Taylor of Wake Forest, and others, in efforts to forestall what to them seemed impending disaster for their institutions.[10]

Several important events helped to precipitate the crisis, which came between 1895 and 1898. Facing the situation just described,[11] friends of the state institutions, including Governor Thomas M. Holt, doubtless added to the discontent of the churchmen by trying to show that the conflict between the church and state institutions was entirely imaginary.[12] Friends of the University refuted the impression that a large amount of free tuition was given at the Univer-

[9] *Minutes Western North Carolina Conference, 1893*, p. 38; *Minutes Baptist State Convention, 1893*, pp. 54–55; *Public Documents, 1893, No. 1*, pp. 30–31.

[10] See below, p. 137.

[11] See above, pp. 133–134.

[12] *Public Documents, 1893, No. 1*, pp. 30–31. In his biennial message to the legislature of 1893, Governor Holt discussed at length the University and church colleges. As a member of the legislature of 1885 he had aided in making the appropriation for the University. Contrary to the prophecy of some at that time that the success of the University would be the destruction of the church colleges, during the eight years that had elapsed every church college in the state had increased its endowment fund, its equipment for instruction, and the number of its students. He prophesied that when the University should come to have a thousand students, every church college would have twice as many as they then had; and he argued that the state of North Carolina needed a University quite as fully as any denomination within its borders needed a college. He thought there was need for both. Illustrating the possibility of being loyal to church colleges and to the University, Governor Holt called attention to the fact that he was a member of the board of trustees and, for a long time, both of the executive committee and of the finance committee of Davidson College. He professed his loyalty to his church college and to the University of his state. He maintained that the University management was free from bias, prejudice or prepossession, political, social, local, or religious, and that the young men of the state were welcomed to its opportunities, "regardless of whether they be rich or poor, Democrats, Republicans or Populists, Baptists, Methodists, Catholics, Hebrews, Friends, Christians, Lutherans, Episcopalians, or Presbyterians."

sity. It was maintained that free tuition was given only to those of the four classes permitted by law, and that only eighteen persons were thus benefited during the session of 1892–93, out of a student body of 317 at Chapel Hill.[13]

The governor's message called for more discussion. At least one member of the legislature called for more facts concerning what the churches wanted, and got them.[14] President Taylor, of Wake Forest, gave his ideas not only to Representative Kitchen but also directly to President Winston, of the University. He complained that as long as the state continued to seek for about the same class of patronage as that desired by the denominational colleges, the latter would have to surrender their hopes of expansion and of vigorous life, or they would have to "purchase success at the cost of constant friction and irritation." He insisted, therefore, upon three changes: (1) the repeal of the free tuition enactment,[15] (2) the taking of no more unsecured notes, and (3) the immediate elevation of the standard of admission into the University and the gradual elimination of the lower studies, so as to complete a system and provide a plan for all the colleges then being "either quietly

[13] There were six sons of ministers, two candidates for the ministry, one cripple, and nine young men intending to teach. It was admitted that the University was unable to obtain cash payments from all of its students and that some gave notes with security when security could be obtained. Of the twenty-two notes taken during the current term, fifteen were secured and seven unsecured, the unsecured being given by persons who had no property and whose parents had no property. There were about seventy scholarships given at the University, this number having been made possible by endowment. There could be nothing unfair about this, for had not a large-hearted man just endowed sixty scholarships at Trinity? (see *State Chronicle*, Feb. 12, 1893, which quoted an unnamed correspondent, who had obtained facts from the annual report of President Winston).

[14] W. H. Kitchen wrote directly to the president of each denominational college for his views on (1) the relations which exist or ought to exist between the University and church colleges, (2) free tuition, (3) educational standards, etc. (*Biblical Recorder*, Jan. 18, 1893).

[15] "... all free tuition at the University ought to be prohibited by the Legislature except so far as it may be provided for by private beneficence" (Charles E. Taylor's letter to W. H. Kitchen, Jan. 11, 1893, published in *Biblical Recorder*, Jan. 18, and in the *Raleigh Christian Advocate*, Jan. 25, 1893).

ignored or tolerated as excrescences upon the present system."[16]

In line with one of President Taylor's demands, "A Bill to Unify the Higher Education in the State and to Elevate the University to the Apex of All Education in the State" was introduced into the legislature of 1893.[17] The provisions of this bill, briefly, were gradually to make the University an institution for graduate and professional work only and to limit the colleges to undergraduate courses, allowing the latter the privilege of awarding bachelor and honorary degrees.[18] The bill got nowhere in the legislature, but it stirred the secular press to write sharply and other friends of the University to ridicule the proposals.[19] Doubtless frightened a bit by the audacity of

[16] "The University should be the apex of the pyramid, the crown of the dome in the State's educational system. . . . For such a university, but not for free education, the General Assembly should make such appropriation as may be necessary (*ibid.*; see also *News and Observer*, Feb. 23, 1893, quoting letter of President Taylor to President Winston, dated Feb. 7).

President Taylor told President Winston that on account of similar curricula at Chapel Hill and Wake Forest, the idea was abroad at Wake Forest that a young man could leave Wake Forest at the beginning of his senior year and take at Chapel Hill the same diploma that he would have received at Wake Forest, this idea creating a ferment at Wake Forest among advanced students ambitious for political preferment. He said there were forty-five fewer students at Wake Forest in the spring semester of 1893 than in the fall of 1892, "due to the energy with which the policy of the trustees of the University has been pressed."

[17] *Senate Journal, 1893*, p. 418. President J. B. Shearer, of Davidson College, is credited with the authorship of this bill, which came to be known as the Apex bill (*University Magazine*, April, 1893, p. 229; Battle, *op. cit.*, p. 479).

[18] *News and Observer*, Feb. 17, 1893; *State Chronicle*, Feb. 14, 1893.

It proposed to abolish the freshman class at the University in eighteen months, the sophomore class four years thereafter, and the junior and senior classes within ten years. The annual appropriation of $20,000 was to be increased $3,000 each year for ten years, so that at the end of the ten-year period the state would be spending $50,000 a year of tax money on its "real" University at Chapel Hill.

[19] *Senate Journal, 1893*, p. 418. The *State Chronicle* branded it "the wildest scheme we have known to be introduced in the legislature in our experience of public affairs" and thought it should be entitled "A Bill to Abolish the University." It argued that there was no institution in America of the sort proposed, that Harvard had sixteen hundred undergraduates, and that there were only five graduate students at Chapel Hill, and that it would be impossible to sustain an institution of learning in North Carolina with higher requirements than those then existing

the proposal, they decided it better to laugh than to cry, and proceeded to laugh the bill out of court. They sought to treat the matter as a joke. An anonymous letter, credited by some to President Winston of the University, pretended to understand the proposal to be to move the institution from Chapel Hill to Apex, a very small village in an adjoining county.[20] The *State Chronicle* declared it would be more sensible and more practicable to move the University to Apex than to do with it as was proposed in the Shearer bill.[21]

---

in Oxford and Cambridge or Harvard and Yale. The people could not pay taxes for such an institution, whose doors would be closed to nine-tenths of the counties of the state. It would be an institution for the few and the rich, supported by the many. Already the University was doing admirable work, with standards of scholarship recognized at Harvard to be equal to the standards of Yale, Columbia, Cornell, and other great universities, and was helping poor boys with scholarships (*State Chronicle*, Feb. 14, 1893).

[20] Battle, *op. cit.*, p. 480.

[21] Feb. 14, 1893. When before a large and select audience, in the office of the Superintendent of Public Instruction in Raleigh, President Shearer set forth the scheme in detail, some sought to make merriment of the occasion. Presidents Shearer, Taylor, and Winston, and others were reported as exchanging sincere compliments, and the fun among the speeches was "enjoyed by all" (*News and Observer*, Feb. 21, 1893). The *University Magazine* (April, 1893, pp. 229–230) made interesting comment on the bill. It declared: "Considerable interest in the University has been manifested recently by college men. The President of Davidson College, after long and profound cogitation, brought forth in Raleigh a plan to 'elevate the University to the *Apex* of the school system of the state.' " "The President of Wake Forest followed the lead of the sturdy Calvinist *haud passibus aequis*. A conference of college presidents was called 'to view' the situation. The conference was said to be long, harmonious, and enjoyable. Everybody was friendly to the University and anxious to help it. This anxiety increased as the Bill for Repairs was introduced. Telegrams passed rapidly and the winged messengers of Jove again summoned the college men together. Greater zeal than ever was manifested for the noble old University. The 'Apex man' was there with increased vigor and *proximus ardet Ucalegon.*' The Joint Committee on Education was amazed to see such desire to build up the University. 'Give it $50,000 a year,' said one college president. 'Put it at the *Apex* of glory and usefulness,' said another. The committee was reminded of the darkey who hugged his sweetheart to death."

In the midst of these discussions there appeared in the *News and Observer* (Feb. 24, 1893) a letter written by Prof. J. L. Armstrong, of Trinity College, which pleased the friends of the University very much. Professor Armstrong decried the repeated contests concerning the University and held that educational leaders

Seeming to get nowhere with their efforts in the legislature of 1893, the church leaders turned to the people. Very definitely, very resolutely, they set out to produce such a "ground swell" of public opinion as to produce an eruption violent enough to make the lawmakers pay attention. The years 1893–94, therefore, were years of continuous agitation and controversy. For these two years both sides pointed to the legislature of 1895. Church papers, especially the *Biblical Recorder*, carried numerous articles and editorials.[22] President Taylor contributed a series of articles to the Baptist paper in 1893, which were commended by the trustees of Wake Forest College and the Chowan Baptist Association, and were, in 1894, reprinted in a forty-six page booklet, entitled *How Far Should a State Undertake to Educate?* and distributed widely over the state.[23] Presi-

could not afford to fall out among themselves. He held that the Israelites in Egyptian bondage did not have such hard conditions put upon them as were proposed for the University, for, said he, "the taskmasters did not require the tale of brick while failing to furnish both straw and clay." He thought it a reflection on the colleges if they could not hold their own with the University.

[22] March 7, 1894. The *Biblical Recorder* resented the statements which some made that the Baptists of North Carolina were contending for the destruction of the University. Baptists had more character and intelligence than to desire its destruction. They were contending for "a principle—broad, well known and clearly defined."

[23] President Taylor's booklet was primarily an appeal to the people. Revealing not only his willingness to trust the people but also his fears for the consequences to denominational colleges if the people should decide against his contentions, President Taylor declared: "Their will, when they have clearly understood the issues, and secured recognition of its expression, will be the end of the complaint and controversy. But, if they shall say that it is right and expedient for the State to occupy the whole field of higher as well as lower education at the present time, and that they believe that the State is competent to do so adequately, then the occupation of many of the colleges will soon be gone, and upon their portals will be written 'Ichabod',—'their glory is departed' " (see his booklet, p. 43). Dr. Durham, chairman of the Baptist Convention's committee on this matter, said his committee decided to fight the question out before the people (*News and Observer*, March 6, 1895).

Twenty-five thousand copies were circulated. These were paid for by Dr. Columbus Durham, who, by surrendering a life insurance policy, financed the publication of these booklets. The Baptist State Convention, in 1895, raised the money and repaid the amount advanced by Dr. Durham (*Minutes Baptist State Convention, 1895*, p. 58).

dent Taylor, Dr. Durham, and others also spoke at various times and places over the state, chiefly to church groups.[24]

Church bodies decided to make another appeal to the next legislature. The Western North Carolina Conference, preferring a proper adjustment to a progressive antagonism, appointed a committee to present a petition to the legislature of 1895 "to establish such an order in the higher schools under its control" as would obviate this conflict of work and interest.[25] The Baptists adopted a similar resolution and appointed a similar committee.[26]

Friends of the state institutions, being concerned chiefly with securing the legislature's favorable vote on appropriation bills, were wise enough, in the main, to be guarded in their statements and movements. The Taylor articles and pamphlets, nevertheless, caused them to be up in arms, and some of them made personal attacks on President Taylor through newspapers.[27] The *Tar Heel*, the University newspaper, sought to rally alumni and students; it was confident

[24] The Rev. T. N. Ivey, prominent member of the North Carolina Methodist Conference, delivering an "Address on Behalf of the Methodist Church of North Carolina" at the inauguration of President John C. Kilgo, of Trinity College, indicated that the Methodist church had no war to wage against institutions. But the denominational college played a part which state institutions could never play. He summed up the Methodist position by declaring: "So North Carolina Methodism, while not fighting any State institution, would plead for a right of way, and with earnestness, discountenance any policy, civil or ecclesiastical, that would devitalize the energies of Christian education through a drastic or unjust competition. So she would say to the State, 'We ask no practical aid from your coffers for Trinity College, but she is your child, and you must throw nothing in her way' " (*Trinity Archive*, Oct., 1894, pp. 25–26). The *North Carolina Christian Advocate* corroborated what Dr. Ivey said. The editor wanted it to be understood that he and his paper were "in nobody's fight." He hoped wise counsel would prevail (*North Carolina Christian Advocate*, Jan. 9, 1895).

[25] *Minutes Western North Carolina Conference, 1893*, p. 38. The committee was instructed to confer with similar committees of other denominations to secure concert of actions.

[26] *Minutes Baptist State Convention, 1893*, pp. 54–55. Instructions to confer with similar committees were also given to this committee.

[27] The *Charlotte Observer*, the *Caucasian*, and the *Economist-Falconer* lent their columns to such attacks. For President Taylor's answer, see the *Charlotte Observer*, Dec. 10, 1894 (see G. W. Paschal, "Public School Advancement in North Carolina," *Wake Forest Student*, Nov., 1929, p. 46).

they would stand by their Alma Mater and hoped the church colleges would lay aside their "nauseating whine."[28] President Winston, of the University, moved and spoke cautiously.[29] In his private correspondence, however, he was not so restrained. In September, 1894, he wrote to a faithful friend of the University that the fight on the University had "degenerated into a war of wind and filth."[30] He was confident, nevertheless, that the fight for state aid had been won.[31]

[28] *Tar Heel*, March 30, 1894; *ibid.*, April 6, 1894.

[29] He continued to speak in behalf of the principle that education is a right, not a charity, and of the belief that universal education means state education, that the state system of education must include the public schools, high schools, normal schools, technical schools for teaching agriculture, mechanics, and engineering, schools for the unfortunate, and, "to cap all," the University with professional schools of law, medicine, pharmacy, engineering, and dentistry. Speaking at the State Agricultural and Mechanical College in Raleigh, for example, he contended for such a state system and reminded his audience that "Washington, the Adamses, Jefferson, and Monroe, all favored State and national aid to universities." He was careful to include a place for denominational colleges, expressing the hope that North Carolina might become an educational center for the South, "with the biggest and best University, A. & M. College, and Denominational colleges in the whole South" (*Tar Heel*, Feb. 9, 1894).

[30] Spencer Papers: Letter of G. T. Winston, Chapel Hill, to Mrs. Spencer, Cambridge, Mass. Sept., 1894.

[31] President Winston added: "We have already won . . . Even the A. & M. is ahead of Wake Forest; as soon as the A. & M. football and baseball teams beat the W. F. boys, as they soon will do, the war will be over" (*ibid.*).

Speaking of athletics, it is perhaps well to note that athletic contests and relationships reflected very definitely the tenseness of the rivalry between the denominational and the state institutions. The reference made by President Winston is significant. A paragraph in President Crowell's report concerning Trinity College to the North Carolina Conference of 1893, also, reveals a great deal in this connection: "I am thoroughly convinced that no event in the entire conference year has so strengthened the self-respect of the college community as the victory over the University football team on the 28th of October. And not only that, but the same event aroused the pride and enthusiasm of the people of Durham to the extent of converting the town to the college as it has never been before" (*Annual Report of President of Trinity College to North Carolina Conference, 1893*).

The rivalry and relationships between the University and Trinity became so tense and strained that from about the middle of the last decade of the nineteenth century to the beginning of the third decade of the present century, a period of approximately twenty-five years, no football games were played between these two institutions. These relationships received a severe jolt in 1893, when, as told

This fight, however, did not come to a crisis until 1895, the one hundredth anniversary of the opening of the State University. And, in the words of a Raleigh newspaper, it was a "battle royal."[32] For strong statements, perhaps uncalled-for imputations, and bad feelings the fight during the session of the legislature of 1895 reached a peak not hitherto attained. And for the next three or four years the warfare continued with progressive and ascending intensity and fierceness, revealing the earnestness and desperation of the church group and the persistence and unbending determination of the friends of the state institutions, and ending only after every inch of the ground had been fought over and over. To understand this crisis of 1895–99, careful attention must be given to (1) the demands of the church group; (2) the principal events in the fight to secure these demands, including (a) the legislature of 1895, (b) the Bailey-Kilgo crusade, and (c) the legislatures of 1897 and 1899; (3) a summary of the arguments (a) for and (b) against these demands; (4) the spirit and intensity of the crisis; and (5) the outcome of the conflicts.

With their backs to the wall, the church leaders definitely formulated their demands.[33] They demanded (1) that for

---

by the University newspaper, Trinity, having defeated the University's crippled football team by the close score of 6 to 4, refused "point blank" to play the second game, whereas it was alleged that there was an agreement for two games, and, if necessary, three (*Tar Heel*, Nov. 2, 1893).

[32] *News and Observer*, March 6, 1895.

[33] The Baptist committee, appointed in 1893, presented to the legislature of 1895, the following long petition:

"1st. While we do not ask for any violent action on your part, we do ask that practical recognition shall be given by your body at this session to the voluntary principle in the support and control of all higher education in our state. We ask that this principle shall be so fully established in the laws of the state as ultimately to put all the institutions of higher learning on the same plane, so far as the principle of their support is concerned. We recognize the necessity for a period of transition. We believe that this period should be reasonable in extent, but definite in limit.

"2nd. That all taxes of the people which are available for educational purposes shall be spent in the better schooling of the children of the State in Public Schools, and that due encouragement be given to the principle of voluntary local taxation for Common School purposes.

the support and control of all higher education in the state the voluntary principle be adopted, (2) that all taxes available for educational purposes be spent on public schools, (3) that no exemption from examination for certificates to teach in the public schools be allowed any person, (4) that no state-supported institution be allowed to use scholarships at the expense of the public purse, (5) that the Agricultural and Mechanical College and the State Normal and Industrial School be required to confine themselves to the work for which they were established, and (6) that no appropriation be made to cover a period greater than the interval between legislatures.[34]

A number of bills and resolutions were introduced in the legislature of 1895 touching the University, including a bill to reduce the salaries of officers and teachers 20 per cent, one regarding the matter of free tuition, and a resolution asking the treasurer for information.[35] Most of these got no further than the committee of the legislature. The one which brought on the battle royal was a bill introduced by Senator Fortune, to abolish appropriations to the University.[36] A hearing arranged by the educational committee

---

"3rd. That no exemption from examination for certificates to teach in the Public Schools shall be allowed to any person.

"4th. That no institution for higher collegiate or university education shall be allowed, while aided by appropriations from the treasury of the State, to issue or use scholarships unless these are based upon an actual annual money income sufficient to pay the regular charges in full for the privileges granted, said income to accrue from sources other than the appropriations made, for the time being, from the State.

"5th. That all institutions chartered by the State for industrial and normal education shall confine themselves strictly to that work so long as they shall be supported in whole or in part by appropriations from the State.

"6th. That no law making an appropriation to any institution shall continue in force, without reenactment, for a longer period than the intervals between the meetings of the General Assembly" (for the memorial and the petition in full, see *Minutes Baptist State Convention, 1895*, pp. 69–72).

[34] The Methodists were in substantial agreement with these demands of the Baptists, although their official formulation of them, with slight variations, was not made until a little later (see below, p. 147, footnote).

[35] *House Journal, 1895*, pp. 230, 382, 603, 836; *Senate Journal, 1895*, pp. 80, 123, 174.

[36] *Senate Journal, 1895*, pp. 91, 211, 507.

of the legislature, turned out to be a rough-and-tumble debate, in which personalities were freely used. Dr. Columbus Durham, for the opponents of state aid, and President Winston, of the University, were the chief debaters.[37]

The legislature of 1895 appropriated the same amount for the University as previous legislatures had done, $20,000.[38] The numerical vote on this measure was not recorded. The *University Magazine*,[39] however, is authority for the statement that "the campaign was of unexampled virulence." And President Winston estimated that if the bill had gone to vote the first two weeks of the session it would have been defeated by a three to one vote.[40] Friends of the University in the legislature had to watch closely every move, moreover, for there were those there who wanted to reduce the amount and one, the representative from Chatham

[37] *News and Observer*, March 5 and 6, 1895. These two issues contain a graphic account of the battle royal before the committee of the legislature. Dr. Durham was aided by W. N. Jones and Dr. Thomas Skinner. Speaking with President Winston were Congressman Harry Skinner, President McIver of the State Normal School, W. A. Guthrie, Charles B. Aycock, Judge D. L. Russell, and Rev. R. H. Leak (Negro).

[38] *News and Observer*, March 15, 1895. This legislature was made up largely of Populists and Republicans, who, according to the *News and Observer*, had been elected by denouncing the "Democratic extravagance in appropriating money to the University." The fact that University alumni held strategic positions in the legislature and the persistent campaigning of the officials and friends of the University enabled them to overcome what appeared to be heavy odds. The Democratic presiding officer of the Senate, the Republican presiding officer of the House, and the Populist United States Senator-elect were all University alumni (*University Magazine*, Jan., 1895, p. 232). Marion Butler, Populist publisher of the *Caucasian*, threw his influence in support of state aid, much to the delight of the University (*Tar Heel*, Feb. 14, 1895).

[39] *University Magazine*, April, 1895, pp. 380–381.

[40] How close the church group came to winning early in the crisis is suggested by statements of President Winston and Professor Alderman of the University. Soon after the adjournment of the legislature of 1895, President Winston wrote a trusted friend that "Even with their aid (that of alumni and friends) we came near destruction. The Baptist flood roared and surged and threatened us . . . Could they have gotten a vote the first two weeks, we had been abolished root and branch by 3 to 1 vote; and even the last two weeks a reduction in our appropriation would probably have been made, if we had come out in battle array" (Spencer Papers: Winston's letter to Mrs. Spencer, April 9, 1895).

County, who, it was alleged, attempted to sneak through a bill to reduce the appropriation from $20,000 to $5,000 a year.[41]

It will be observed that the Baptists did most of the fighting in the contest of 1895, the Methodists following a more pacific and conciliatory course.[42] And although President Winston thought the battle was all won in 1895, the Baptists refused to believe that they had been defeated. Reinforced by the Methodists, under the aggressive, dynamic leadership of President John C. Kilgo, recently come into the state to direct the destinies of Trinity College, the opponents of state aid and advocates of the voluntary principle in higher education continued, with renewed determination, the contest till near the close of the century.

"The Baptists are not quitters. In the same spirit that our fathers bore stripes and imprisonment and infamy and death for religious freedom, the separation of Church and State, the Baptists of North Carolina are called upon to stand for the voluntary principle in higher education," wrote, in 1896, the young Baptist editor, Josiah William Bailey, who a short while before had succeeded his father on the *Biblical Recorder*.[43]

[41] *Ibid.*, March 9, 1895; *House Journal, 1895*, pp. 568, 894.

[42] The *North Carolina Christian Advocate*, noticing a Raleigh correspondent's observation of the apparent lukewarmness of the Methodist committee, represented the attitude of the conference as being not one of demand for withdrawal of appropriations to the University but of desire for a proper adjustment of relationships by the legislature that would obviate the conflict between the institutions of church and state. Obviously the Methodist editor was not so greatly exercised nor quite so determined as were the Baptists. This Methodist paper, nevertheless, persistently pointed out to its constituency the "benefits of training in Methodist schools," the "reproach of North Carolina Methodists that, during the past year, at least two State Schools had each as many or more Methodists as any Methodist school in the State," that many of the Methodists at state institutions were "simply bought with the price of free tuition or such terms as could not be duplicated by denominational institutions," and that the state should reconstruct its educational policy so as to confine itself to the work of the common school, the university proper, and to technical education (*North Carolina Christian Advocate*, Jan. 30, July 17, and Aug. 21, 1895).

[43] *Biblical Recorder*, Nov. 11, 1896. Through his fearless fight in this contest and subsequent public enterprises, Mr. Bailey won for himself such public notice

We fought this battle (1895) and lost it by the knavery of men who were trusted ... Baptist associations throughout North Carolina have within the last ten weeks endorsed unanimously the efforts of the representatives of the denominations to correct this great wrong.... We go up now into Convention. For two years this body has declared itself. In the spirit of the fathers it will not quit in a hundred years until the right is established and the wrong dethroned. It is an opportune season. We stood alone under the leadership of the stalwart Durham two years ago before the General Assembly. Before the Assembly chosen last week, to meet in January next, there will be gathered leading men of other denominations, particularly the Methodists. The occasion demands a united, a determined, a strenuous effort.[44]

With such ringing words the young Bailey plunged into the fight and pulled Baptists and Methodists alike in with him.[45]

Editor Bailey and the Baptists obviously were greatly encouraged by the happenings in the Methodist camp. President Kilgo, who found the state press not too friendly and the Methodist Church papers too little inclined to fight with the abandon and vigor characteristic of his nature, had established, in 1896, the *Christian Educator*. Through this newspaper he could have untrammeled approach to the people. And with the closest sort of co-operation from the

---

that he soon entered prominently into state politics and finally, in 1930, won his way into the United States Senate. That Editor Bailey intended to bring the issues to a crisis is indicated by an editorial (*ibid.*, March 11, 1896) in which he declared "one grand, united effort will establish the (voluntary) principle for good and all." President Kilgo, likewise, established himself as such an able and fearless leader of his church that, in 1910, it elected him one of its bishops.

[44] *Ibid.*, Nov. 11, 1896.

[45] *Minutes Baptist State Convention, 1896*, pp. 61–62; *Biblical Recorder*, Nov. 18, 1896; *Christian Educator*, Nov., 1896, Vol. I, No. 10.

The Baptist State Convention, in 1896, resolved to "reaffirm its opposition to state aid by taxation to higher education" because it was "wrong, unjust and unwise ... wrong against the people, who cannot receive the benefits of such appropriations; unjust to the private and corporate and denominational institutions voluntarily supported; unwise because the people of North Carolina are now inadequately provided with public schools for their children and need every cent of their taxes that can be spared for that purpose."

editors,[46] he was saying a plenty. After a year of agitation and education through the columns of his paper, and otherwise, President Kilgo had led the North Carolina Methodist Conference, in the fall of 1896, to take almost the identical position taken by the Baptists two years earlier.[47]

[46] The editors of the *Christian Educator* were Dr. W. I. Cranford and Professor R. L. Flowers, members of the Trinity faculty. Editor P. L. Groome, of the *North Carolina Christian Advocate*, was regarded as only lukewarm, even as defending the University mildly. Editor W. L. Grissom, who succeeded Groome in July, 1896, was against state aid but apparently did not fight vigorously enough to suit President Kilgo (*Biblical Recorder*, July 15, 1896; July 22, 1896).

[47] Following the recommendation of a committee, composed of E. A. Yates, J. N. Cole, and John C. Kilgo, the conference adopted resolutions, introduced by President Kilgo, which varied only slightly from the memorial presented to the legislature of 1895 by the Baptist committee. The Methodists combined in their point 2 both 1 and 2 of the Baptist paper, substituted a strong statement in favor of Christian education for the Baptists' objection relative to the certification of teachers, and omitted altogether point 6 of the Baptist position concerning the continuity of appropriation laws. The resolutions, in full, except the preamble, are as follow:

"1. That we commit ourselves uncompromisingly to Christian education and insist that our people in their homes teach their children the doctrines of Christ and patronize those schools whose influence will not be harmful and patronize those colleges that have given positive instruction in the truths of the Bible.

2. That we regard the free public schools as a necessity to the State and we declare ourselves fully in sympathy with them. These schools are for the people and should be made efficient. That within the constitutional limits of taxation we recommend an increased appropriation for common schools. That while we do not think it the function of the State to teach religion in its colleges, and while we recognize the fact that there are many citizens who do not wish to patronize church colleges, and while we have no disposition to exterminate or do injury to State colleges, yet as citizens of North Carolina, as well as members of the Methodist Episcopal Church, South, we do not believe that it is just to the Church to tax its members to carry on an educational work to the injury of the Church colleges or to put the State colleges in unfair competition with the Church colleges.

3. We believe that it is out of harmony with the principles of government, and morally wrong for the State to undertake to furnish free higher education to the few at the expense of the many, and therefore that all tuitions in the State University, in so far as they are based upon the appropriation of public moneys, should be discontinued. That we request the legislature to discontinue the appropriation of public money for free scholarships and tuitions at the University.

4. Knowing that the income from the tuitions is not sufficient to meet the current expenses of a college or University, we are not opposed to the appropriations to the University, but we think these appropriations should be limited to such amounts as are necessary to meet the deficiency in current expenses after

Editor Bailey and President Kilgo conducted their crusade with all the zeal of Richard the Lion-Hearted. Endowed with dynamic personalities, gifted in public debate, and armed with newspapers which they virtually controlled, they threw everything they had into the contest and led an offensive against what seemed to them as real an enemy of as righteous a cause as ever existed.

The methods of these crusaders were not unlike those used by Dr. Durham and the Baptists in the fight of 1893–95. The chief difference was not of kind but of degree of intensity and of bitterness. Briefly told, their plan of attack seemed to be to arouse and hold as large a following as possible among the church people and then to impress the opposition and the legislature with the righteousness of their cause and with their certainty of its ultimate success. They made sure, first of all, that their respective churches, in their official capacity, were solidly back of them.[48] Then they used their newspapers, the daily press insofar as it was available for their use, and other periodicals open to them, for a continuous campaign of propaganda.[49] They wrote voluminously themselves and encouraged others, including prominent pastors, general secretaries,

---

tuitions have been collected from all students, except those to whom private scholarships have been given.

5. That as the aim of the State in the establishment of the Normal and Industrial College at Greensboro, N. C., and the Agricultural and Mechanical College at Raleigh, N. C., was to provide technical and not higher literary education, we declare ourselves in sympathy with them as long as they adhere to their original purpose, but we are opposed to any policy that will in any way divert them from this aim" (*Minutes North Carolina Conference, 1896*, pp. 14–15; *Christian Educator*, Dec., 1896).

The alumni of Trinity College, at the 1896 commencement, adopted a resolution declaring for Christian education and against state aid; and the *Biblical Recorder* took "fresh courage" (*Biblical Recorder*, June 17, 1896).

[48] *Minutes Baptist State Convention, 1893*, pp. 54–55; *1897*, p. 64; *Minutes North Carolina Conference, 1896*, pp. 14–15. Several Baptist associations in the fall of 1896 protested against state aid, including the Atlantic and the Central associations (*Biblical Recorder*, Aug. 5, Sept. 2, and Oct. 21, 1896).

[49] The *Biblical Recorder* was filled with controversial articles from the pen of Editor Bailey and others (see files from 1895 to 1900). The *Christian Educator*, published for three years, was devoted almost entirely to this controversy.

and bishops, to contribute articles on the subjects under controversy.[50] They reprinted materials which each other had written, and came to each other's rescue when either seemed to be under intense or threatening fire.[51] They sought to have elected to the lawmaking body candidates favorably disposed to their side of the conflict.[52] They wrote directly to this body.[53] They made trips to Raleigh. They spoke on many occasions and at many places. They were alert to sense the weakest points in the personalities and arguments of their opponents and to attack with all the force of their powerful pens and their tongues. They sought to employ good strategy. They tried to turn from a defensive contest to a vigorous offensive. They championed the cause of the common people—the common schools,[54] and they maintained that the state was unable to give truly higher education; the church possessed an inherent monopoly of Christian education.[55]

[50] G. W. Flowers, "A Word of Protest," *Christian Educator*, May, 1897. President Kilgo secured from Bishop E. R. Hendrix, Dr. W. A. Candler, and others definitions of Christian education (see letters of E. R. Hendrix to J. C. Kilgo, Sept. 3, 1897, and of W. A. Candler to J. C. Kilgo, Sept. 1, 1897).

[51] See *Biblical Recorder* and *Christian Educator* files for numerous examples, particularly, *Biblical Recorder*, March 17, 1897. For another specific example, see article, "At Least Consistent," from the *Sunday School Magazine*, reprinted in the *Biblical Recorder* and again reprinted in the *Christian Educator*, Nov., 1897.

[52] For testimony on this subject see the account of the debate before the educational committee of the legislature of 1895, in the *News and Observer*, March 5 and 6, 1895. Also article, "Public School System," by Dr. C. C. Wood, in *St. Louis Christian Advocate*, March, 1897. Reference in this article is to the Baptist Church getting control of the legislature, "which they have practically done." See also *Biblical Recorder*, Sept. 30, 1896, urging Baptists to pledge candidates on their attitude toward state aid.

[53] For an open letter of President Kilgo to the legislature of 1897, see the *Christian Educator*, Jan., 1897.

[54] Mebane invited Dr. Kilgo to Raleigh and promised that the Methodists and Baptists of the state should have a hearing. He added: "I shall not endorse any system of supervision that will open the way for the 'University gang' to control the public school system of North Carolina. . . . I want to assure you that I am and have been aware of the force of Denominational Colleges, and want your support for public schools" (letter of C. H. Mebane, State Superintendent-elect, to J. C. Kilgo, Jan. 14, 1897).

[55] To the crusaders, Christian education was the only really higher education.

The friends of the state institutions used the University publications, the *Tar Heel*, the *University Record*, and the *University Magazine*, to some extent. The secular press of the state, in the main quite friendly, was relied upon for defending the University and hurling occasional darts in the direction of the crusaders.[56] They also got help even from the press outside the state.[57] Their strategy in the legislature was one of their most effective weapons. They acted on the theory that the best defensive is a strong offensive; they asked for increased appropriations.[58] Furthermore, in the words of President Winston himself, they pursued the Fabian policy.[59] They managed to delay voting when to vote seemed dangerous. They refused to come out in battle array. They professed their love for the common schools and pledged their support to measures designed to provide more money for them. They were accused of delaying the vote on appropriations to common schools until after the institutions of higher learning had first been cared for.[60] The presidents of the State University and of the State Normal and Industrial School are said to have spent weeks around the rooms of the legislature lobbying for their measures.[61]

The arguments used in the period of the crisis were not new. Practically all of them had been employed previously and have been discussed in connection with other phases of

[56] *Tar Heel*, Feb. 22, 1896. See also the files of the Raleigh *News and Observer*, the *Charlotte Observer*, the *State Chronicle*, *Webster's Weekly*, and other leading state papers.

[57] The Charleston (S. C.) *News and Courier* and the *Richmond* (Va.) *Times* gave space to this controversy. See *Richmond Times*, Dec. 25, 1895, and *Biblical Recorder*, July 28, 1897.

[58] *House Journal, 1897*, p. 714.

[59] Spencer Papers: C. T. Winston's letter to Mrs. Spencer, April 9, 1895.

[60] *Ibid.* See also J. W. Bailey's letter in *News and Observer*, March 11, 1897; and B. W. Spillman, "Who Proved Themselves Friends of the Public Schools," *Biblical Recorder*, March 17, 1897; April 14, 1897.

[61] C. H. Mebane, "Statement of the Superintendent of Public Instruction," *Biblical Recorder*, March 17, 1897. President Winston was succeeded by Dr. E. A. Alderman as president of the University in 1896, Dr. Alderman being inaugurated in Jan., 1897. Dr. Charles D. McIver was president of the Normal School.

this study. In this summary of the arguments used in the crisis, therefore, one has, in effect, a summary of the arguments employed in the numerous conflicts between church and state in higher education in North Carolina.[62]

Most of the arguments for the voluntary principle in the support and control of higher education and for the other related demands of the church leaders[63] may be summarized under three main heads:

(1) It was *not right* for a state to undertake to supply all the demand for higher education.

(2) It was *not expedient* for a state in the condition of North Carolina at that time, to undertake to do so.

(3) It was *not possible* for a state to supply the kind of training desirable for its youth without committing itself to some special form of religious belief.[64]

1. In support of the argument that it is not right for a state to undertake to supply, at the expense of the people, all the demand for higher education, it was argued that to do so (a) would lead to *paternalism*, (b) would be *false economy*, (c) would be *unwarranted favoritism*, and (d) would be exceeding the requirements of the constitution.

Concerning paternalism, state aid was like protective tariffs, great pension systems, and the establishment of religion in state churches. It would lead to unlimited interference by the state in every department of business.[65]

[62] So numerous and oft-repeated were the arguments for and against the demands of the denominational leaders that only a summary is possible here. And they overlapped each other at so many places that it is not regarded either practicable or necessary to separate them according to the specific demand or demands they were intended to support or defeat.

[63] See above, pp. 142–148.

[64] Under these headings, used by President Taylor in his pamphlet on *How Far Should a State Undertake to Educate?*, p. 7, who virtually summarized the principal arguments used previous to his writing and current at that time (1893), are included the arguments of others who wrote since the publication of the pamphlet, bringing the summary up to date.

[65] "The public mind seems much opposed to trusts and monopolies, but never was any monopoly organized upon so gigantic a scale and with such daring effrontery as the educational monopoly of the State, built up with the money of the very

In support of the argument of false economy of state aid, it was held that all the needs of the state for higher education could be abundantly supplied by private and corporate enterprises, without cost to the state. Those who objected to sending their sons or daughters to church colleges might do what the church people did—build colleges and universities to their liking.[66] Even the great majority of teachers and many of the leaders of the state had not come out of state colleges.[67]

---

citizens whose schools they seek to ruin by unfair competition. The Sugar Trust, the Standard Oil Trust, the Nail Trust, may have wrecked many smaller enterprises by underselling, yet this was done with individual capital, but this trust seeks to wreck other like enterprises, and make the ruined corporations foot the bill. Nothing is clearer than that in the South, West, and Northwest the States are striving to monopolize higher education . . ." (J. C. Kilgo, "A Ringing Endorsement," *Southern Christian Advocate*, reprinted in *Christian Educator*, March 1897).

"If a State may furnish education below cost to the recipient, . . . why may it not furnish to its citizens blankets, agricultural implements and other articles of utility and comfort?" To be consistent, it would have to do so. A state should not become the rival of her own citizens in any enterprise (Taylor, *op. cit.*, pp. 9–12).

Bishop H. N. McTyiere lent strength to this argument by referring to what had happened in South Carolina in 1894. He said: "The act of the Legislature at Columbia was passed, granting $37,000 for the support of the University and the Military Academy—an amount, I was informed, sufficient, not only to cover free tuition in both, but free board in one of those institutions" (*Christian Educator*, Oct., 1896).

[66] *Christian Educator*, Sept. and Oct., 1896, quoting Bishop Haygood and Bishop McTyiere. Bishop McTyiere said: "There is a class, not without activity and influence, who affect breadth and elevation, and in the face of this axiom of political economy cry out: 'What, must a great State be dependent on sectarian and private benevolence for the higher education of its sons!' Their exclamation goes for argument, ignoring the fact that the best literary institutions of our country have had that origin. The anti-Church sect is the most bigoted and intolerant of all the sects. These gentlemen have a way of getting into the management of public trusts, and of dispensing or enjoying the patronage. If they wish godless and unsectarian colleges and universities, this is a free country; let them build and run them at their own expense. It is asking too much of a Christian people to do this for them."

[67] Taylor, *op. cit.*, p. 9. President Kilgo, writing on this point, thought it "strange that a college graduate should thus (by free scholarships) be induced to make a living" (Kilgo, "Education of the Poor Boy," *Biblical Recorder*, July 15, 1896). The *Biblical Recorder*, Dec. 9, 1896, declared: "The University does not supply teachers for our common schools. If there is a reader of this paper who knows of a University graduate who is one of the 7,000 common school teachers of this state, we would be glad to hear from him."

It would be unwarranted favoritism to supply to the few the "luxuries of education" while the many did not enjoy the privilege of even common schools.[68] To boast that one's son had a free scholarship would be to admit that one had unloaded the son on the public, a thing not to boast of as a great relief.[69] It was contended, furthermore, that the use of public funds to give free tuition at a state college to ministerial students and sons of ministers was a class distinction.[70]

The constitution did not require the state to provide higher education. The article relating to higher education was not mandatory but permissive. The legislature, therefore, should carry out the wishes of the people, which, it was

[68] Kilgo, *op. cit.;* Taylor, *op. cit.*, p. 12. Dr. Columbus Durham, in the debate before the committee of the legislature in 1895, referred to a statement published in the Raleigh papers and signed by President Winston, in which twenty University students made a declaration concerning their financial condition. "These twenty students," said Dr. Durham, "are the worst off in the University, and out of these only four receive scholarships. If we could receive the names of the holders of the scholarships, we would find them the sons of the most well-to-do citizens of the state" (*News and Observer*, March 6, 1895).

President Kilgo, writing in 1897, said: "The 'poor boy' has already been much in evidence in the speeches of legislators in North Carolina and South Carolina. He is a great fellow, but he never goes to college, and scores of college professors never saw him in his real home. He cannot get work and does not aspire to a college diploma just now, but is much concerned about a shirt and a pair of shoes. For him the State had better build factories and give out free clothing, instead of proposing free tuition in a college, otherwise set off by an impassable gulf" (Kilgo, "A Ringing Endorsement," *Southern Christian Advocate*, reprinted in the *Christian Educator*, March, 1897).

[69] *Christian Educator*, July, 1896. "A pauperized manhood is a poor substitute for a college diploma" (from Address by President Kilgo reported by the *Charlotte Observer* and reprinted in the *Christian Educator*, Aug., 1896). For similar argument see also item by C. W. Blanchard in the *Biblical Recorder*, Aug. 26, 1896, and Ellwood P. Cubberley, *Public Education in the United States*, pp. 139–147.

[70] "This spurious, unsought and undesired State charity toward the churches sounds a little insincere among so much state denunciation of 'sectarian education.' A state college that advertises free tuition to ministerial students as a specialty, should hush its wild ravings against sectarianism, or else quit paying public money to educate the leaders of these sects. Such a cheap bid for the ministry of the church is humiliating to every noble impulse of the true ministry. The churches are not just quite ready to accept such generosity at the expense of the taxpayers of the State. It is time for the Legislature to stop this wild misappropriation of the people's money" (Kilgo, *op. cit.*).

contended, were against state aid.[71] It would be better for the state and for state institutions if these institutions could be free from all political relations and controlled by self-perpetuating trustees under liberal charters and amply equipped by their alumni and the friends of education. The University had prospered for a long time on such support. The disestablishment of state institutions of higher learning, therefore, was urged, an idea by no means so startling, it was held, as was the proposition to sever the connection between church and state.

2. Supporting the contention that it was not expedient for the state to undertake to monopolize the field of higher education, the church leaders (a) lifted up the elementary and secondary schools for more consideration at the hands of the state, (b) warned of the danger of destroying the motive of individuals to strengthen existing colleges or build new ones, (c) pointed out the folly of weakening or destroying church and private institutions comparatively free from the element of inherent instability in the life and working of all state institutions under political control, and (d) denied the alleged expediency of subsidizing institutions for the training of teachers and other men for social and political leadership.

Every cent of money raised by taxation available for educational purposes should be expended in increasing the efficiency of the elementary and secondary school system. It was maintained that there was valid reason for free schools in which all citizens had an opportunity for securing that degree of education necessary to the intelligent discharge of civic duties.[72] Only one person in five hundred

[71] Taylor, *op. cit.*, p. 14.

[72] "These schools do not rest on the same basis as State colleges, nor do they involve the same civil policy. The defenders of the misuse of public money in giving free tuition to a few are adroitly striving to make public common education and State higher education identical in claims and necessity. It is the old trick of unloading a bad enterprise upon a sound one . . . These graded schools are no more State schools than a city mule and trash cart are State property" (Kilgo, "Education of the Poor Boy," reprinted in *Biblical Recorder*, July 15, 1896, and

was able, either financially or intellectually, to enter a college or university, and to pursue the policy of strengthening the latter at the expense of the elementary schools would mean the rich would become richer, the poor poorer, the educated more educated, and the ignorant more ignorant.[73] It was regarded as a "preposterous absurdity" to offer free tuition in higher institutions when free common schools of the lowest grade could run hardly four months in the year.[74] The Baptist State Convention felt the force of this situation so strongly that it memorialized the legislature to correct it.[75] The $74,161 appropriated annually for higher education in the state would enable the state to support the four months' school term, and the $20,000 a year given the University would provide an excellent system of supervision for public schools or provide an adequate number of teachers' institutes.[76] The church leaders, no doubt genuinely in-

---

Christian Educator, Aug., 1896; *Christian Educator*, Jan., 1898). The Baptists favored state support of elementary schools "as a concession to the emergency upon which we have fallen" (Report of Central Baptist Association in *Biblical Recorder*, Aug. 5, 1896). They took into account, also, the point that teachers could not afford to make a profession of elementary instruction, "for the reasons that in many cases their pupils will be very poor, and their youth always makes the remuneration small." They could make elementary instruction their profession if the state should assure them a competence (*Biblical Recorder*, Jan. 10, 1894).

[73] *Biblical Recorder*, Feb. 24, 1897.

[74] *Christian Educator*, Oct., 1896, quoting Bishop McTyiere.

[75] *Minutes Baptist State Convention, 1898*, p. 77. This memorial reaffirmed a position previously taken by the Baptists. The position of the Baptists had excited the attention of the *Philadelphia Record*, which was quoted by the *Biblical Recorder* of Nov. 25, 1896, as saying: "The N. C. Baptist Association [Convention], with only two dissenting votes, has reaffirmed its opposition to higher education, for the reason that the people are inadequately provided with public schools for their children. Such a protest is in the nature of a higher education in common sense for the legislators everywhere. Expenditure of State funds for the finishing schools while the primary schools are unprovided for is an injustice and a piece of folly. It is Buddensieck building, and can only end in a collapse."

[76] *Biblical Recorder*, Dec. 23, 1896; Jan. 13, 1897. The contrast between the state's care for common schools and the University was graphically stated as follows: Referring to an advertisement announcing 47 teachers and 413 students at Chapel Hill, it was remarked that there were not quite nine students to a teacher, while the free school teachers of the state were expected to teach from 40 to 50

terested in and sincerely devoted to the common schools, found it a very popular if not a very effective weapon to speak much and often in support of state appropriations for common schools. President Taylor, in 1893 and 1894, had given the cue and set the pace for the common school argument. Editor Bailey and others in his camp, as well as Methodists, kept up the campaign until there are those who regard him as entitled to more credit than McIver, Alderman, or even Aycock for popularizing public education in North Carolina.[77]

It was held to be bad political economy for the state to charge itself with doing that which, if let alone, religious zeal and private munificence could and would do as well and even better.[78] If the tendency toward state maintenance and control should culminate, the gifts of individuals to private institutions probably would be, in the future, few and small.[79]

---

pupils at $30 a month. And then the comment: "Good old North Carolina, doing big things for Education—working the University faculty to death to educate our people. One Professor to eight boys. The State ought to give them a pension when they wear out in this work" (L. J. Holden's letter to J. C. Kilgo, July 7, 1897).

[77] Paschal, "Public School Advancement in North Carolina," *Wake Forest Student*, Nov., 1929, pp. 31–40. Also *Biblical Recorder*, 1893 to 1900; The *Christian Educator*, 1895–1898; and the *North Carolina Christian Advocate*, 1893–1900. For the Methodists, the *Christian Educator* championed the doctrine that education works up, not down. "There is no falser doctrine than that education works down, and hence higher education is of supremest value. The State has acted upon this false doctrine, and has achieved very little. It has made pets of its higher institutions, and left preparatory education [meaning, one would suppose, elementary and secondary education] to the accidents of low educational sentiment. Instead of its being true that education works down, the reverse is true, it works upward. It is time that preparatory education should be regarded as the supreme factor in our educational work. And no men need to learn this more than college men" (*Christian Educator*, March, 1896).

[78] *Christian Educator*, Oct., 1896, quoting a letter from Bishop McTyiere. See also President Kilgo's letter to the legislature of 1897 in *Christian Educator*, Jan., 1897.

[79] Taylor, *op. cit.*, p. 19. On this subject Kilgo said: "Suppose every young man and woman in the Church and private colleges of the State would leave them and claim free tuition, or even attend the State colleges and pay tuition, at once this overwhelming increase of patronage would necessitate an appropriation of

It was held, furthermore, that it was inexpedient to build up colossal, overshadowing state institutions to the destruction of the smaller colleges. State institutions, it was maintained, were not of the people, by the people, and for the people. A state college had its own constituency as clearly defined as a Methodist or Baptist college.[80] The political influence of state institutions was unwholesome. They were at the mercy of partisans and demagogues. Education ought to be free from partisan politics.[81] Freedom was best conserved by church colleges. Being free from political patronage, they could teach without fear of forfeiting any political favor.[82] The best, if not the only, safeguard of a state university, was the healthful existence of a similar institution under denominational patronage.[83] There were

---

$100,000 instead of $21,000. This supposition shows what a burden the Christian colleges have taken from the shoulders of the tax-payers and put on those who are directly benefitted. Yet legislators talk of these colleges and their friends as being unpatriotic, and educational enemies. It is a new type of patriotism that makes a traitor out of a father who assumes the burdens of his son's education, and a patriot of the man who unloads them on the taxpayers, regardless of color or condition" ("A Ringing Endorsement," *Southern Christian Advocate*, reprinted in *Christian Educator*, March, 1897).

[80] *Christian Educator*, April, 1897.

[81] *Ibid.*, March, 1897; *Biblical Recorder*, Aug. 31 and Sept. 14, 1898. The Baptist editor did not like to hear it boasted that a foreign minister's appointment was secured by the University, that this office or that could not be filled except by a University man, that one of the requisites to the "good places" in city schools was connection with the University. Such work was beneath the dignity of an educational institution, "even though it is a State-aided one" (*Biblical Recorder*, June 17, 1896). "The trustees of the State college may be good men; but not always. An outcast Baptist preacher, Rev. T. W. Babb, was not long ago made by politics a trustee of our State University, and others with him whose reputations are by no means shining. At best, they are elected by politicians in the General Assembly; and, if the General Assembly of North Carolina is a sample, we may lay it down for a fact that General Assemblies elect trustees who, regardless of character, are in their political party. It is Party not character, spoils not humanity, that they are most concerned for. One can never tell whom a political party will put in as a trustee, or what a political party will do with a State institution" (*Biblical Recorder*, Aug. 31, 1898).

[82] *Ibid.*, Aug. 31, 1898; *Christian Educator*, July, 1897.

[83] *Christian Educator*, Oct., 1896, quoting Bishop McTyiere on the bad atmosphere that infected certain state universities before denominational institutions arose "to shame them into propriety."

dangers, also, which sooner or later might manifest themselves in a state which had a large colored population. Such dangers could not threaten the Christian or other private institutions.[84]

Church leaders denied the contention that the control and support of higher education by the state was rendered expedient by a necessity for a supply of teachers and social and political leaders. The law of supply and demand would take care of this matter without any care of expense to the state. Better pay and longer terms would create the demand for teachers, and the supply then would take care of itself. So far as North Carolina teachers had had higher education at all, the majority had received it at Christian and other private colleges. The more of the higher education a man or woman received, the less likely it was that he or she would ever teach in a public school.[85] With a good public school education given by the state, a person with real capacity for leadership and a worthy ambition could get the rest under the voluntary as well as under the state-support system.[86]

That the state could not provide all useful learning was stoutly and ardently maintained by denominational leaders, who relied chiefly upon two propositions: (1) the desirable education must contain religious elements, and (2) the state was debarred by its fundamental law from furnishing these religious elements.[87]

[84] Taylor, *op. cit.*, p. 19.

[85] President Caldwell is quoted (Taylor, *op. cit.*, p. 25) as saying: "To educate a young man in a college is to disqualify him almost with certainty for the permanent business of an elementary schoolmaster . . . To educate a youth in college is to spoil him for the occupation of a primary schoolmaster . . . He will soon be tired of being an abcdarian, if he can teach Virgil and Homer, or hope for distinction in one of the learned professions. His tastes, his desires, his habits, the scope of his mind, his expenses and modes of living, have all been formed entirely at variance with the ends proposed."

[86] *Ibid.*, pp. 24–26; also *Biblical Recorder*, Oct. 25, 1893, and Jan. 10, 1894.

[87] Taylor, *op. cit.*, pp. 29–43; *North Carolina Christian Advocate*, Aug. 21, 1895. They argued these propositions so persistently that they were accused of making "a heartless attack upon university and public education," which, of course, they

Mere moral instruction or the presentation of ethical truth was not enough; this would not satisfy the deeper needs of the nature. Infidelity had "hid itself in science and enthroned itself in colleges and universities, and by a distorted and incomplete idea of education" had done great harm. Along with all education should go a purpose to build up a faith in God, "the only secure foundation for national and individual life," without which the worst results were to be expected from education.[88]

In an effort to show that the state had no right to furnish education containing religious elements, many churchmen argued at length.[89] Some admitted that very much of really valuable Christian education had been given by state institutions, and agreed that the University of North Carolina was for many years virtually a Presbyterian institution. The University of Georgia had been largely under Baptist influence. The results were good, but the means were unjustifiable. Christian education was always and everywhere a good thing. But no state had any right to give or authorize it. Unless state institutions were made absolutely secular, they would almost inevitably drift under the influence of one or another of the religious denominations. If a system of education were to be framed embracing the doctrines of all sects, furthermore, these would be found so mutually antagonistic that only a skeleton of natural regli-

---

denied (G. F. Kirby, "In Defense of Dr. Kilgo," *Christian Educator*, Nov., 1897; also editorial from *Biblical Recorder* reprinted in *Christian Educator*, July, 1897).

[88] *Minutes Western North Carolina Conference, 1893*, p. 59; *Minutes North Carolina Conference, 1894*, p. 33; *1895*, p. 13; *1896*, pp. 14–15; *Christian Educator*, Dec., 1896; Report Central Baptist Association, in *Biblical Recorder*, July 15, 1896; *Minutes Baptist State Convention, 1897*, p. 64.

[89] "Christian institutions are the only institutions for the sons and daughters of Christian mothers and fathers. Let every Baptist, every Methodist, every Presbyterian, every Christian, every Friend, every Reformed, every one who follows Christ rally around the banner of Christian education. Our cause is impregnable. It will not die so long as Christ is the same, yesterday, today, and tomorrow. We are reviled; he was. We are sneered at; he was. We are misrepresented; he was. He withstood and conquered; we shall" (*Biblical Recorder*, July 21, reprinted in *Christian Educator*, July, 1897).

gion would remain; and if, on the other hand, the state should frame a system which rejected the peculiar doctrines of all sects, nothing would remain as an object of belief. If a state took any cognizance of sects, the disciples of Comte, Haeckel, and Ingersoll would be as much entitled to recognition as Protestants, Catholics, or Jews. A state was not at liberty to favor one form of religion more than another.[90]

They offset the Constitution[91] with the North Carolina Declaration of Rights.[92] Whenever the state undertook to teach or uphold by its authority any religious opinions which were not held by some, or even a few, of its citizens, it *interfered* with the rights of conscience. When the state used tax money for giving instruction or exerting influence, directly or indirectly, which antagonized the religious opinions of any, it *controlled* the rights of conscience; for a citizen was not at liberty to decline to pay the taxes which were so used.[93]

[90] Taylor, *op. cit.*, pp. 30–31. Baptists admitted these arguments applied alike to common schools as well as to colleges and universities, but thought common schools offered very little practical difficulty, inasmuch as the child was at home most of the time and could easily receive religious instruction there. The position was taken that neither prayer nor the reading of the Bible could be allowed in any school supported by general taxation. Such a position seemed necessary in order to meet the Catholic's demand for a division of public school money (*ibid.*, p. 31).

[91] "All useful learning shall be duly encouraged and promoted in one or more Universities."

[92] "No human authority should, in any case whatever, control or interfere with the rights of conscience."

[93] J. S. Bassett, "Shall a Church Have a College?" *Christian Educator*, May, 1897; Taylor, *op. cit.*, p. 34. The following statement is typical of the position taken by Baptists and Methodists: "The State cannot give higher education according to its essential idea as understood by thoughtful Christian people, for such higher education involves indirectly, if not directly, the inculcation of the Christian religion, inculcating Christian ethics. Our State Constitution very properly prohibits the use of public moneys for sectarian purposes. From the point of the State the Christian religion is a sect of religion, as much as Judaism or Mohammedanism.... We speak of our government sometimes as a Christian government, but in strictness we are not entitled to a Christian government. Or, we may say, that according to Baptist idea, which has largely prevailed in this land, of entire separation between Church and State, the only really Christian government is that government which does not concern itself with religion as

The conclusion of this point, with the method by which it was arrived at, was summed up in the following syllogism:

Now, the education provided by a State must either include some religious elements or exclude all religious elements.

---

religion, but only with people who happen to be religious, as having certain rights which must be respected, but not more so than the rights of other men. The Church idea and the State idea are distinct. The last appeal of the State is to the sword. The first and last appeal of the Church is to the Cross. The State may bear the sword. It cannot preach the Cross. The State cannot do the work of the Church in higher education, because if she is consistent with herself she must ignore the Cross of Christ. The State can consistently teach only a defective system of ethics, certainly not Christian ethics; her teaching of history cannot be acceptable to Catholic and Protestant alike; she could treat the Bible only in a cold scientific way as literature, a treatment which would be well nigh disgusting to any real believer in its unique mission. . . .

"Which really is the higher education—that education which is obtained in the cold, neutral atmosphere of consistent State institutions, or that which is offered in an atmosphere of untrammeled Christian influences, where mention of the name that is above every name is not only not forbidden, but is expected and invited?

"If it be true that Jesus Christ has given us the highest type of Christian manhood—the one perfect human character—it must be true that the type of character fostered by the Christian religion is superior to all others. And if it is true that the highest thing in higher education is the soul-life that should dominate it, the higher character that sanctifies it by giving it purity, motive and energy, then it is also true that however highly the State may cultivate intellect she must, if she is consistent, necessarily and avowedly fail to furnish a higher education that is worthy of the name. When she says that she cannot teach religion, she virtually says that she cannot inculcate Christian character. It is not right for the State to attempt to give higher education, for she cannot do it.

"Those evangelical Christians who hold . . . that higher education should be in the hands of the State rather than those of the Church, and that religious influences may be sufficiently secured in the State institutions through the lives of Christian teachers and other like indirect means, render themselves the subjects of just criticism by Catholics, Jews and agnostics, and might some day be practically driven from their position by a majority of such people or even an influential minority as a factor in politics. Christian advocates of higher education by the state may not find fault with State institutions so long as they are run to suit their own religious ideas, but when they are run to give influence to the religious ideas of other people the case becomes different. And such Christians will then be forced back to denominational or private institutions, thus giving a practical demonstration that the State cannot be depended upon to give higher education with a religious soul of the right stamp" (Dr. C. P. Erwin on "Free Tuition" in *Christian Educator*, Jan., 1897).

But if some religious elements are excluded, the Constitution is violated.

Hence, the education provided by the State must either be in violation of the Constitution or imperfect.

But a State must not violate the Constitution.

Therefore, the education provided by a State must necessarily be imperfect; or, in other words, the State cannot provide "all useful learning."[94]

Building on the argument that desirable education must have religious elements which the state could not give, the church leaders contended for a state policy which would not tend to destroy the denominational colleges. Without such a policy "there shall be no education except Godless and Christless education in North Carolina." "It means that unless we struggle persistently, Wake Forest and Trinity and Davidson and the other colleges must be changed into Theological Seminaries for the training of preachers."[95]

When the friends of the State University claimed it was teaching Christianity but not denominationalism, the Methodist and Baptist leaders branded the claim as "a supreme piece of arrogance." "The University has done enough talking about 'broad Christianity' and 'narrow churches' to either hush such gab or produce its 'broader Christianity.'"[96] President Kilgo told the friends of Christian

[94] Taylor, *op. cit.*, p. 34.

[95] *Biblical Recorder*, Jan. 6, 1897; J. S. Bassett, "Shall a Church Have a College?" *Christian Educator*, May, 1897.

[96] *Christian Educator*, June, 1897.

"These 'narrow churches' have sent out all the missionaries and built all the churches in this and other States. Thank God the world is not dependent on this 'broader Christianity' crowd. If the University can and wishes to teach Christianity, let it do it, and quit its abuse of the Christian denominations who have made this land and redeemed this people. Christian education is more than the donation of a Bible to each graduate, or else Mr. Ingersol is a saint" (*ibid.*).

The *Biblical Recorder's* comment on this point was as follows: "The *Wilmington*

education that "It is the verdict of all the churches in America that the necessity to occupy, at least, the field of higher education is upon them . . . . The effort of state colleges to claim equal rights with church colleges to promulgate Christian religion, creates a suspicion among all who have the least knowledge of the genius of American institutions."[97]

Friends and leaders of state institutions, facing the denominational crusaders in the crisis of 1895–99, also called to their aid arguments used in previous contests. As in the case of the church leaders, the state leaders advanced hardly a new argument. In summary, they maintained (a) that the Constitution demanded the maintenance of one or more state universities; (b) that as head of the public school system of the state, the University was educating many poor boys, training teachers, and rendering other services which the church colleges were not prepared to render; (c) that the University cost the state so little that the money put into it would extend the elementary schools very little; (d) that state institutions were not, by free tuition, enticing students away from the church colleges; (e) that the University was religious but non-partisan and non-sectarian; and (f) without state-aid state institutions

---

Messenger remarks innocently: 'By the way, we hear of an important step to be taken at the University in behalf of an increase of interest in the matter of "Christian education"—not a pretense or humbug sort, but the pure and genuine. Time will reveal the work.' Well, well, one would have thought a few weeks ago that what of Christian education our University did not have had not been discovered. We await the revelation of time. It may be that we are to be treated to a systematic theology of the new gospel of the State. At any rate it is refreshing to know that our University has at last recognized that it is not the head of the churches of North Carolina; and we doubt not that as its eyes open time will tenderly reveal to it what has long since been revealed to others, that there can be no such thing as a Christian State, and that a Christian State institution is a pretence and a sham" (reprinted in *Christian Educator*, Jan., 1898).

[97] Kilgo, "An Open Letter to the Friends of Christian Education," *Christian Educator*, Sept., 1897. See also Kilgo, "Christian Education: Its Aims and Superiority" (Trinity College Pamphlets) and his article on "Education and Crime, *Christian Educator*, Oct., 1896.

could not exist.[98] In a word, the state was not endeavoring to crowd out denominational institutions but to perform a service required by the Constitution.[99]

"In our own State the different Christian denominations have done and are doing a great work in this noble cause," said Governor Carr, "and I am sure you will join me in grateful recognition thereof. If the Church was able to provide for the education of all the people we might trust this great work to it; but we know that it is not. Its capacity for good is limited, notwithstanding its divine origin, to the numbers, ability, and disposition of the human beings who constitute its membership. Knowing, then, the inability of the Church to provide schools for all the people, and knowing, too, that the future of the State is to be largely affected and influenced by the education of her children, the duty of the State to take part in this work becomes clear and imperative. We must know—we do know—that there are a large number of boys and girls whose education cannot be provided for in the denominational schools and colleges, to say nothing of the thousands whose inclinations do not lead them to these schools. . . . "[100]

The common school system was born in the University, and the destruction of the University would not add a day and a half to the terms of these schools.[101] Private philan-

[98] Battle, *op. cit.*, pp. 481–493. President Winston's brief, presented to the legislature of 1893, is a good summary of the arguments of the state-aid group. Governor Elias Carr's message to the legislature of 1897, moreover, is another good summary of state-aid arguments (*Executive and Legislative Documents, 1897, No. 1*, pp. 42–49; *University Record*, Jan. 27, 1897, p. 36).

[99] It was held that the right of the state to aid higher education was given by the Constitution of North Carolina, that it was a universally recognized principle of government throughout the union and among all civilized people, "from the time when Moses and Daniel were fitted for the duties of higher citizenship by their respective governments, to the time when Jefferson founded the University of Virginia and Washington proposed a National University," and that the denial of this right was the denial of the state's right to establish any school (*ibid.*, p. 490).

[100] *Executive and Legislative Documents, 1897, No. 1*, p. 47; *University Record*, Dec., 1896, p. 2.

[101] *Ibid.*, p. 43. "The University and the Public School System in North Carolina," *University Magazine*, March, 1899, pp. 212–219; June, 1899, pp. 312–316.

thropy, moreover, could not be expected to put money in an institution if the state should formally declare the institution unworthy of support.[102] By its general influence in behalf of education, by sending out men of influence favorable to education, by supplying teachers, by maintaining a summer school for teachers, and by educating at least sixty teachers annually, the University, the head of the state school system, was deserving all it received from the state.[103] "All the forces of the University have worked, are working, and shall ever work" for an adequate system of common schools.[104]

As to competition with the church colleges, it was argued that there were about twenty colleges in the state and one university, that there was room for all, that the state aided them all by releasing them from taxation, that the state sought no monopoly in education nor could it yield any, that church institutions had prospered since the reopening of the University, receiving increased endowment and students, and that the University was in the field long before any college in the state.[105]

On the question of the University's taking boys from other colleges by giving them free scholarships, emphatic denial was made. Neither did the University give scholarships to rich boys. All scholarships controlled by the institution

[102] Battle, *op. cit.*, pp. 490–491.

[103] *Ibid.*, p. 492; *University Record*, Feb., 1897, p. 16.

[104] *University Magazine*, June, 1899, p. 316; *University Record*, Jan. 27, 1897, pp. 38–40.

[105] Battle, *op. cit.*, p. 491. In his inaugural address President Alderman declared: ". . . . the University has no desire to limit or curtail the usefulness of any educational institution. It recognizes the value and services of its fellow colleges in North Carolina. . . . The University asks for no monopoly, and it will yield none. The University is here to stay. It will always attract men of all denominations. The various denominations should rally around the State University and avail themselves of its educational facilities. Might not the denominations well promote their interests by coming to the seat of the University and creating dormitories and halls to take care of the home and religious life of the University students of their faith and giving in these halls such moral training and religious instruction as they may deem for the best interests of their respective denominations?" (*University Record*, Jan. 27, 1897, pp. 37–38).

were given to boys of talent, character, and poverty. And no scholarships were provided out of state funds.[106]

On the question of the University's right to be religious, its friends and leaders made much of the "marriage of Christianity and democracy" and "the Christian State,"[107] of the "atmosphere of religion and refinement at Chapel Hill,"[108] and of "Christian education—the rule at Chapel Hill."[109] President Alderman's ideal for the University was described as a place "where the life and teachings of Jesus furnish forth the ideal of right living and true manhood."[110]

President Alderman admitted that the voluntary principle was "a noble and beneficent idea" when "united with and stimulated by state action." He insisted, nevertheless, that to remove the energy of the state entirely and rely exclusively on the voluntary principle would lead to "aristocracy in education pure and simple." In addition, he held that it would kill the voluntary spirit by removing the stimulus.[111]

The most interesting part of the crisis, in some respects,

[106] Battle, *op. cit.*, p. 492. It was stated that tuition fees were charged at state institutions in only six states, the North Carolina fee being $60, South Carolina $40, Iowa $25, Missouri $20, Oregon $10, and South Dakota $9 (*News and Observer*, March 12, 1897). Governor Carr stated that in 1896–97, sixty-five students at Chapel Hill had free tuition under the state laws, and seventy-four had tuition by private philanthropy.

[107] President Alderman in his inaugural address (*ibid.*, p. 539; also *University Record*, Jan. 27, 1897, pp. 25–30).

[108] See report of visiting committee, in *ibid.*, p. 552.

[109] *Ibid.*, p. 569; *University Record*, April, 1897, pp. 31–32.

[110] *Presbyterian Standard*, Feb. 14, 1900. Charles B. Aycock, then a United States district attorney, who later became famous as North Carolina's educational governor, did not understand this contest when the church leaders were saying: "We love the University, God bless it, therefore we will take away the appropriation." He argued that there was no competition in education and wanted to let the state run the University, the Baptists Wake Forest, the Methodists Trinity, and the Episcopalians their own schools. Aycock's reference to the Episcopalians and their schools touched off an explosive; Dr. Skinner wanted to know where the Episcopalians had a college. Aycock answered, in part, "Let them build one of their own," and then went on to say: "I know what was in the Doctor's mind, but it shall not find utterance through me. I went to the University without religion, and I came away a Christian and a Baptist. All religions stand on the same footing at the University" (*News and Observer*, March 6, 1895).

[111] *University Record*, Jan. 27, 1897, p. 36.

was not the arguments made for and against the University and other state institutions, however, but the exchange of accusations, insinuations, and epithets, which help reveal the spirit and intensity of the crisis. President Kilgo of Trinity College, who was made the object of a virulent attack, was accused of making "a heartless attack upon university and public education" and a "very eloquent plea for ignorance."[112] So concerted was the attack on President Kilgo that his friends regarded it as an attempt to drive him out of the state.[113] He is said to have been branded as a "buffoon, a blasphemer, a ranter, an ignoramus, a tool of the trusts, a deceiver, and a sycophant."[114] President Winston of the University, furthermore, is said to have threatened, as a means of arousing prejudice against church colleges, to show how Wake Forest, through its endowment fund, was allied with the Standard Oil Trust and Trinity with the American Tobacco Trust.[115] Friends of the church

[112] Dr. Cyrus Thompson, in *News and Observer*, Oct. 19, 1897.

[113] *Christian Educator*, July, 1897, quoting an article, "They Shall Fail," from *Biblical Recorder*, July 21, 1897; G. W. Flowers, "A Word of Protest," *Christian Educator*, May, 1897.

[114] *Ibid.*, Aug., 1897, quoting "A Plain Statement of Facts" from the *North Carolina Christian Advocate.*

[115] *Richmond Times*, Dec. 25, 1895. Concerning this alleged threat, the *Christian Educator* (Aug., 1897) had much to say: "*The Educator* has had this threat in its possession ever since it was published, and has held to it, at the same time watching the drift of things. Dr. Winston's plan has been followed very closely. Every attack made on Trinity during the summer has been made by a University man, and in the name of defending the University, and the so-called defence has been to attack Trinity because of its benefactions. The real issue has not been the benefactions, but Trinity, as the other bodies who have received benefactions have gone unnoticed. Nor does this objection arise from a holiness that revolts at the use of these benefactions, as some of the parties opposing their use at Trinity have sought them for their own use. . . .

"Now much has been said about attacks on the University and its friends have played the baby act to a high degree of perfection. The efforts of the University to center the impression that it is the innocent victim of a vicious attack by the church colleges would be amusing if the falsity of it did not make it so serious. The University never ceases to make war on the church colleges. Its policy is to fight them and at the same time pretend to be as innocent as 'Mary's Little Lamb.' Its methods are to shoot from ambush and turn all political prejudices against the church colleges, as Dr. Winston threatened to do, as his followers are now doing."

colleges, in turn, charged the University's friends with hurling prejudice against Trinity and with making "war on the church colleges." An "educational ring" had determined to "drive all church colleges to the wall."[116]

The legislature of 1897[117] marked a turning point in the crisis. What transpired there did not completely or immediately harmonize the discordant elements, for Editor Bailey, President Kilgo, and their allies continued to fight. Their fighting spirits remained undaunted for months after the legislature had adjourned, but their followers were beginning to admit the futility of fighting.[118] The church press made a heroic effort to keep the forces in fighting spirit, but the handwriting was on the wall.[119] How completely the state-aid group had control of the legislature of 1897 is revealed by the defeat of three measures sponsored by the church group. The denominational colleges regarded as unfair the provision in the charter of the State Normal and Industrial School which made a diploma from that institution a life-time certificate to teach in the public schools of the state without further examination by the supervisors.[120] Instead of correcting this alleged un-

[116] *Christian Educator*, Aug., 1897. Indicating further the fury of the fight are the following phrases taken more or less at random from the writings of this period of the controversy: "Irritable," "pugnacious," "impudent," "insolent," "discourteous," "narrow," "dogmatic and sectarian rather than Christian," "sneer," "spurious, unsought, and undesired state charity," "ravings against sectarianism," "buy students," "shoot from ambush," "not fit to feed swine," "traitors to their country and their God," "religious pigmies."

[117] State aid was one of the issues in the election of this legislature. At any rate, the *Biblical Recorder* (Sept. 30, 1896) urged Baptists to pledge candidates on their attitude toward this question.

[118] Editor Bailey and the *Biblical Recorder* kept up its criticisms of the University as late as Aug. 16, 1899: "Power unlimited to issue scholarships, a lobby in the Legislature to increase appropriations every year, and a perfectly plain policy of tolling off all the students possible will have its effect unless the Christian people stand by Christian institutions." Obviously, however, its hopes were rather to win patronage to denominational colleges than to remove the reasons for these criticisms. The *Christian Educator* suspended publication in 1898.

[119] J. C. Kilgo, "Dogmatic Criticism," *Christian Educator*, Feb., 1897; *Biblical Recorder*, March 17, 1897.

[120] *House Journal, 1891*, pp. 135, 159, 167, 802; *Senate Journal, 1891*, pp. 156,

fairness, the legislature, in 1897, gave to The Normal and Collegiate Institute at Asheville, a Northern Presbyterian school, the same exemption from examinations for teachers' certificates, but denied it to the graduates of Wake Forest, Trinity, Davidson, the University, Greensboro Female College, Peace Institute, and St. Mary's Female Institute.[121] Then, in order to find out exactly how the tax money was being spent at Chapel Hill, an attempt was made to compel the bursar of the University to make regular reports; but this attempt also failed to get by the legislature.[122] Again, as in 1895, a bill was introduced to repeal the appropriation to the University, but this bill did not get out of the committee.[123] Instead of withdrawing the University's appropriation, the amount was increased to $25,000, an advance of $5,000; and the appropriation to the State Normal School was likewise raised to $25,000, an amount exactly double that which was formerly appropriated to the institution at Greensboro.[124]

Notwithstanding the relentless efforts of the Bailey-Kilgo crusaders, the "University gang,"[125] as State Superintendent-elect Mebane called the supporters of state aid, had won by a wide margin.[126] Perhaps the church group did

---

133, 353, 413; *News and Observer*, Jan. 26, 1899; *North Carolina Christian Advocate*, Jan. 23, 1895; *Biblical Recorder*, April 7 and July 28, 1897.

[121] *House Journal, 1897*, pp. 261, 527, 606, 647, 890; *Senate Journal, 1897*, pp. 431, 440, 550, 592.

[122] *House Journal, 1897*, p. 315.

[123] *Ibid.*, pp. 562, 612.

[124] *Ibid.*, pp. 714, 770, 771, 815; *Senate Journal, 1897*, pp. 463, 469, 470, 548; *News and Observer*, March 4, 1897.

[125] The officials of the public schools were not opposed to the University as such, but were, of course, zealous for the public schools and doubtless jealous because the University and other state institutions of higher learning were receiving what seemed to them an unfair proportion of tax money. This fact tended to ally them with the church group and perhaps caused Mebane to refer to the ardent supporters of the University as the "University gang" (C. H. Mebane's letter to J. C. Kilgo, Jan. 4, 1897).

[126] The bill increasing the University's appropriation was passed in the Senate with only ten dissenting votes (*News and Observer*, Feb. 26, 1897). Editor Bailey explained that the bills providing for increased appropriations were brought

not have opportunity to show its full strength, as was alleged; but even so, their opponents had driven a wedge into their ranks and succeeded in taking the heart out of some of them. Some began to say, "See what you have done! You are in a worse condition than if you had kept your mouths closed." A few began to fear that the increase in the appropriations was the result of the recent agitations. A number got comfort out of the fact that although the legislature did not wipe out entirely the free scholarship provision at state institutions, the legislature did not broaden it.[127]

One thing the legislature did was very pleasing to the denominational leaders, who had made it one of their special demands and had worked for its passage. The legislature made available $50,000 for common schools, just half as much as the church leaders and other friends of the public school system had requested.[128] Having been so active in support of common schools, the church leaders regarded this appropriation a signal victory. The amount for public schools was increased to $100,000 in 1899 and to $200,000 in 1901.[129] These provisions for the public schools came not only as a boon to the common people but also tended to bridge over the gap between common schools and colleges, to make a greater demand for colleges because more students would be prepared to go to college, and therefore also to decrease the competition between the institutions of church and state.

---

before the committee when those who opposed them were absent, and no opportunity was given to speak against them before the committee. He did not think it fair to advertise that the bills were unanimously approved when actually half of the committee were absent (*Biblical Recorder*, April 14, 1897).

[127] "The Real Status of the Question," *North Carolina Christian Advocate*, reprinted in the *Christian Educator*, May, 1897.

[128] *House Journal, 1897*, pp. 1066, 1107; *Senate Journal, 1897*, pp. 736, 737, 758, 825.

[129] *House Journal, 1899*, pp. 479, 567, 1151, 1199, 1257; *Senate Journal, 1899*, pp. 356, 542, 752, 931, 961, 985; *House Journal, 1901*, pp. 1136, 1140, 1219; *Senate Journal, 1901*, pp. 812, 835, 857.

For months after the legislature of 1897, Editor Bailey and others sought to keep up their courage and their crusade and to stand by President Kilgo when attack was made upon him; but they soon found their support disintegrating and were therefore disposed, at the turn of the new century, to fall in line with the era of conciliation and co-operation which was to follow.[130]

It is interesting to observe, again, that when the legislature, in 1897, came to fill vacancies in the board of trustees, laymen were put in the places of the ministers whose terms expired at that time, marking the complete secularization of the control of the State University.[131]

[130] The *North Carolina Christian Advocate* refused to concede defeat: "The sacred cause, heedless of laugh and sneer and argument of worldly might will advance, and God will brush aside men and parties and legislatures and parliaments to perpetuate its progress" ("The Real Status of the Question," reprinted in *Biblical Recorder*, March 17, 1897).

Editor Bailey's letters to President Kilgo are interesting. For example:

July 14, 1897: "We must not let them put us on the defensive. They are fighting you just as they fought Dr. Durham. They made him mad, and he lost his head. Beware. We are solid. The rank and file of the Methodists are with you . . . John White and I will stand by till the morning . . . I will make the fight hotter in the *Recorder* from now on. . . ."

July 16, 1897: "I want to caution you to be as careful as possible. You know I want you to be aggressive; you must be; but guard your utterances. The Pharisees are watching you. Get out your pamphlet . . . But don't go for old Kingsbury, Caldwell, or Webster. There is nothing to gain by it. We can't waste ammunition on sparrows and flies."

August 6, 1897: "You killed Kingsbury; John White flayed Caldwell; and I am going to beat the brains out of the *News and Courier*. It appears we are winning."

November 9, 1897: "Cy Thompson says you are a meteor. And you must be destroyed . . . I told him his points in the *News and Observer* were every one those of a fool or a knave . . . And as for Abernathy and Holt—what a pair to draw to—a blatterskite and a skunk; a nice match for sissy; after McIver's own heart; and twin sisters to Joe Daniels and Thompson . . . Three dollar pop guns!"

Superintendent Mebane wrote President Kilgo (letter of Aug. 17, 1897) expressing great concern over "the mean attacks made upon you by the secular press."

Editor Bailey found President Kilgo "entirely too quiet" in March, 1898 (Bailey's letter to Kilgo, March 24, 1898).

[131] See above, pp. 130–131.

V

Relationships in the Realm of Elementary and Secondary Education

THE framers of the Constitution of North Carolina laid the foundation for a state system of elementary and secondary education;[1] but it took the legislature over sixty years to give elementary schools to the children of the state and over a century to make even a good beginning at establishing state high schools. And whereas only thirteen years after provision for it were put into the fundamental law of the commonwealth, the legislature chartered the University of North Carolina,[2] generations of children and youth grew up with no help from the state in securing even the elements of knowledge or the preparation for admission to the University before the state ever undertook seriously to do anything for them.

Why the state acted so promptly in establishing a university has already been considered.[3] Why it delayed so long before establishing schools of lower rank is a question calling for consideration here. Several factors operated to hold the state back. One was the uncertainty as to what kind of schools, other than one or more universities, the Constitution meant for the state to establish. Some people interpreted it to mean that public schools should be created by the legislature, while others regarded it as intending that existing academies should be aided or new ones set up.[4]

[1] Article 41, Constitution of 1776 (see above, p. 3).

[2] See above, p. 3.

[3] See above, chap. i.

[4] W. K. Boyd, "The Finances of the North Carolina Literary Fund," p. 4. Numerous bills were introduced in the legislature to aid academies, but none ever became law (*ibid.;* see also Coon, *Public Education in North Carolina: A Documentary History, 1790–1840*, I, xxii-xxix, 14, 25, 28, 43, 44, 46, 49, 50).

Hatred of taxation, sparsely settled communities, very primitive means of communication, the pressure of slavery, the feeling that public aid smacked of charity, and the educational destitution of the people have likewise been advanced as reasons why it was almost impossible to win popular support for public schools in North Carolina during the first half-century of its statehood.[5] The lack of a common religion, and the educational activities of the leading denominations, which established their own elementary schools and academies, may also have been powerful factors in delaying the day of a state-supported public school system. A consideration of the part the churches played in retarding or aiding this system is the purpose of this chapter.

Before the state became earnestly and actively interested in public schools, practically all of the elementary and secondary education was supplied by private and denominational schools. According to the census of 1840, there were then in North Carolina "141 academies and grammar schools and 632 primary schools of all kinds," and enrolled in the academies were 4,398 and in the primary schools 14,937 pupils.[6]

In 1772, when Organ and St. John's Lutheran churches sent commissioners to Germany in search of a pastor, they were instructed also to secure a schoolteacher. When they returned, in 1773, they brought both with them; and since that time the work of the church and that of the school have been closely identified in the polity of the Lutheran Church in North Carolina.[7] A Lutheran congregation without its school was hardly thought of. It was sometimes without a pastor but rarely without its teacher.[8]

The story of the work of the early Presbyterians in North Carolina, particularly in academies, is unquestionably the

[5] Coon, *op. cit.*, p. xxi.

[6] C. H. Wiley, *North Carolina Reader, No. III*, p. 3.

[7] G. D. Bernheim and George H. Cox, *History of the Evangelical Lutheran Synod and Ministerium*, p. 64.

[8] Prof. R. A. Yoder, private letter, quoted in "Views from Different Sources," *Christian Educator*, Oct., 1896.

brightest page in North Carolina's educational history before 1840.[9] "As soon as a group was settled, preparations were made for religious services, and when the log church was erected, it became also a schoolhouse, a community center, and the foundation of a nation."[10] So powerful was the Presbyterian influence in the educational life of the state that a roster of the leading schoolteachers of the state from 1790 to 1840 resembles a section from the list of graduates of Princeton College. In this period, Presbyterian preachers were especially active in establishing academies.[11] The Presbyterian system of education provided for three grades of institutions, including (1) parochial schools, (2) academies, and (3) colleges and universities.[12] Although how content were they with their own schools one cannot say with confidence, yet one suspects that the fact that this group of educationally minded people were supplying the needs of their own children with even a fair degree of satis-

[9] W. H. Foote, *Sketches of North Carolina*, pp. 517–523. A good account of Presbyterian activities in education. Another good account is C. Alphonso Smith, *Presbyterians in Educational Work in North Carolina since 1813;* also Cornelia Shaw, *Davidson College*, *passim;* and C. L. Raper, *Church and Private Schools of North Carolina.*

[10] Shaw, *op. cit.*, pp. 1–4.

[11] C. L. Coon, *North Carolina Schools and Academies, 1790–1840*, pp. xiii–xxxiii. Coon's introduction to this volume gives a concise picture of the activities of the Presbyterian preachers and others, including a few Methodist and Episcopal preachers, who served as principals and teachers of early schools and academies.

[12] *Minutes Synod of North Carolina, 1847*, pp. 25–27. The report adopted by the Synod of 1847 described the three grades of institutions as follows:

1. Parochial Schools under the care of the Church Sessions, including all schools for elementary instruction (infant-schools, Sabbath schools and Bible classes, or common schools).

2. Academies, under the care of the Presbyteries, comprehending all existing institutions of this grade (grammar schools for classics, high schools, gymnasiums, institutes, normal schools for training teachers, female schools, and seminaries, and female colleges).

3. College and University under the care of the Synods. The College "... imparts the discipline, the science and the literature, fitting young men to enter upon the study of either of the learned professions." The University "... provides for all parts of a College, with the munificence of a State; and, above a College, it sustains the several Professions;and furnishes facilities for the augmentation of learning" (*ibid.*, pp. 26–27; see also Sherrill, *Presbyterian Parochial Schools, 1846–1870*).

faction helped to delay the coming of the state's public school system.

The Baptists, before 1840, on the contrary, were not greatly interested in education and, therefore, did very little for it. Although organized primarily to promote missions and education, the Baptist State Convention, at its twelfth annual meeting, recorded the fact that education, for some years past, had occupied "for scarcely a moment" a place in its deliberations.[13] When once aroused, however, as will appear later in this discussion, this great body of people became very active in the interest of common schools and other educational agencies. The absence of schools of their own seems to have made it quite easy for them to support the movement for free schools. The Methodists, very much like the Baptists, were not noted for their educational activities before 1838, due, in part perhaps, to the fact that their state organization was not formed until 1838.[14] The Quakers, Moravians, and other small sects showed marked interest and activity in education.[15]

In addition, there were many Sunday schools which taught children, including children of the poor, to read and write and "in the habits of moral reflection and conduct." In the legislature which created a school fund, an effort was made to secure state aid for Sunday schools on the ground that they instructed children who otherwise would be brought up in ignorance and vice.[16] This effort was re-

[13] *Minutes Baptist State Convention, 1842*, pp. 14–15. See also above, pp. 4–5.

[14] See above, p. 6.

[15] Zora Klain, *Quaker Contributions to Education in North Carolina*, pp. 280–281. There were nine schools under the care of Quakers and fifty-three to which Quaker children went in 1839–40, according to the records of the North Carolina Yearly Meeting.

[16] *House Journal, 1825*, p. 170. The Orange County Sunday School Union was the leader of the movement for state aid to the Sunday schools throughout the state. Its memorial, in part, was as follows: ". . . the Sunday School Union of Orange County has under its care 22 schools in which are instructed from 800 to 1000 children, many of whom, . . . the children of the poor, who otherwise would have been brought up in utter ignorance and vice, have been taught to read and trained to habits of moral reflection and conduct. The schools have been heretofore supplied with books for the most part by the charity of the public, and it is

peated two years later.[17] Both legislatures, however, regarded the proposals as inexpedient.[18] Nevertheless, even for a long time after the public school system was established, Sunday schools continued to supplement the work of the state system, both in the low country and in the mountains.[19]

The state system of free schools, as they were called then, started in the fall of 1840, although for a decade there was no organization or administration resembling a modern school system.[20] The state initiated its plan of support of public schools in 1825, not by direct taxation, but by establishing an endowment known as the Literary Fund.[21] In 1836, during the last days of President Jackson's administration, this fund was greatly enlarged by the treasury of the United States, which distributed at that time its surplus revenue among the states.[22] In 1839 a law was passed by the state legislature making the proceeds of the Literary Fund available for schools, providing for the division of the counties into school districts, and making it the

---

to furnish the necessary books that your memorialists pray for such aid, as that the sum of 25 cts. per annum may be paid for every Sunday School learner under their care, out of the public taxes, in such manner and to such persons for their use, as in your wisdom you may deem best. And your memorialists would further pray a similar provision for all the Sunday schools formed, or which may be formed within the limits of our County and throughout the State" (Coon, *op. cit.*, I, 283–284).

[17] *Senate Journal, 1826–1827*, p. 86; Coon, *op. cit.*, p. 339.

[18] *Ibid.*; *House Journal, 1825*, p. 170.

[19] C. H. Wiley, *Alamance Church* (pamphlet), p. 27; "Sabbath Schools and Common Schools," from the *Connecticut Sabbath School Journal*, in *Biblical Recorder*, Dec. 15, 1838; "Sabbath Schools Related to Common Schools," *North Carolina Journal of Education*, Oct., 1858, pp. 308–309.

[20] W. K. Boyd, *History of North Carolina*, II, 243.

[21] The chief sources of this fund were (1) dividends from the stock owned by the state in certain banks and navigation companies; (2) license taxes paid by liquor dealers and auctioneers; (3) a balance in the Agricultural Fund, established in 1822, and (4) income from vacant swamp lands and lands vacated by the Cherokee Indians through treaties of 1817 and 1819 (Boyd, *op. cit.*, pp. 6–7).

[22] *Ibid.*, pp. 9–10; J. A. Blair, *Reminiscences of Randolph County*, pp. 29–30. North Carolina's share of this federal money was $1,433,757.40, of which $300,000 was applied to the Literary Fund.

duty of the county courts to call an election to ascertain whether or not the people wanted free schools.[23] Each district which voted for schools simultaneously taxed itself $20 on condition that it receive $40 from the Literary Fund. By the fall of 1840, nearly every county in the state had voted in favor of schools.[24] This, in brief, is the story of how the state's system of free schools began. By 1860 over $3,000,000 had been thus spent on elementary schools in North Carolina.

In the state-wide campaign of 1839–40, and the years following, when the fate of the state's free schools was in the balances, the churches had their first big opportunity to show their attitude toward state schools for the masses. The Quakers had already expressed themselves in most convincing fashion. In 1834 their Yearly Meeting sent a memorial and petition to the legislature wherein they not only protested against certain repressive slave laws, including one making it a crime to teach a slave to read and write and one prohibiting slaves and free Negroes from exhorting and preaching, but declared boldly that "it is the indispensable duty of the Legislature of a Christian people to enact laws and establish regulations for the literary instruction of every class, within its limits; . . . ."[25] Thus the Quakers went far ahead of their times, for about as far as anyone else at that time had gone was to talk about the "education of the poor."[26] They, therefore, were doubtless

[23] Boyd, *op. cit.*, p. 242.

[24] Blair, *op. cit.*, p. 30. By 1846 all the counties had taken advantage of the opportunity provided by the law of 1839 (see Boyd, *op. cit.*, p. 18).

[25] See "Memorial and Petition" signed by Jeremiah Hubbard, Clerk, in Coon, *op. cit.*, II, 675–676.

[26] Concerning even the slaves, the Quakers declared: "And lastly, your Petitioners would respectfully submit to your consideration, not only the repeal of those laws before mentioned, but *the enacting of other laws and regulations for the general instruction of Slaves*, in the doctrines and precepts of the Christian religion, and in so much of literary education at least, as will enable them to read the Holy Scriptures, which would undoubtedly tend to the improvement of their general character, and condition, and greatly lessen if not wholly remove, the apprehension of danger from them." It was the habit in old Presbyterian families, and doubtless also in others, to teach the slaves to read and to furnish them with Bibles (Wiley, *Alamance Church*, pamphlet, p. 31).

ready to support the efforts of the state which were made five years after their memorial and petition.

The Baptists, through their church paper and their convention, supported the state whole-heartedly in its efforts to establish free schools. In fact, it was General Alfred Dockery, a charter member of the board of trustees of Wake Forest College, who introduced a resolution in the senate which opened the way for the operation of the state's elementary schools.[27] And soon thereafter Wake Forest included in its curriculum a course intended to train teachers for these public schools.[28] The *Biblical Recorder and Southern Watchman*,[29] moreover, gave publicity to the act of the legislature of 1839 and advocated, through its editorial columns and otherwise, its adoption by the counties.[30] It

[27] *Senate Journal, 1834*, Feb. 6.

[28] G. W. Paschal, "Public School Advancement in North Carolina," *Wake Forest Student*, Nov., 1929, p. 40.

[29] This paper was called simply *Biblical Recorder* after 1839.

[30] *Biblical Recorder*, Feb. 2, 1839; July 20, 1839; July 27, 1839. In these issues, effort was made to "rouse up the minds of the people . . . to their duty, respecting the School Laws" passed by the last legislature. One L. Simmons, writing from Simmons' Tan Yard, N. C., urged Editor Meredith to help get the people to vote "School." Among other interesting things, he said: "You that live in town, may think that no man in his senses would vote against a School; but believe me, there are a great many in the country of the ignorant people, that are determined to vote 'No School.' I have often heard my Father speak of the fine herds of deer and buffaloe that induced the Pennsylvanians and Virginians to move to this country for the sake of the game which they could procure with so much ease; now you know that it is the most ignorant kind of people that will leave their agricultural pursuits to procure a subsistence by hunting game—so that this country was first settled by a very ignorant and unlearned people, and this is what has kept N. Carolina under the weather . . .

"And now, my dear friend, you can do a great deal of good by stirring up the minds of the people, especially ministers of the gospel, who have a powerful influence over the people. There should be a sermon delivered on the subject in every congregation in the State, previous to the election. . . .

"Only get a majority to vote for a School, and N. Carolina is a made State. You know the Legislature have made considerable ado about Internal Improvement for years past, (for which I am a strong advocate) but when they passed the school law, they struck at the very root of internal improvement;—and had this law been passed twenty years ago, I have no doubt that N. C. at this time would be worth a million more than it is" (*ibid.*, July 20, 1839).

was found necessary to overcome the impression that the schools were to be charity schools to which the children of the poor only were to be sent. The Baptist paper helped to counteract this impression and to make it clear that these schools were to be "the people's schools, paid for with the people's money."[31] It also sought to remove the fear that the tax would be an enormous amount.[32] And then, in 1842, when the state's schools were still under suspicion and treated with indifference in many counties, the Baptist State Convention threw its full support to the state's enterprise. Its report on education that year declared that "Our brethren must be impressed with the importance of educating their children, and with the duty of providing Institutions suitable for accomplishing this object." It urged "that our free schools should receive the special attention of ministering brethren," who should become "the guardians of these schools." The convention deplored the fact that, according to the 1840 census, of the state's 209,685 white population over twenty years of age, 56,609 could neither read nor write. With enthusiasm the Baptists voted to help remove this blight from the state's record; and from 1842 to the present day, as will appear, the leaders of the Baptists have strongly espoused the cause of common schools.[33] They reiterated their stand in 1843 and from

[31] *Ibid.*, July 27, 1839. The editor quoted the *New Bern Spectator* to the effect that the income from the Literary Fund was nearly $100,000 a year and would be applied to the purposes of general elementary instruction of the children of all classes.

[32] *Ibid.*

[33] *Minutes Baptist State Convention, 1842*, pp. 14–15. One of the most interesting paragraphs of the report of 1842 is as follows: "Your committee remark, then, that our Free Schools should receive the special attention of ministering brethren. These schools are just going into operation. We are unaccustomed to them. The system itself is undoubtedly imperfect, and for this reason requires attention. If its defects be observed and pointed out, they will soon be remedied. In our denomination no person will be found to attend to this unless our ministering brethren do it. And they should make it a point of duty to do so. They should visit every school in their respective section or in any way connected with their churches. Teachers need encouragement. It will give them great pleasure

time to time since then have not failed to let the state know how strongly they favored common schools.[34]

No similar declaration is found in the minutes of the Methodist Conference before 1840; but the Conference was not formed until 1838, and it was doubtless too much occupied in setting its own house in order to give much thought to state education. We do know, however, that the Methodists were friendly to common schools, and their Normal College, which later became Trinity College and Duke University, was devoted to the training of teachers for common and high schools.[35]

The Presbyterians did not oppose efforts of the state to develop its common school system. In fact, they not only contributed a fine educational background to the state but furnished the leader who did more to popularize and to develop the state school system than any other man or group of men. The Presbyterians gave Calvin Henderson Wiley as the state's first superintendent of common schools.[36] And his character and statesmanship did more to win and to hold the confidence and esteem of the people, not only of his own church but also of all the denominations, than everything else the state did to secure their confidence and support. In 1852 Wiley was elected as head of the public school system of the state, which office he held until 1865 when he was regarded as one of the foremost educational leaders in the United States.[37] Concerning the development of the state's schools under his leadership more will be said later. Suffice it to point out here that the state

---

to see that there is someone at least who sympathizes with them, and who appreciates in some degree the importance of the services they are rendering the community. The students can be conversed with and encouraged in habits of virtue. It should never be forgotten that in a few years they will make the community. From these, too, will be formed the churches and the ministry."

[34] *Ibid.*, *1843*, p. 9.

[35] L. S. Burkhead, *Centennial of Methodism in North Carolina*, pp. 180–181.

[36] He was ordained a Presbyterian minister in 1866 (Smith, *op. cit.*, p. 15).

[37] Smith, *op. cit.*, p. 14.

showed real wisdom in the choice of this trusted leader of the strongest group, educationally, in the state.

As willing as the churches seemed to be to encourage the state's venture in popular education, wise strategy demanded that special efforts be taken to show the private and denominational schools, academies, and colleges their interest in the free schools and to enlist the hearty sympathy and active co-operation of the preachers. Wiley himself recognized that "the common school system, from the very nature of things, had been imperfectly understood; it had not received that respect to which it was entitled, and there were doubts and gloomy forebodings pervading the public mind."[38] Governor Bragg explained that, for fifteen years or more after the beginning of the state's activities in elementary education, an opinion prevailed to some extent that the common schools had been of little benefit and that their small benefit had been more than counterbalanced by the injury resulting therefrom to other schools.[39] There was obvious jealousy on the part of "old field" schools and academies, which were numerous in the state in 1850.[40]

Wiley proved to be just the man to deal with such jealousies and forebodings. He was a Presbyterian of the Presbyterians. And, as has been suggested, Presbyterians had more primary schools and academies than anybody else and therefore more to fear from the standpoint of competition. Wiley emphasized religion in education and sought to establish a deep religious purpose in the public schools of the state. He was responsive to the demands of the religious leaders, who were pleased with his ideals and leadership.[41] He was able to convince them that attention would

[38] Wiley, *op. cit.*, No. III, p. 4.

[39] *Executive and Legislative Documents, 1856–57* (*Governor's Message*), pp. 22–23. Governor Bragg admitted that inferior schools in most counties had been superceded by the common schools.

[40] E. W. Knight, *Public School Education in North Carolina*, p. 150; Boyd, *op. cit.*, p. 246.

[41] *Biblical Recorder*, March 11, 1853. See letter of "Quaestor," written from Duplin, N. C., Dec. 23, 1852, to Wiley, printed in this issue of the *Recorder*.

be given to the manners and morals of the pupils, based upon the teachings of the Scriptures, as nearly every school of the period of 1790 to 1840 claimed to do.[42] He declared, in 1855, that a great work had been done, "under the guidance of Providence," in planting steady habits and "Bible principles" and expressed the conviction that "universal education based on the revealed and eternal Word of God, and drawing its life and energy from it," would help to make North Carolina "a lasting abode of Peace, Liberty, and Happiness." He observed that the common schools had become more hopeful and registered his determination to see that "the true principles of Christian progress received their fullest political and personal development."[43] Wiley regarded religion to be "the only sure foundation of national prosperity" and felt that his position on this point was "destined to become a fixed elementary principle of political economy."

> The object of all education, therefore, should be not to learn to dispense with the agency of God, in our affairs, but to lead us more directly to Him. . . . Education is only a blessing as a means of leading to these results, and the improper prejudice raised against it are due to the fact that promoters of "vain babblings, and oppositions of science, falsely so called," have, in certain places, confounded the means with the end.[44]

Wiley not only heartily approved the use of the Bible in the schools but commended the practice of some county boards of common schools of distributing Bibles among the schools of the county.[45] He insisted, furthermore, that

[42] Coon, *op. cit.*, pp. xxxvi–xxxvii.

[43] Wiley, *op. cit.*, p. 5 (Preface).

[44] *Annual Report Superintendent of Common Schools, 1858–1859*, p. 42. This report contains a good presentation of Wiley's philosophy of education. See also the *North Carolina Journal of Education* (established in 1858 largely through Wiley's instrumentality), Jan., 1858, pp. 14–20; Feb., 1858, pp. 33–35; May, 1858, p. 147; Aug., 1858, p. 245; Oct., 1858, pp. 308–309; May, 1859, p. 148; Jan., 1862, pp. 9–11.

[45] *Annual Report Superintendent of Common Schools, 1858*, Exhibit H, No. 3. Wiley included in his report the following letter from A. A. Scroggs, Chairman of the Wilkes County Board of Common Schools, referring to a county educational

school committees appointed to examine and pass on the qualifications of those wishing to teach in the common schools should construe strictly the constitutional provision which made it impossible for those "who deny the Being of God, or the divine authority of the Old or New Testament" to hold any civil trust.[46] He admonished that committees should exclude immoral and infidel teachers from the schools. "It is your right and your duty rigidly to enforce this rule without exceptions, for any cause." He felt that they could do this "without acting in such a way as to cause or countenance sectarian agitation." In addition to excluding infidel teachers, direct religious influence should be exerted by example, by precept, and by admonition.[47]

---

meeting: "I then called over the names of all our Committee men, *invited the ministers of the Gospel* and the teachers and magistrates to come forward and take seats (as by an article in our constitution they are already members by virtue of their office.). . . .

"After the president took the chair, and our association was fully organized, I submitted a few suggestions concerning the introduction of the *Bible* in our schools—having ascertained that this matter had been so neglected that it amounted almost to a prohibition—premising that I had obtained, partly by donation and partly by purchase, a sufficiency of books to give one copy of the *Bible* and 10 copies of the Testament *to every school district in the county*. I urged with earnestness and zeal the great importance of this movement—enjoined it upon the teachers to attend to this matter—and called upon the committees to help us carry forward the plan. My remarks were listened to with profound attention on this point; and I have reason to believe will not only command the approbation of all our school officers, but will contribute something toward the accomplishment of this much needed measure."

[46] *Annual Report Superintendent of Common Schools, 1860,* Letter of Wiley to the committees: . . . "I cannot conclude this letter, gentlemen, without solemnly reminding you of the infinite importance of a constant and anxious care on your part as to the personal character of those whom you endorse as fit instructors of the youth of our land.

"You should permit no possible consideration to induce you to grant certificates to any who do not prove an unexceptionable moral character; . . . . and while I would not have you pry impertinently into the general speculative opinions of candidates, I would remind you *that none who deny the Being of God, or the divine authority of the Old or New Testament, are allowed to hold any civil trust under the Constitution* of our State. And in this connection, I may add that all who counsel resistance to the powers that be, resist the ordinances of God; and that if you will keep these plain tests in view, you cannot be accused of attempting to exercise any unjust authority over the rights of conscience."

[47] *North Carolina Journal of Education,* May, 1859, p. 148.

Wiley also very tactfully recognized all the denominational colleges and helped to bring them to the attention of pupils in the public schools. For example, of Wake Forest College he said, in his *North Carolina Reader, Number III*, that its "buildings are elegant and substantial, the country healthy, and board cheap," and that it reflected credit on the Baptist denomination. Of the Methodists he said they were "doing God and their country good service," particularly in the education of women.[48] "Episcopalians, Methodists, Baptists, and Presbyterians are engaged in a generous and well-contested struggle to see who can do most for education; and the Society of Friends, or Quakers, find it not against their conscience to take part in this sort of warfare."[49] In summary, the state system of public schools under Wiley took over much of the spirit, purpose, materials, and methods of the church schools and academies.

It is no wonder, therefore, that Wiley was able to report, in 1858, that there was manifest, everywhere, a greatly improved feeling, and that "ministers of the gospel of all denominations, professional men of every class, professors in all colleges, and politicians of every party" were "laboring heartily, cheerfully, hopefully, and harmoniously on the platform of the Common Schools."[50] Even three years earlier he was able to say that "colleges, academies, and high schools have been induced to lend their influence in *favor* instead of *against* this great system (of common schools), and politicians and parties have come to recognize it is the great hope of the country."[51] As early as 1855 he

[48] His reference was to Greensboro Female College, the first college for women chartered in North Carolina.

[49] Wiley, *op. cit.*, Lesson XXVIII, pp. 74–75. The Baptist Convention (*Minutes, 1855*, p. 35) and the Presbyterian Synod (*Minutes, 1857*, p. 25), in the educational reports, referred to the common schools as being of high order. The Presbyterians called special attention to the "paramount importance" of fostering and encouraging "our admirable system of popular education."

[50] *Annual Report Superintendent of Common Schools, 1858–1859*, p. 9.

[51] *Executive and Legislative Documents, 1856–1857*, No. 9, p. 39.

called attention to the fact that colleges and common schools had been placed "on a more intimate, friendly, and honorable footing with regard to each other."[52]

So impressed was Governor Ellis with the harmonious relationships existing in 1859 that, in his inaugural address, he declared, "Our educational system is but an index to the state of religion and morals among our people." He referred to the "rich fruits of that free and universal religious toleration" and added: ". . . . instead of jarring of conflicting sects, we have the harmonious action of all denominations of Christians, in teaching the great truths of practical religion, and introducing that moral training among the people, which is an essential preparation to their exercising properly the functions of self-government."[53] And in his message to the legislature in 1861, Governor Ellis declared that "the natural friends of education are to be found among those who are engaged in the advancement of religion and morals."[54]

This fine co-operation brought forth almost phenomenal growth in schools. Whereas in 1840 there were only 141 academies and grammar schools and 632 primary schools of all kinds, with fewer than 20,000 pupils, in 1855 there were at least 200 academies and grammar schools and about 3,000 primary schools, with at least 120,000 children attending, an increase of approximately 600 per cent since 1840.[55] Wiley reported, in 1855, that nine-tenths of the children of the state attended the common schools "at some time or other."[56] In 1857 there were enrolled in the common schools 150,000 children out of a school population of 220,000. Several thousand more were enrolled in private schools and academies and in Sunday schools.[57] In 1853 there were 800 teachers in the public schools of the state; in 1860 there were 2,286. In 1853 the receipts for common

[52] Wiley, *North Carolina Reader, No. III*, p. 5.

[53] *Raleigh Register*, Jan. 8, 1859.

[54] *Executive and Legislative Documents, 1860–1861*, p. 17.

[55] Wiley, *op. cit.*, p. 3.

[56] *Annual Report Superintendent of Common Schools, 1855*, p. 7.

[57] Knight, *op. cit.*, p. 174.

schools were $192,250; in 1860, $408,566. In 1858, we are told, North Carolina had a larger school fund than Georgia, Virginia, Maryland, New Jersey, Massachusetts, or Maine.[58]

The second major opportunity for the churches to show how they felt toward public schools came in the period of Reconstruction and the years immediately following. During the period of the Civil War, Superintendent Wiley had succeeded, almost singlehandedly, in preserving to the uses of public schools the Literary Fund, notwithstanding numerous efforts to apply it to war purposes, thereby keeping the public schools open. With the collapse of the Confederate government, however, the stock of the banks in which the Literary Fund had been largely invested became worthless. In 1866 the total income from this fund was $776.[59] The collapse of the public school system, therefore, was in sight. The legislature of 1865–66 abolished the office which Wiley had held since 1852. It refused to restore the Literary Fund, and made local taxation for schools optional.[60] The Constitution of 1868[61] placed public education on the basis of taxation rather than endowment, a fact calling for the development of a willingness to be taxed and of a conviction and policy as to where the tax money should be applied. In this task the churches were destined to play an important part.

Although in 1869 the office of superintendent of public instruction was revived, Wiley was not restored to office.[62] A new regime, with S. S. Ashley, a "carpetbagger," as superintendent, took charge.[63] So unpopular was the whole Reconstruction program that education under it tended also to become unpopular. The legislature of 1869 appropriated $100,000 "out of any moneys in the Treasury

[58] Smith, *op. cit.*, pp. 14–15.

[59] Boyd, *The Finances of the North Carolina Literary Fund*, p. 21.

[60] *Ibid.*, pp. 21–22; *Laws of 1865–1866*, chap. 34.

[61] Article IX, Sec. 2.

[62] School Laws, 1869, sec. 63–70.

[63] *Ibid.*, p. 4. Ashley defeated Braxton Craven, the Democratic nominee (Hamilton, *Reconstruction in North Carolina*, pp. 176–184, 254).

not appropriated otherwise" for the support of the four-months school term provided in the Constitution of 1868;[64] but there was very little available for schools. Taxes in North Carolina were increased fourfold,[65] but there were practically no schools. Schools were closed. The poverty of the people, the dissipation of public funds, and the agitation to educate the Negroes, and the threat of both races attending the same schools tended to retard the restoration of schools even for the whites.[66] The Presbyterians, who had always stood in the front ranks of those who had sought to promote secular education,[67] expressed doubt, in 1869, as to the value of state education of all kinds.[68] The Methodist paper also questioned the control of public schools by civil authorities. It held that "since our people have become so mixed; so diversified in tastes, habits and sentiment—so divided into sects, parties, and cliques—and since especially, the idea is, that the prevailing party or sect is the State," it would be impossible to work

[64] *Ibid.*, sec. 53; Constitution of 1868, sec. 3.

[65] *The South in the Building of the Nation*, IV, 608–617.

[66] In 1874 Governor Curtis H. Brogden indicated, in his annual message, two impediments to a vigorous system of common schools: "First, our comparative poverty as a people; and secondly, the so-called Civil Rights Bill." There was no law in the state forbidding Negro children from attending any public schools. By general consent, and by the erection of separate schoolhouses for the two races, they have always been separated (see *Executive and Legislative Documents*, 1874–1875, pp. 14–15). The constitutional convention of 1868, however, had refused to require separation of the races (see Hamilton, *op. cit.*, p. 244). The opposition to taxation for public education in North Carolina continued throughout the century, on three grounds: (1) robbery to tax one man to educate another's children; (2) burden upon an already impoverished white population to educate the Negroes, who paid so small a proportion of taxes; and (3) "educate a negro you spoil a field hand" (*Report State Superintendent Public Instruction, 1887–1888*, p. xl).

[67] *North Carolina Presbyterian*, March 26, 1868.

[68] *Ibid.*, Oct. 13, 1869; see also above, pp. 66–68. They mistrusted it on the ground that it tended to official corruption and consequently to a general demoralization of the people and that it tended to infidelity. Whether they were the only reasons for mistrusting state education is doubtful. The disrepute of the Reconstruction officials doubtless was also an important consideration. It may be, too, that the chief opposition to higher education by the state was used as a basis for opposing all state education (see above, chap. iii).

any system of education kindly and beneficially to all.[69] In general, the churches reflected the popular distrust of the new regime. Some of them, therefore, began afresh in 1869, to emphasize the importance of private and denominational schools.[70] In a word, the churches relied upon the state to maintain elementary schools so long as the state administration was, in their judgment, representative of the people and able financially to support them but, when contrary conditions prevailed, undertook to step in to supply, insofar as possible, what was lacking in public education.

Presbyterians evidenced concern for the education of the children of soldiers dying in the military service of their country; but just how much was actually done beyond calling the need to the attention of the sessions is not apparent.[71] North Carolina Quakers, assisted by Friends of other Yearly Meetings, including the Baltimore, London, and Dublin, did more not only for the education of freedmen but also of whites than perhaps any other agency in the state during the Reconstruction period.[72] For example, in 1865, they maintained thirty schools for an average of over four months, enrolling nearly as many children not of their own faith as of their own.[73] By 1869 there were forty-four Quaker schools, with an average term of over six months, and with an enrolment less than half of which were children of Quaker families.[74] As meager as those Quaker schools

[69] *Raleigh Episcopal Methodist*, Nov. 24, 1869.

[70] *Ibid.*; *North Carolina Presbyterian*, Oct. 13, 1869.

[71] *North Carolina Presbyterian*, Aug. 24, 1864, printing resolutions unanimously adopted by the Fayetteville Presbytery in April, 1863, and subsequent resolutions on the subject.

[72] *Minutes N. C. Yearly Meeting of Friends, 1866*, pp. 9, 13; *1867*, pp. 9, 14, 15; *1868*, p. 9; *1869*, pp. 12, 13; *1872*, pp. 18–20; *1873*, pp. 15–16; *1875*, p. 15; *1879*, p. 27.

[73] *Ibid., 1866*, p. 13.

[74] *Ibid., 1869*, pp. 12–13. "The opening of these [Quaker] schools attracted attention. The State Superintendent of Public Instruction was in frequent communication with the Friends' Superintendent, the local authorities frequently inquired concerning the operations of the schools, and the newspapers of the State gave favorable comment" (F. C. Anscombe, *The Contributions of Quakers to the Reconstruction of the Southern States*, p. 28).

were, compared with the needs of the state, this system of Quaker schools was the only one in the state at all corresponding to public instruction.[75] In 1872 the state contributed $3,000 and the Peabody Fund $6,000 to the Quaker schools.[76] Smaller amounts of public money were contributed to these schools at other times.[77] By this time North Carolina had largely recovered from the turbulence of Reconstruction, and the state was assuming increasing care of the educational system. In 1875 the superintendent of Quaker schools in the state reported "a more general patronage of free public schools."[78] By 1883 the public schools had practically absorbed the elementary educational work of the churches.[79]

A number of churches co-operated with the state in provisions for the education of the freedmen. Some idea of the nature and extent of this co-operation is had from the annual report of the Reverend J. W. Hood, assistant superintendent of public instruction, who, in 1869, went into detail concerning the "Educational Work Among the Colored Population of the State."[80] Most of the Negro

[75] *Ibid.*, pp. 31–34. Two good volumes on the educational work of the Quakers are Zora Klain, *Quaker Contributions to Education in North Carolina*, and Anscombe, *op. cit.* One must not get the impression, however, that private schools even began to supply the needs of the children. Not over 7 per cent of the children ever attended private schools in any one year (*Biennial Report Superintendent Public Instruction, 1894–1896*, pp. 4–5).

[76] *Ibid.*, p. 38.

[77] *Minutes N. C. Yearly Meeting of Friends, 1873*, pp. 15–16, referred to "public money used" amounting to $2,000, and *1879*, p. 27, to "received from Public School Fund, $351.91."

[78] *Ibid., 1875*, p. 15.

[79] "The apparent lack of interest in education, which is only apparent, not real, is owing to the fact that the funds which have been at our disposal in the past are exhausted and the public schools have well nigh absorbed the education of our children in the common schools. If you could secure the services of some one who is efficient to go over the Yearly Meeting with funds at his disposal for extending the length of the schools, and stirring the pure minds of the people on education with a view to preparing and furnishing students for Friends' school at New Garden, the true interest and mission of North Carolina Yearly Meeting would be subserved . . . " (*ibid., 1883*, pp. 18–19).

[80] *Annual Report Superintendent Public Instruction, 1869*, pp. 16–22. Hood was a Negro, who became a bishop in the A. M. E. Zion Church.

schools were those aided by the American Missionary Association and the American Union Freedman's Commission, which supplied teachers, erected buildings, and aided the freedmen themselves in building.[81] Twenty-five Quaker schools for Negroes were reported in the state.[82] Eight Episcopal parish schools were included in Hood's report.[83] The Presbyterian parochial schools for Negroes constituted the fourth class of Negro schools in the state in 1869.[84] The state encouraged these religious groups, especially to supply teachers, for the wages the state offered were so small as not to attract a sufficient supply.[85]

[81] *Ibid.*, p. 17. The American Missionary Society insisted that teachers should be members of some evangelical religious denomination; the Union Commission deemed this immaterial.

[82] Concerning the Quaker schools, Hood said: "While these are placed second in order in this report, they are second to none in character. In educating the Freedmen the Friends are doing a work of praiseworthy benevolence. Without expectation of fee or reward; without attempting to teach the peculiar tenets of their faith; without any apparent desire to advance the interest of their own denomination, they are laboring to dispel the mist of ignorance which has so long hung over the colored people of the South. The Bible is introduced into all of their schools, but is read without comment.

"The teachers are selected without regard to sex, sects, section, nativity, or complexion. They are particular, however, respecting the moral character of the teachers. They require of the teachers as much care for the moral as for the intellectual improvement of their pupils . . ." (*Minutes N. C. Yearly Meeting of Friends, 1870*, p. 21; *1871*, p. 20; and *1872*, p. 31, for additional facts concerning Quaker schools).

[83] Of them Hood said: "With one exception they are good schools of the kind. If members of particular denominations choose to support denominational schools and to have their children's time largely occupied in studying the doctrines and forms of the Church, it is their own matter. . . ."

[84] "The Presbyterian Church is making great efforts to establish a system of parochial schools, and I believe is meeting with satisfactory success. To this end, they have taken the initiatory steps to establish a College at Charlotte, in which they propose to have a Normal Department. By securing the best material that can be obtained, it is hoped that this department will furnish teachers for the Parochial Schools. . . . The Government through the Bureau has appropriated $10,000 for the erection of buildings for this institution. I learn that it is proposed to give free tuition to any whom it is desirable to train for teachers in the common schools; provided the Board of Education will make an appropriation for their board and room rent . . . They have 5 other schools in Mecklenburg County, three in Cabarrus, three in Rowan, one in Iredell, one in Davie, one in Davidson, one in Guilford, and one in the City of Wilmington" (*ibid.*).

[85] *Annual Report Superintendent Public Instruction, 1869*, p. 27.

The most effective work of the churches in behalf of elementary schools under state auspices was done in the period between 1880 and 1900. By 1880 the state had sufficiently recovered from the aftermath of the Civil War to resume its educational activities in earnest. The struggle of this period was largely one as to whether the state should educate "from the bottom up" or "from the top down." The church leaders, especially Baptists and Methodists, as has been indicated in our discussion of higher education,[86] advocated educating "from the bottom up"; they espoused the cause of common schools.

In the contest of 1881, for example, the church colleges advocated more generous state support for common schools.[87] They called emphatic and repeated attention to the fact that only one-third of the children of the state were in school, that the school term was only about ten weeks, and that the state gave only eighty-one cents for the education of each child for a whole year. From 1881 to the close of the century, church conferences and conventions and the church press held up continuously before the people the plight of the public schools and urged upon the state the necessity for establishing and maintaining an adequate system of elementary schools.[88] They even went so far as to advocate persistently that all taxes available for educational purposes should be spent "in the better schooling of the children of the State in Public Schools."[89]

The arguments offered by the church leaders for state support to common schools, though often repeated and given with varying degrees of emphasis, were, in the main, quite simple and easily understood. They fitted perfectly into the denominations' defense of their higher institutions and also into the Baptists' and the Methodists' interest in the

[86] See above, pp. 153–156, 170.

[87] "A Memorial in Behalf of the Denominational Colleges of the State," *Biblical Recorder*, Feb. 16, 1881; *Minutes N. C. Yearly Meeting of Friends, 1881*, p. 22.

[88] *Ibid., 1898*, p. 45; *Biennial Report Superintendent Public Instruction, 1904–1906*, p. 11.

[89] See above, p. 154.

masses. For the smaller denominations, Presbyterian for example, parochial schools were possible, although even in their cases, it is doubtful if parochial schools were ever very generally used or highly successful in North Carolina.[90]

The report of the committee on education adopted by the Baptist State Convention in 1901 perhaps illustrates the philosophy which helped the Baptists and Methodists in particular to favor common schools. This report referred to common schools as serving the masses, "a position to which the very democracy of our Baptist policy commits us," and to this fact as making the Baptists the "heartiest supporters and sympathizers of the general educational revival" then in progress among the people of the state. Attention was called to the commendable effort of the state to make suitable provision for the education of the 439,000 white children of school age then in the state "and among which number our Baptist people must have a large per cent."[91] Baptists and Methodists claimed among their number "the rank and file" of the people of the state, all of whom needed a common school education but very few of whom, they thought, could ever aspire to a college or university education.[92]

It would hardly be fair, therefore, to assume that the interest of churches in public schools was based merely upon a hatred of the University. Even as early as 1871, the *Raleigh Christian Advocate*[93] was pleading that the legislature put free schools on "a solid and permanent basis." Regardless of their motive, the fact remains that the churches were, as a rule, quite friendly to public schools.[94]

[90] Sherrill, *op. cit.*, pp. 79, 224.

[91] *Minutes Baptist State Convention, 1901*, p. 55.

[92] The agitation for common schools was a part of the democratic movement in North Carolina in the nineties, known as the Populist movement. In 1894 the Republicans and Populists had a majority in the General Assembly, and in 1896 fused and elected Daniel L. Russell governor (Hamilton, "North Carolina, 1865–1909," *The South in the Building of the Nation*, I, 507).

[93] Feb. 8, 1871.

[94] "The question has been raised by some of our exchanges as to whether the

The question of motive and credit for the passage of the public school bill[95] in 1897 arose almost immediately following its passage. When the Raleigh *News and Observer* gave credit for the passage of the bill to President E. A. Alderman of the University and President McIver of the State Normal, leaders of the Baptist denomination immediately took issue. They charged the Raleigh paper with "misrepresenting everything that has to do with our Baptist people," accused the presidents of the two state institutions with selfishly delaying the passage of the public school bill until appropriations had first been made to "their own infant industries which were unable yet to stand alone," and gave the credit to Editor Bailey of the *Biblical Recorder* and President Taylor of Wake Forest College.[96] Editor Bailey himself

religious denominations in North Carolina are opposed to public education or not. For the Baptists we can answer most assuredly that they favor public education. It is *the hope of many thousands of the children of Baptist parents throughout the State. The files of the RECORDER for fifty years are open for inspection, and will show that the Baptists as citizens have been, and are now, the strongest friends of our public schools to be found in North Carolina.* . . . We are in favor of public schools, and wish to see them multiplied and improved" (*Biblical Recorder*, May 27, 1891).

The *Raleigh Christian Advocate* made similar denial for the Methodists. "*The country places have no better provision for education than they had when the public school system was revived after the war.* There has been no progress in our system of public education except in the centers. The politicians will still beat time on this question till the people rise up and demand something. Such reforms can only come by taxation . . . " (*North Carolina Christian Advocate*, Nov. 27, 1895).

"We believe thoroughly in popular education, and that our public school system should be enlarged and strengthened as rapidly as possible. We therefore respectfully petition the next General Assembly to make a special appropriation of not less than $200,000 for this purpose. We direct that the secretary of this Conference present this action of that body" (*Minutes Western North Carolina Conference, 1900*, p. 33).

See also *Biblical Recorder*, Jan. 26, 1881; April 29, 1885; July 4, 1888; Oct. 25, 1893; Jan. 10, 1894; Aug. 5, 1896; May 5, 1897; Jan. 27, Feb. 3, Feb. 17, Feb. 24, March 17, March 31, May 12, July 28, Aug. 25, Oct. 25, 1897; Oct. 5, 1898; *Minutes Baptist State Convention, 1900*, pp. 57–58; "The Work of the Churches for Education in North Carolina," *Biblical Recorder*, Aug. 23, 1905; John Franklin Crowell, "A Program of Progress: An Open Letter to the General Assembly of North Carolina of 1891," *Trinity College Publication No. 3; Christian Educator*, Nov. 1896; Jan., 1898; *North Carolina Christian Advocate*, Jan. 31 1900.

[95] See above, p. 170; *House Journal, 1897*, pp. 1066, 1107; *Senate Journal, 1897*, pp. 736, 737, 758, 825.

[96] "Now that the bill has become a law, the people should know who proved

denied that the credit should go to President Alderman and President McIver.[97] Superintendent Mebane was inclined to give the ministers of the gospel much credit for influencing parents with reference to their duty to their children and doing much for the cause of education. He thought they had helped popularize education to the point where politi-

---

themselves the friends of the common schools. For there were several days when its fate was doubtful in the Senate, and but for the untiring, effective work of President Alderman and President McIver, who came down from Chapel Hill and Greensboro, and staid till this bill was passed, and Superintendent Howell, and Professor Holmes, this act to appropriate $50,000 to the common schools, would have died in the Senate, and never been resurrected" (*News and Observer*, March 10, 1897). For the Baptist side of the issue, see the following: B. W. Spillman, "Who Proved Themselves the Friends of the Public Schools?" *Biblical Recorder*, March 17, 1897; "An Unseemly Bid for Credit" (editorial), *ibid.;* L. Johnson, "Honor to Whom Honor Is Due," *ibid.;* G. W. Paschal, "The Truth as to the Public School Advancement in North Carolina," *Wake Forest Student*, Nov., 1929, pp. 31–40.

[97] "President Alderman and President McIver opposed the original bill appropriating $100,000 to the public schools. They stated to the committee of the House in the presence of a *News and Observer* reporter that they had nothing to say on this measure; and then went on to suggest an appropriation based upon the condition of local taxation—a condition which they will not agree to apply to the institutions for which they are respectively the presidents.

"2. Neither President Alderman nor President McIver made any effort at all for an appropriation for the public schools before they had gotten increased appropriations to their institutions. . . .

"3. President McIver and President Alderman promised officials, legislators and individual friends of the public schools to work for this bill. They knew it would not do for them to come to Raleigh and get increase for themselves and leave the public schools in their distressingly needy condition.

"4. President McIver and President Alderman did a great deal of work after the success of the bill had been partially assured. . . .

"5. Superintendent Mebane wrote the original bill. He spoke before the committees. At one time he saved the bill, when neither President Alderman nor President McIver was present. At this time they were looking after their institutions. . . .

"For my part I am content to know that the needs of the public schools have been recognized; and that something to better them has been done. I have no fear that the credit of this will be stolen. It is not like public money. Neither lobbying, nor newspaper misrepresentation, nor playing to the grand stand, nor heroic running to the rescue after the rescue has been made, will avail. The people shall know who are and who are not the friends of their schools" (J. W. Bailey's letter in *Christian Educator*, May, 1897).

cians were speaking "long and loud for the dear children."[98] When the educators of the state wanted, in 1902, to get more tax money for education, they confidently relied on "the full co-operation of all the churches of the state" and appealed to the pulpit to "inculcate the supreme duty of universal education."[99]

During the last twenty years of the nineteenth century there was among Methodists and Presbyterians a lively interest in parochial schools, although apparently the Methodists did very little to establish them. From 1881 to 1895 the Methodists agitated in behalf of such schools.[100] In 1888 the Presbyterian Synod outlined a plan of parochial schools and preparatory schools.[101] By 1890 there seems

[98] *Biennial Report Superintendent Public Instruction, 1898–1900*, pp. 31, 59. Concerning the issue raised by the *News and Observer*, Superintendent Mebane said: "Let those who do work for the Public Schools have credit for what they do. I honor and respect Drs. McIver and Alderman. They are doing and have done great things for the educational interests of the state, but they are not the only friends of education, and not the only men who deserve credit for the educational acts of the last General Assembly of North Carolina" (*Biblical Recorder*, March 17, 1897).

[99] "Address to the People. . . . by Conference of Educators, Held in the Governor's office in Raleigh, Feb. 15th, 1902," reprinted in the *Guilford Collegian*, 1902, p. 115.

[100] The Rev. L. L. Nash, in *Raleigh Christian Advocate*, May 3, 1882, advocated the establishment of parochial schools. The North Carolina Conference (see *Minutes, 1887*, p. 51) urged Methodist people "to put forth still greater efforts to build up and support primary and academical schools." The *Raleigh Christian Advocate*, Aug. 17, 1892, believed that "every church ought to have a parish school" (see also *Minutes North Carolina Conference, 1881*, p. 22; *1895*, p. 42).

[101] "The churches are encouraged to establish wherever practicable and desirable, parochial schools, for primary and classical instruction, under their supervision. Recommendation that educational conventions be held soon in all our churches, where 'steps should be taken to establish, wherever practicable or convenient (1) in every church one or more primary schools for the younger children, under twelve years of age, to be taught by some approved Christian woman or man, in which shall be taught reading, writing, the four primary rules of arithmetic, with primary geography, etc., and also the Bible and the Catechisms of our Church; said schools to be *free* to all the poor of our Church, and, if practicable, *free* to all. (2) In every church, or in each suitable group of contiguous churches, when convenient, it is recommended that steps be taken to establish a classical or high school, as preparatory to the college or university.' It is recommended that three or more trustees be appointed by the sessions, to hold office for one year,

to have been among the Presbyterians of a number of states a "conversion from State-schools to Church-schools."[102] By 1895 Presbyterians in North Carolina were making concerted efforts to revive their parochial schools. That year Orange Presbytery declared that

> The free or public schools in our country districts by reason of limited funds and constant change of teachers are very imperfect and inadequate—a very poor substitute for the parochial or church school of former years. Yet they are the only schools available in many sections.
>
> Let us return to the system of our fathers, and plant the school house by the side of the church and give to the children of our churches and of their neighborhoods an elementary as well as a liberal Christian education.[103]

Orange Presbytery deplored the fact that "through oversight or neglect" Presbyterians were "leaving the primary and formative education of their children to the State or relegating them to ignorance." This presbytery, therefore, overtured the synod to devise the best method of "advocating, establishing, and fostering parochial schools throughout the bound of the Synod."[104] This same year the Presbyterian Synod declared that parochial schools were growing in favor and were more ardently advocated than for many

---

to raise funds, secure school-houses, employ teachers, take general control of the schools and report to sessions semi-annually" (*Minutes Synod of North Carolina, 1888*).

[102] Sherrill, *op. cit.*, p. 224.

[103] *North Carolina Presbyterian*, Sept. 19, 1895; see also *ibid.*, Oct. 3, 1895.

[104] *Minutes Synod of North Carolina, 1895*, p. 341. In response to this overture the Synod of 1896 recommended:

"1. It is both proper and desirable for the Church to control and direct primary and preparatory education of her children, male and female, as far as circumstances may permit.

"2. To this end we recommend to the consideration of all Churches, the establishing of Parochial Schools in every parish or congregation, which shall either be independent of or supplementary to public or private schools already in existence" (*Minutes Synod of North Carolina, 1896*, p. 73).

years past.[105] The number of such schools had greatly increased.[106]

Some were regarded as supplemental to the public schools; and so far as the record shows, there was nowhere friction between the parochial and the public schools.[107] Some of them even received state aid.[108] The *North Carolina Presbyterian* noted a model parochial school which received an appropriation from the state school fund.[109] Northern Presbyterians also received state aid for some of their schools in the mountain counties. From 1890 to 1900 or 1905 they had about seventeen scattered through the counties of Madison, Buncombe, and Yancey. The terms of the public school then were from three to six months. The public school committees allowed the Presbyterians to furnish the teachers, and the Presbyterians supplemented the terms so as to give these communities an eight- or nine-months school. The county boards of education paid the salary of the teachers for the length of the public school term, and the Presbyterians paid for the supplemental term. To comply with the laws, the Presbyterians gave the county boards a lease for their buildings.[110] The laws allowed school committees to contract with the teacher of certain private schools to give instruction in subjects taught in the public schools.[111]

[105] *North Carolina Presbyterian*, Nov. 14, 1895; *Minutes Synod of North Carolina, 1895*, p. 406.

[106] No record of the number was given. Reference to further increase was noted in 1897 (*ibid., 1897*, p. 263).

[107] *Minutes Synod of North Carolina, 1895*, p. 405.

[108] Baptists protested against this practice (*Biblical Recorder*, Aug. 17, 1898).

[109] This was conducted under the auspices of the Davidson church, managed by board of trustees selected annually by the congregation from membership of church, thus keeping school under control of church. "Three teachers are employed and ample salaries paid them out of the tuition fees *supplemented* by the appropriation from the State school fund, so that for three months in the year the tuition is absolutely free. Cannot some such combination of Church and State [perfectly legitimate] be adopted in all our country communities and guarantee to our children a thorough *primary* education . . . ?" (*North Carolina Presbyterian*, Nov. 28, 1895).

[110] Letter of W. E. Finley, White Rock, N. C., to L. L. Gobbel, July 5, 1933.

[111] Chap. 15 of the Code as amended by Laws of 1885, 1889, 1891, 1893, 1895

The provision in the law, and in practice as it related to the Presbyterians and to the state, aroused a storm of protest. The Baptists denounced this relationship as contrary to the principle of separation of church and state. They called upon the Presbyterians to "take their hands off the public purse and the public schools" and suggested that they ought to refund all the money received from the state.[112] So prominent an issue did this become that the

---

and other statutes, Sec. 2591, p. 35, provided: "In any school district where there may be a private school, regularly conducted for at least nine months in the year, the school committee may contract with the teacher of such private school to give instruction to all pupils between the ages of six and twenty-one years in the branches of learning taught in the public schools, as prescribed in this chapter, without charge and free of tuition; and such school committee may pay such teacher for such services out of the public school funds apportioned to the district, and the agreement as to such pay shall be arranged between the committee and the teacher: *Provided*, any teacher so employed shall obtain a first-grade certificate before beginning his work, and from time to time make such reports as are required of other public school teachers under this chapter: *Provided further*, that the Board of Education of the county (Bd. of Commissioners) and the County Supt. (Chairman of Comrs.) shall have the same authority in respect to the employment and dismissal of teachers under this section and in every other respect as is conferred in other sections of the law: and *Provided further*, that all contracts made under this section shall designate the length of the public school term, which shall not be less than the average length of the public school term of the county of the preceding year." Superintendent Scarborough's note: "This section is intended to harmonize the public and the private school interests, but it does not permit the pupils of any one district to be divided among the different private schools that may be located within its limits. The general law provides that districts must be laid off and definite territorial lines established and a public school house provided, at which all the pupils within such lines are to attend school. If, however, the committee think best, they can employ the principal of a permanently established private school to teach all the schools of the district, following the spirit and letter of this section.

"The object of the above section is not to destroy the public school, but to make it better, to emphasize the fact that good public schools, well filled public schools, will mean well filled academies and colleges . . . I have tried to have all our schools—the State, the denominational colleges, and the private schools—to realize more than ever that there is one subject, one work, upon which we can unite our forces, and that is the work and progress of our public schools" (*Biennial Report Superintendent of Public Instruction, 1896–1897*, pp. 49–50).

[112] "A Sectarian Hand on Our Public Schools," *Biblical Recorder*, Aug. 17, 1898: "Little did we dream that the example of Rome would ever be followed in North Carolina, and that the battle for separation of Church and State would have to be fought out again in this State, and against a Protestant church. But slowly

State Superintendent of Public Instruction interpreted the law to exclude denominational or church schools from the right to claim its benefits. In a letter to the county supervisors, written the next day[113] after the protest broke out in the columns of the *Biblical Recorder*, Superintendent Mebane ruled that the spirit of the laws seemed to be "against combining Church and State in any way."[114]

---

silently, and almost stelthily, the Presbyterians (Northern) have gotten their hands into the treasuries of our public schools in Western North Carolina; and today . . . that church has promulgated a school system in some of our mountain counties whereby it gets the public school money for running its own institutions. This is the Roman Catholic idea identically. It is union of Church and State without defense or apology." Editor Bailey led the Baptist State Convention to reaffirm its opposition to state aid to denominational schools in 1903 (*Minutes Baptist State Convention, 1903*, p. 46).

[113] Aug. 18, 1898.

[114] *Biennial Report Superintendent Public Instruction, 1896–1898*, pp. 98–99. The letter to the county supervisors declared:

"I have had numerous inquiries recently in regard to combining the public schools with denominational schools, and therefore write you that you may have my opinion on this subject.

"I think it best for the committee always to provide a public school lot and building.

"The spirit of the laws seems to be against combining Church and State in any way.

"When the public school is combined with a denominational one, the best interest of the public school can rarely, if ever, be secured.

"We cannot have the support of all the poeple when the public school is united with the church school.

"The public schools are for all the people, supported by all the people, and must serve all the people in enlightenment without regard to any denominations or churches.

"*The law provides for combining public schools with private, but I do not think that this, in any sense, means denominational or church schools.*

"I am aware that these schools have well-prepared teachers, but notwithstanding this, the primary object for which they are employed is to benefit the Church that sends them out, and in every community we find some parents who will not send their children because the school is under other church influence than their own.

"Let us not have any hindrance in the way of united support in the schools, which must have the support of all our people if they are ever what they should be."

See also letters of C. H. Mebane, Superintendent of Public Instruction, to Rev. Charles L. Greaves, Pittsboro, N. C., June 29, 1898, and to Rev. G. C. Shaw, Oxford, N. C., Aug. 8, 1898, in *Biblical Recorder*, Aug. 17, 1898; and *Biennial Report Superintendent Public Instruction, 1898–1900*, pp. 95, 237.

Superintendents T. F. Toon and J. Y. Joyner, who, in order, succeeded to the leadership of the public school system of the state, likewise ruled that "there was no legal authority to contract with any strictly denominational or sectarian school to use public school funds and conduct the public school in connection therewith."[115] Considerable pressure was brought upon the state superintendent to reverse this ruling and to instruct county boards of education to have public schools taught in connection with certain denominational schools; but he firmly stood his ground.[116] In addition to their objection on the doctrine of separation of church and state, the Baptists' academy principals held that the conditions upon which an academy might receive state money were unfair to the academies.[117]

[115] *Biennial Report Superintendent Public Instruction, 1902–1904*, p. 200: "I have ruled that the term *private school* does not include sectarian and denominational schools. There is, therefore, no express authority for making any contract with these schools for the use of public school funds. Without express authority such contracts would be illegal. Letters on file in this office show that this has been my ruling. Captain John Duckett, chief clerk in my office, informs me that this was also the ruling of my predecessor, General T. F. Toon."

[116] *Ibid.*, pp. 240–241; *1906–1908*, p. 234.

[117] M. A. Adams, "The Plight of Secondary Schools," *Biblical Recorder*, Dec. 2, 1903: "This new law has simply legislated the heart's blood out of our private academies . . . It simply requires the academy to teach the whole curriculum to the district, to all who are under 21 years of age, regardless of what that curriculum may be, and then the school boards do not pay one cent more than before. In other words, the man who runs an academy is forced to pay tribute for so doing and fleeced out of his tuition-rate, whatever he may teach, provided he teaches the public school in connection with his academy. That is the encouragement given to establish schools of high grade. In order to make all doubly sure, they will not allow the academy man to use the same grade of teachers as any ordinary public school. They must all be first-grade and fully up to date, whereas the teacher of public schools may have only a second-grade certificate and the assistant needs only a third. The manifest object of all this is to legislate the life's blood out of our private schools, or force them to do obeisance for a song. Some years ago we fought a battle for our higher institutions of learning, but now we are called upon to fight for both our higher institutions and our secondary schools also. If we do not have the secondary school, all is lost. A more covert attack at private effort has never been made. You may fear the alliances which may in any possible way compromise our schools with the State. It is time for us to know that the State cannot do our work, and we cannot do the State's work." See also *Biblical Recorder*, Jan. 13, 1904.

There were very few state-supported high schools in the state before 1900.[118] Practically every voice of all the churches had spoken in unison for the spending of tax money for the purpose of giving an elementary education at public expense to every child. Concerning secondary schools they were not so united. Many churches maintained academies as feeders to their colleges.[119] And as has been shown, they were sensitive about what they regarded as unfair competition when the State University and the Agricultural and Mechanical College admitted students of "almost any degree of preparation."[120] They held the state responsible for closing many preparatory schools.[121]

Private and denominational high schools were attempting to supply the demand for secondary education.[122] Even so, they were inadequate. There existed a gap between

[118] There was no high-school system, as such. A few of the larger cities and towns maintained "graded schools." According to the report of Superintendent John C. Scarborough, there were only five before 1881. "The following cities and towns of the State have established graded schools and graded school systems for the education of the children within their respective limits: Charlotte, Salisbury, High Point, Greensboro, Wilson, Rocky Mount, New Berne, and Wilmington, making thirteen . . . The course in most of them is arranged to prepare the pupils for entrance into the regular classes of our State University and of the best colleges in this and other States" (*Report State Superintendent Public Instruction, 1881–1882*, p. 48).

[119] *Biblical Recorder*, Sept. 20, 1855: article by E. Dodson; *ibid.*, Nov. 9, 1904, for a list of Baptist Schools in North Carolina.

[120] See above, p. 23; Kilgo, "Our Educational Condition," *Christian Educator*, Oct., 1897.

[121] *Biblical Recorder*, Jan. 22, 1896: article by C. W. Blanchard. "In our office last week a brother counted on his fingers eight schools in a certain county in this State which have closed up: and the suspension of every one of them could be partially traced to the drastic competition of the State," wrote the editor of the *Biblical Recorder*, who alleged that at the University there was, so far as he could see, "no bar of age or education to entrance" and at the State College of Agriculture and Mechanic Arts the only bar the editor knew of was one of age—the matriculate had to be thirteen years of age (*ibid.:* Editorial).

[122] Superintendent S. M. Finger reported in 1887–88: " . . . perhaps as many as 25,000 of our young people are in these (private) schools, many of whom have passed beyond the facilities now afforded by the public schools and are seeking further educational advantages in these private institutions" (*Report Superintendent Public Instruction, 1887–88*, p. xxxix).

the college and the public schools.[123] And in the midst of the increasingly intense competition between the colleges of the churches and of the state in the nineties, the churches set out to reopen "the long-closed doors of the church academies" and to establish an extensive system of preparatory schools.[124] The Methodists undertook to maintain at least one high school in every presiding elder's district. The Baptists sought to establish at least one preparatory school in each association.[125] In 1893 the Presbyterians reported the growth and increase of a number of preparatory schools for boys under distinct Presbyterian control and support, "without any ecclesiastical connection mentioned."[126] The Methodists of the Western North Carolina Conference were gratified, in 1893, that "notwithstanding the general depression of the country and the multiplication of graded schools and other institutions receiving large appropriations from the State" attendance upon their schools was good. Yet they viewed with alarm "the growing encroachment of the State upon the legitimate work of the Church in the education of her sons and daughters."[127] The state superintendent of public instruction, furthermore, is reported to have received not a few letters complaining that there was "friction" between the private and public agencies of lower education.[128] The principal of one academy is said even to have declared that the free

[123] J. F. Crowell, *Annual Report of the President of Trinity College to the North Carolina Conference, 1893* (pamphlet). See also *Trinity College Bulletin*, Supplement, Dec. 1, 1890, No. 8.

[124] *Minutes Synod of North Carolina, 1892*, Appendix; *Minutes Baptist State Convention, 1894*, p. 47; "A Model Report on Education," *Biblical Recorder*, Aug. 5, 1896; *ibid.*, Sept. 2, 1896.

[125] *Raleigh Christian Advocate*, Jan. 6, 1892; Aug. 17, 1892; Sept. 14, 1892; Oct. 12, 1892. *Biblical Recorder*, Aug. 5, 1896; *Minutes Baptist State Convention, 1896*, p. 64.

[126] *Minutes Synod of North Carolina, 1893*, p. 191.

[127] *Minutes Western North Carolina Conference, 1893*, p. 59.

[128] "The Province of the Family, the State, and the Church in Education," *Biblical Recorder*, Jan. 10, 1894.

schools would be a curse from which twenty years hence Baptists would pray to be delivered.[129]

The fact that now and then some worthy individual found himself facing the loss of a livelihood and made personal protest, however, should not obscure the major fact that the church held the line until public reinforcements arrived. On the whole, there seemed to be a disposition on the part of the churches to retire even from the field of secondary education as soon as the state was ready to occupy it.

In summary, one finds that the relationships between church and state in the realm of elementary and secondary education were friendly and co-operative. Church and private schools occupied the field until 1840, when the state came in to supplement the work already being done. The state took over much of the spirit, purpose, and materials of the church institutions. When, after the Civil War, the state system of public schools broke down, it was the churches which kept alive interest in education. And when the economic and political conditions of the commonwealth regained their equilibrium, the churches threw the full weight of their influence back of a movement for a state-supported system of common schools. In general, the church institutions retired as the state advanced to occupy the field. In some instances, the state contracted with denominational schools to give public education. The Baptists protested so strongly, however, that this practice was soon abandoned. The churches and private agencies supplied practically all secondary education prior to the twentieth century. There was some feeling among the churches, particularly academy principals, that even in public schools, the state was encroaching upon the legitimate work of the church. They were sensitive of the danger

[129] "Against Public Schools," *Biblical Recorder*, May 5, 1897. This sentiment was not representative of the Baptists. The Baptist editor decried such opposition to public education.

that the state might destroy the feeders of their institutions of higher learning. The state high-school movement did not get under way until near the close of the first decade of the present century. How the churches and state got along when the state undertook in earnest to put secondary education in reach of every boy and girl will be considered, with other twentieth-century problems, in the next chapter on the twentieth century and the present *modus vivendi*.

VI

The Twentieth Century and the Present *Modus Vivendi*

THE twentieth century has been an era of conciliation and co-operation between the forces of church and state in North Carolina. Most of the issues which caused misunderstanding and conflict in the preceding century, particularly the last decade of it, had been, by the turn of the century, either removed or adjusted. Practically all agencies of church and state turned from bickerings and unwholesome rivalry to promoting a spirit of amity and good fellowship. There have been, of course, a few notable exceptions. To discover (1) the underlying causes and (2) the agencies promoting this conciliatory attitude; to note (3) examples of co-operation and (4) instances and areas of conflict; and (5) to indicate how the forces of church and state get along together at the present time, are the purposes of this closing chapter.

The causes underlying this twentieth-century spirit of conciliation are not hard to find. Some of them have already been indicated.[1] Church colleges began to receive means of survival and were therefore not so prone to oppose state aid to state institutions. From January, 1897, to December 1, 1900, more money had been given to colleges and more spent for school buildings and equipment than ever before during so short a period.[2] Trinity College increased $335,000 in property and $202,000 in endowment. Wake Forest added $36,379 to its holdings. Approximately $650,000 were added to the eight principal denominational colleges during this period. The Vanderbilts, Rockefellers, and Dukes were beginning to pour some

[1] See above, p. 170.

[2] *Biennial Report Superintendent of Public Instruction, 1900*, p. 60.

of their money into educational institutions. North Carolina denominational institutions received some of it and hoped for more.[3] They were beginning to offer scholarships themselves and were hopeful of establishing more of them.[4]

The common schools were being recognized and supported by the state.[5] This fact not only removed the argument of aristocracy in education, favoritism to the wealthy, and the rest which the church leaders used against appropriations to the University, but provided education for the masses and created a demand for higher education. Thus in the educational revival under Aycock and in the years following, practically all educational institutions found very little difficulty in securing students.[6] In fact, from 1897 to 1900 practically all of the colleges reported from 8 to 70 per cent increase in enrolment.[7] In 1905 the University, reporting the greatest enrolment of any previous year, had its appropriation increased from $25,000 to $45,000 a year and received also from the legislature $50,000 for a chemical

[3] *North Carolina Christian Advocate*, June 27, 1900; *Biblical Recorder*, July 5, 1905.

[4] During the presidency of J. F. Crowell, through the liberality of B. N. Duke, there were sixty scholarships a year offered at Trinity College to meritorious men. (Each Presiding Elder selected two "bright, pious, poor young men, if they could stand the entrance exam.") These were withdrawn in 1896. "But it has been recently announced that 50 of the scholarships have been restored and would be awarded by the faculty only for proficiency in learning." The editor entered a plea for fifty scholarships each for Weaverville, Rutherford, Davenport, and Brevard (*North Carolina Christian Advocate*, June 27, 1900).

[5] See above, p. 170.

[6] *Biennial Report Superintendent Public Instruction, 1902*, p. 14; *Proceedings: Inauguration of President Gaines* (April 25, 1928), p. 56.

"Reports from the denominational colleges and the private high schools and academies of the State . . . indicate an era of unprecedented prosperity for those worthy institutions of learning, these most important and necessary factors in our educational life. In these prosperous conditions of all educational institutions in the State may be found additional evidence that stimulation of educational interest, agitation of educational questions, and cultivation of educational sentiment must in the very nature of the case help all educational institutions of every proper sort" (*Biennial Report Superintendent Public Instruction, 1902–1904*, p. 15).

[7] *Ibid., 1900*, p. 60.

laboratory—all without protest from the other institutions.[8] The church group had surrendered the notion that all girls and boys should be sent to church institutions.[9]

Many agencies very purposefully promoted a spirit of conciliation. The Presbyterians, as usual, were prominent in the role of peacemaker and defender of the University. They were still in the saddle at Chapel Hill. The *Presbyterian Standard*[10] took editorial notice of the election of Dr. F. P. Venable, a Presbyterian elder, to succeed President Alderman, a choice which had "met with hearty approval from all parts of the state." In fact, quite consistently, with one or two important exceptions which will be discussed later,[11] the *Presbyterian Standard* and the Presbyterian Synod stood by the state institutions against all comers.[12] It was voted that "the official organ of its synod had been the most conspicuous defender of the right of State institutions to exist and be supported by the State."[13] The Presbyterians refused to allow Davidson College to be drawn into controversy.[14] Some of them were willing to "fight to the death" the man who should oppose any appropriation to the University.[15] They felt the one thing North Carolinians needed more than any other was to leave "the narrowness" that had "characterized the life of the State for more than one hundred years" regarding the institution at Chapel Hill.[16]

Although it required three or four years after the be-

[8] Battle, *op. cit.*, p. 647.

[9] *Biblical Recorder*, July 27, 1904.

[10] July 18, 1900.

[11] See below, p. 222.

[12] *Presbyterian Standard*, July 13, 1899; July 17, 1901; July 8, 1903; Dec. 11, 1907; Feb. 1, 1911; Jan. 27, 1915; *Minutes Synod of North Carolina, 1921*, pp. 560, 562, *1923*, p. 214.

[13] *Presbyterian Standard*, July 17, 1901.

[14] *Ibid.*, July 13, 1899.

[15] "The Paradoxes of the Century," a sermon preached in Second Presbyterian Church, Charlotte, N. C., Dec. 30, 1900, published in *Presbyterian Standard*, Jan. 9, 1901.

[16] *Ibid.*

ginning of the century for Baptists and Methodists to become fully reconciled to the established policy of state aid to higher institutions, they fell in line. By 1904 the *Biblical Recorder* was writing on the "Progress of the University of North Carolina," recognizing and commending its "excellent work,"[17] and soon was also praising the work of the Agricultural and Mechanical College at Raleigh.[18] The Baptist State Convention commended the efforts of "our Christian Governor and Superintendent of Public Instruction" (Aycock and Joyner, both Baptists) in making possible the educational awakening.[19] It recorded a hearty desire "not only for a spirit of amity between the "State and denominational colleges, but also of good fellowship and co-operation in the great task which is common in part to both."[20]

The Methodists were not very outspoken after 1900 about state institutions of higher learning, although in recent years the official organ of North Carolina Methodism has befriended the State University in several instances.[21] About common schools they were enthusiastic. The North Carolina Conference of 1902 called upon its preachers and people to do all they could "to improve the quality of common school education." It also discouraged the organization of secondary schools under the direct management of the church and recommended that the church give support to efforts to establish strong secondary schools, whether as private schools, community schools, or graded schools.[22] The Western North Carolina Conference thought

[17] *Biblical Recorder*, Feb. 10, 1904; March 23, 1904.

[18] *Ibid.*, Sept. 6, 1905.

[19] *Minutes Baptist State Convention, 1905*, pp. 70–71.

[20] *Ibid., 1917*, p. 78.

[21] For example, this church paper opposed the reduction of appropriations to the University in 1933, calling attention to the fact that already the support had been decreased from $894,429 received by the institution from the state in 1928–29 to $504,700 for the current year, a decrease of 43.6 per cent in a period when student enrolment had increased 22.9 per cent (*North Carolina Christian Advocate*, Jan. 19, 1933; *Durham Morning Herald*, Jan. 21, 1933).

[22] *Minutes North Carolina Conference, 1902*, p. 51.

the state was doing a great work in education.[23] It thought pastors should take an intelligent interest in public schools; yet it deprecated sectarianism in making up public school boards. It advised that church buildings and parsonages be placed adjacent to school buildings wherever practicable. This body of Methodists felt that the homes of the preacher and the teacher should be alongside the church and school buildings.[24]

Leaders of the state joined in the efforts to promote harmonious relationships between church and state in education. The governors of the state, superintendents of public instruction, and presidents of the State University were conspicuous in such efforts. President Edward Kidder Graham, President H. W. Chase, and President Frank P. Graham of the State University; State Superintendents J. Y. Joyner, E. C. Brooks, A. T. Allen, and Clyde A. Erwin, and most of the governors on several occasions, revealed attitudes of genuine friendliness toward denominational institutions.[25] For example, President E. K. Graham, speaking at the inauguration of President Brewer of Meredith College in 1916, declared:

> . . . we greet you today, not under the impulse of a momentary surge of friendliness, preliminary to a relapse into unsympathetic competition; we greet you as our colleague and we come to do unaffected honor to you today and to pledge to you, through the length of days, the co-operation, understanding, and loyal support of men and women who pray that no personal or partial good

[23] *Minutes Western North Carolina Conference, 1910*, p. 45.

[24] *Ibid., 1915*, pp. 39–40.

[25] *Biennial Report Superintendent Public Instruction, 1906–1908*, pp. 17–18; 1914–1918, pp. 40–41; *Meredith College Bulletin* (Inauguration Number), Jan., 1916, pp. 39, 55; E. K. Graham, *Education and Citizenship* (address delivered at the inauguration of Dr. Charles E. Brewer as President of Meredith College, Feb. 3, 1916), pp. 192–197; *Proceedings: Inauguration of President Gaines, Wake Forest College, April 25, 1928*, p. 30; *Proceedings: Inauguration of President Walter Lee Lingle, Davidson College, June 3, 1930*, p. 15; *Letters and Papers of Governor Cameron Morrison*, pp. 147, 179; *Papers and Letters of Governor Angus Wilton McLean*, pp. 360–361, 382–387, 394–398, 434–438.

may obscure the highest good for which we all labor, and without which all labor is in vain.

In this atmosphere of friendliness, the churches were inclined to promote their own institutions without fighting the state institutions.[26] Frequent reference was made to the work which the state was doing in education, not to suggest that it should do less but to arouse their own constituency to do more. All the denominations were agreed that state institutions could never take the place of church schools.

This spirit of amity was expressed, furthermore, in several very definite co-operative enterprises, among which were (1) numerous experiments in moral and religious instruction in the public schools and in the State University, (2) recognition of church colleges as teacher-training agencies and state subsidy of teacher-training work in Negro church colleges, (3) state contracts with church schools for public school teaching, (4) state purchase of church school buildings for housing public schools where the church desired to abandon the work to the state, and (5) state support for orphanage schools.

The Bible as a textbook has not been generally used in the public schools of North Carolina since Wiley's day. Yet there have been, in recent years, numerous experiments in moral and religious instruction in the public schools and in the State University. Some of the denominational leaders, particularly Presbyterians, have insisted that the Bible should be used as a textbook.[27] Widespread dis-

[26] Annual Report of Executive Committee of Schools and Colleges of the Presbyterian Church in the United States, May 21, 1908; *Presbyterian Standard*, Aug. 19, 1908; Sept. 20, 1916; Dec. 15, 1920; *Minutes Baptist State Convention, 1917*, p. 80; *1918*, p. 76; 1920, p. 87; *Guilford College Bulletin*, Vol. XVI, No. 4, 1923; *Minutes North Carolina Yearly Meeting of Friends, 1900*, p. 26.

[27] *North Carolina Presbyterian*, March 22, 1894; *Presbyterian Standard*, Feb. 2, 1910; Dec. 28, 1910; July 12, 1911; Dec. 6, 1911; Nov. 5, 1913; Dec. 15, 1920.

Methodists have gone on record as favoring "a complete program of moral and religious training in the primary and high school grades of the public schools" and "optional courses in religious and moral subjects . . . in the State colleges and in the State University" (*Minutes North Carolina Conference, 1922*, p. 51).

agreement among the churches on this issue, however, has resulted in its elimination from the regular curriculum, except under special experimental arrangements.[28] One arrangement, worked out by the several co-operating denominations and the local school boards, permits pastors or other teachers representing the churches to go to the public high school once each week for a period of teaching. A modification of this plan permits the pupils to use public school time in which to go to their respective churches for religious instruction. In some cases, high-school credit is given; in others, it is not.[29] In some places local churches have united to pay the salary of one or more teachers of Bible in the public schools, and the local board of education furnishes the room.[30] In a number of places instruction in Bible, ethics, and morals has been given "in connection with other courses."[31] In a few places public-school credit has been allowed for work done in the Sunday school.[32]

The University of North Carolina and most of the denominations of the state, moreover, co-operated for two years in maintaining a chair of Bible at the University.[33] The financial support was provided by the churches. At the call of President Chase of the University, a conference

[28] The Baptists have been as much opposed to the use of the Bible in public schools as the Presbyterians have favored it. President W. L. Poteat of Wake Forest, Rev. R. T. Vann, and Dr. J. Y. Joyner, state superintendent of public instruction, prominent Baptists, appearing before a committee of the legislature, opposed a measure designed to prohibit the exclusion of the Bible from the public schools. President Poteat is quoted as saying, "The intolerance of the Protestant majority in North Carolina today would be more odious than the intolerance of the Catholic majority in Spain in the fifteenth century" (*Presbyterian Standard*, Nov. 5, 1913).

[29] L. L. Gobbel, The Present Status of Moral and Religious Instruction in the Public Schools of North Carolina (1927), pp. 8–11.

[30] *Ibid.*, pp. 9, 11–12; *Presbyterian Standard*, Sept. 23, 1925; P. H. Gwynn, Jr. "The Bible in the Public Schools," *Presbyterian Standard*, Oct. 22, 1924. In at least one instance the teacher of Bible was employed "just as any other teacher is employed" and was "paid his salary in the same way" (Gobbel, *op. cit.*, p. 9).

[31] *Ibid.*, p. 10.

[32] *Ibid.*, pp. 5, 13–14.

[33] Professor M. Thornburg Workman was the one chosen for this experiment.

of the representatives of the leading denominations was held at Chapel Hill in April, 1923. At this time it was proposed that the Protestant bodies of the state unite in support of teachers of Bible, of their own choice, whom they should nominate to the trustees of the University and other state colleges.[34] Subsequent meetings were held in Greensboro and Chapel Hill. The church representatives agreed upon a proposal,[35] which was submitted to the University authorities for their consideration.[36] The University authorities agreed to the general principle that the

[34] *Journal Protestant Episcopal Church, 1923*, p. 95; *Minutes Synod of North Carolina, 1923*, p. 187; *ibid., 1924*, p. 33; *Presbyterian Standard*, Oct. 17, 1923; *Minutes Western North Carolina Conference, 1924*, p. 56; *Minutes North Carolina Conference, 1924*, p. 60; *1925*, p. 61.

[35] The following resolutions were adopted by the Greensboro Conference:

"1. It is the sense of this body that the Bible should be taught in connection with our State institutions of higher learning.

"2. It is the sense of this body that it should be taught by the denominations concerned through their own agencies, either separately, or co-operating.

"3. It is the sense of this body that the five institutions be requested to give credit for Bible study under proper conditions; and that the chair appoint a committee to confer with the authorities of these institutions, and to work out with them a plan for such work.

"4. That this committee report back to this body whatever seems feasible" (*Journal Protestant Episcopal Church, 1924*, p. 39).

[36] On Feb. 5, 1924, a committee representing the Episcopal, Presbyterian, Baptist, Methodist Episcopal (South), Methodist Protestant, Christian, and Lutheran churches met with President Chase and a committee of the faculty of the University. The following plan was submitted to the University authorities for their consideration:

"1. That the Bible should be taught in the University of North Carolina.

"2. That it should be taught under the auspices of the religious denominations co-operating as follows:

(a) That those who teach the Biblical courses shall be elected through the regular channels of the University, on the nominations of the churches participating.

(b) The salaries and expense of such teachers shall be provided either through private gifts, or by the churches co-operating, and not through taxation or from public funds.

(c) It is understood that such teachers should hold their position subject to the approval of both the University authorities and the committee representing the participating organizations.

(d) The course of study to be offered shall be arranged by the University, after consultation with the above standing committee, representing the participating bodies" (*ibid.*, p. 40).

Bible should be taught in the University and that the chair should be supported by funds other than those coming from public taxation. The matter of divided control was questioned on the grounds of legality, sound educational policy, and principle.[37] The churches, therefore, modified their plan. They simply requested the University to establish a chair of Bible and to elect a professor and agreed to pay the salary. This arrangement was to continue for a period of two years.[38] Professor Thornburg Workman was employed in 1926, as indicated, and served for two years. The experiment was then discontinued.[39] Numerous factors entered into the discontinuance.[40] For one reason, the money for the support of the chair was not forthcoming. Back of this fact doubtless lay the additional fact that the University did not grant credit for the courses, which, therefore, were not generally elected. Then, too, some members of the faculty were not in sympathy with the project. And it was impossible for one man to be a Methodist, a Baptist, a Presbyterian, an Episcopalian, and everything else at the same time.

The spirit of co-operation expressed itself, furthermore, in the realm of teacher-training. Instead of continuing the irritating condition which permitted church colleges to feel that they were being discriminated against in that the graduates of certain state institutions were given life certificates to teach in the public schools of the state,[41] Superintendent J. Y. Joyner, in 1907, worked out a plan whereby the state accepted the statement of the colleges concerning work done by their graduates as a basis for granting certificates to teach in the schools of the state. In 1919 Superintendent E. C. Brooks, who had previously served as head of the department of education in Trinity

[37] *Ibid.*

[38] *Ibid.*

[39] See Walter Patten's letter to L. L. Gobbel, April 20, 1934; also editorial of *Tar Heel*, May 5, 1928.

[40] *Ibid.*

[41] See above, p. 143.

College, inaugurated a state system of certification.[42] That system contemplated the issuance of certificates upon the basis of college training. It became necessary, then, to set up standards by which to know the value of the work done at the various institutions. Growing out of that need, the North Carolina College Conference was organized in 1921 and through it standards were set up.[43] These standards have been applied alike to both state and private or denominational institutions.[44] Since 1921, therefore, it has not been a question of whether the institution was a state one or a denominational one. All institutions, including the state teacher-training colleges, whose charters made their diplomas life certificates, have been expected to meet a few specific teacher-training requirements. No teacher is now certified by virtue of any special privilege which the institution from which he or she was graduated may have had.[45] All of the changes in certification of teachers that have been made by the State Department of Education within the past fifteen or eighteen years have been made by the state superintendent and the director of certification in conference either with summer school direc-

[42] At the invitation of Superintendent Brooks, a conference met in Greensboro during the month of October, 1921. The conference was composed of the president and one member of the faculty of each college in the state, and was called mainly to secure harmony of opinion and concert of action among the state and denominational institutions. At this meeting the following resolutions were adopted:

1. "... that a mere promise to teach for a term of years is not sufficient ground on which to issue a scholarship by the State;

2. "... that such scholarships as are issued from State funds should leave the holders, or beneficiaries free to use them in any accredited institution of their choice;

3. "... that it is the sense of the body that some generally accepted definition of a standard college as a working basis in North Carolina should be agreed upon and adopted" (*Minutes Baptist State Convention, 1921*, pp. 106–107).

[43] These standards approached those found in the larger regional associations, such as the Southern Association of Colleges and Secondary Schools, or the North Central Association of Colleges and Secondary Schools (Educational Publication No. 76, State Department of Education, 1925, p. 5).

[44] Letter of James E. Hillman, Director, Division of Curriculum Construction, State Department of Education, Raleigh, to L. L. Gobbel, April 19, 1934.

[45] *Ibid.*

tors or with the North Caroline College Conference. At these meetings the denominational colleges have usually had a majority of those present participating in the conference.[46]

With the larger church schools for Negroes in North Carolina, moreover, the state has co-operated, through the good offices of N. C. Newbold, Head of the Division of Negro Education in the State Department of Education; and from them the state has received excellent co-operation in the preparation of teachers for the state. Very definitely the state has sought the co-operation of the church and private schools for Negroes in training a sufficient number of teachers.[47] This co-operation progressed to the point that, from 1921 to 1931, North Carolina made appropriations to Negro church colleges; the state paid $15,000 a year on salaries. It sent the money directly to the president of the church institutions to be applied to the work of the professor of education in the institution.[48]

In elementary and secondary schools, both white and Negro, there have been interesting instances of co-operation. As has been indicated in the preceding chapter, in the nineties the state aided a number of the schools of the Presbyterians, especially those of the Northern Presbyterians, in the mountain counties of the western part of the state.[49] After vigorous protest on the part of the Baptists, and after the spirit of local pride in schools arose to the point where the counties desired to have their own schools, the Presbyterians, in 1910, turned over these schools to the local boards.[50] The public school authorities purchased many of the buildings, and the Presbyterians retired their workers.[51] In more recent years similar purchases have

[46] Letter of Holland Holton, Director, Summer School of Duke University, to L. L. Gobbel, March 12, 1931.

[47] *Biennial Report Superintendent of Public Instruction, 1914–1916* (Section, by N. C. Newbold, V, f, on Negro Rural Schools: Teacher Training).

[48] Information given directly by N. C. Newbold from his office in Raleigh, N. C., in Feb., 1933.

[49] See above, p. 197.

[50] Letter of W. E. Finley, White Rock, N. C., to L. L. Gobbel, July 5, 1933.

[51] *Ibid.*

been made from other denominations.[52] About 1930 the state returned to a policy similar to that of 1890–1905, when it assisted in paying the salaries of teachers in denominational institutions.

For example, Mountain Park Institute in Jefferson County, founded by the Baptists, found itself lacking in boarding students and therefore began to take in local high-school students. Inasmuch as the latter were responsibilities of the state, the state paid into the institute budget an amount sufficient to pay the salary of the number of teachers required, under the state schedule, to take care of the local high-school students, the amount thus paid counting as a part of the county's allotment for public school purposes.[53] Buies Creek Academy, in Harnett County, and Fruitland Institute, Hendersonville, also Baptist institutions, have a similar working agreement with the state.[54]

A series of interesting examples of co-operation relate to certain Negro schools in Vance County established by the Freedmen's Board of the United Presbyterian Church. In 1891 this board purchased property and built a school building at Henderson and for nearly forty years operated a school purely as a missionary effort in the interest of

[52] Examples: The Elise High School, at Hemp, until 1932–33 was operated by the Presbyterians. In 1933 the county took over the property from the Presbyterians and are operating it as the Hemp School. Liberty Piedmont Institute (Baptist), Davidson County, closed after the session of 1925–26. The county bought the building and made it a unit of the county high-school system. A similar example is the Yancey Collegiate Institute, Burnsville (information given directly by A. B. Combs from office of State Department of Education, Raleigh, Feb., 1933).

[53] The public high school, in other words, uses the buildings of Mountain Park Institute, which is designated in the Surry County budget as Bryan High School, getting its name from the public elementary school at that place. The elementary school building is owned by the county. The school has other teachers privately paid. Three or four teachers are paid by the State, allotted on the basis of the average daily attendance of pupils actually living in the district (information given directly by A. B. Combs from the office of State Department of Education, Raleigh, Feb., 1933).

[54] *Ibid.*

the Negroes. In 1930 a co-operative plan was put into effect. The city paid the tuition of all high-school students at that time residing in Henderson Township, for the county then had no standardized four-year high school. In 1932 the city and county paid the salary of four teachers in this Presbyterian school, the Freedmen's Board paying the salaries of the other teachers required for the work. Then a fire destroyed the administration building. Immediately a co-operative plan was worked out by the church and state by which the church board donated the site and eight thousand dollars and the city and county contributed ten thousand dollars toward an eighteen-thousand-dollar building. This means that the administration building is owned now by the Board of Education of Henderson Township, the other property—two dormitories, a library, a gymnasium, an athletic field, and other small buildings—by the church board.[55] In 1933 the city and county paid the salary of seven of the teachers, the church paying the salary of the others. In the same county, about twenty-five years ago, this same church established and for about twenty years maintained, independently of the county and state, an elementary school for Negro children. Then it was taken over by the county as to salaries for teachers and control. The property, including the school building and teachers' home, owned by the church, are still being used by the county without cost.[56]

Concerning the orphanage schools in the state, most of which are church institutions, there has been developed a very definite co-operative arrangement. These orphanage schools, Baptist, Methodist, Presbyterian, Catholic, all, have, in effect, joined the state school system. Since 1931 these schools,[57] including both the elementary and the

[55] Letter of J. A. Cotton, Henderson, N. C., to L. L. Gobbel, Feb. 10, 1933.

[56] *Ibid.*

[57] A modification of the plan is in effect touching the Methodist Children's Home in Winston Salem and the Methodist Orphanage in Raleigh. The high-school boys and girls from the Children's Home are simply sent to the Winston Salem high school. The Orphanage children are sent to the Raleigh city schools

high school, have been run as a part of the city and county school systems. The state pays the current expenses, including the regular salaries of teachers, coal, and other items; the orphanages furnish the buildings, and pay to the teachers that part of the salaries, if any, in excess of the state schedule. The course of study must be the same as that offered in the city schools.[58]

In summary, it may be said that in the realm of elementary education the churches in North Carolina, except the Catholic, have always seemed ready to retire from the field as soon as the state became ready to supply the needs of the children. Since the beginning of the state system of public schools, following the Reconstruction period, the churches, in the main, have followed the policy of opening their schools in remote sections where there were no state schools. As the educational facilities of the state increased, the church schools have gradually withdrawn. In a few instances there have been a few teachers paid by the state because the churches had well-equipped buildings and the state had not seen fit to invest heavily in building and equipment.

Concerning secondary schools, the same may be said, with reservations. With the coming of a few public graded schools before 1900, as has been shown,[59] there was a disposition on the part of more than one denomination to resent this alleged encroachment upon the legitimate work of the church. When, in 1907, the state took its first major step toward a state system of high schools,[60] there was not mani-

---

for two years of high school. The state has offered to take over all four years of the high-school period. The high-school principals preferred to have the pupils for all four years, if any; but the Orphanage elected to keep the pupils for two years in order that they may work part of the time.

[58] Information given directly by A. B. Combs from office of State Department of Education, Raleigh, Feb., 1933 (see also *Literary Digest*, Sept. 2, 1933, p. 23).

[59] See above, pp. 201–203.

[60] The state appropriated $45,000 to aid in the establishment of public high schools. Counties and school districts were required to contribute an equal or greater amount than that received from the state fund, and no town of over twelve

fested quite such resentment. The Baptists, however, had set out, in 1906, to give "most earnest support to every effort to establish a splendid system of preparatory schools all over the state." They observed that the state system of education failed to furnish the majority of children the opportunity of adequate preparation for college. They felt that private and denominational academies could do this preparatory work better than public schools.[61] They did not oppose the public high schools. Neither did they allow the state's efforts to establish high schools to turn them away from their plans. Persistently, until 1921, they labored to establish and maintain preparatory schools in all sections of the state.[62] The more the state did for secondary education, it appeared, the harder the Baptists worked for their schools. In 1909 they put an educational secretary in the field in the interest of secondary schools.[63]

In the meantime, the State Superintendent of Public Instruction, a Baptist, was telling the state that "No one Church is able to support enough of these high schools to place high-school instruction within reasonable reach or within the financial ability of more than a mere handful of

---

hundred inhabitants could share in this fund at all. A total of 156 high schools were established the first year (*Biennial Report Superintendent Public Instruction, 1906–1908*, p. 8).

[61] *Minutes Baptist State Convention, 1906*, pp. 57–58. J. Y. Joyner, State Superintendent of Public Instruction, was a member of the Baptist Committee on General Education, which made this report.

[62] They admitted, in 1907, that with fewer than thirty denominational high schools, they had only been experimenting with the question. "The State has already begun the establishing of high schools in every county of the State, possibly on account of our failure to do our duty in this regard. The schools are free to all of a certain grade. Shall we now falter, shall we give up our God-given mission, shall we play Jonah and allow ourselves to be thrown overboard and spend a period in midnight darkness rather than go forward in the discharge of our duties? Let us stand by our institutions . . ." (*Minutes Baptist State Convention, 1907*, p. 53).

[63] They believed that "to delay united effort longer would be disastrous" (*ibid., 1908*, pp. 63–64). Their secretary began work May 1, 1909 (*ibid., 1909*, pp. 64–65).

boys and girls in rural districts."[64] Although claiming the equality of Baptist high schools with state high schools, by 1915 the Baptists were beginning to doubt if many of their schools could long maintain "their unequal contest" and admitting that "unless our schools offer something better than can be found in the State schools, we cannot reasonably expect our people, however loyal, to continue paying their own schools for what the State schools will offer freely."[65]

In 1921 they observed that some of their most prosperous schools suffered decided losses from competition with state institutions. They concluded that these losses were "not accidental" but "permanent." The situation gave them "grave concern" and led them to suggest that they "reflect seriously before proceeding to establish any others."[66] The Baptists henceforth were to rely less and less upon their own preparatory schools and more and more upon the public high schools.

In this era of conciliation and co-operation, which since

[64] *Biennial Report Superintendent Public Instruction, 1906–1908*, pp. 17–18. The same statement on this subject was repeated in the reports of 1908–1909, 1909–1910, 1914–1915, and 1915–1916. Superintendent Joyner added:

"The Church High School could hardly hope for the patronage of more than the children of the families accepting its tenets or inclined to its doctrines. For a complete system of high schools, therefore, that would reach all the children, it would seem to be necessary for each denomination to maintain a system of high schools in every county and to have as many systems of high schools in each county as there are denominations in that county. The impracticability and expensiveness . . . must be apparent. . . .

"The church high school and the private high school will still find a place and an important work in our educational system, but they can never take the place or do the work of the public high school for the masses of the people. . . . God speed the work of the Church and the private high school in this common battle against ignorance and illiteracy. There is work enough for all to do; but surely, in a republic like ours, . . . friends of the church high school and of the private high school will never undertake to say that all the people must get out of the way of a few of the people, and that the many public high schools, supported by all the people for the benefits of all the children, must get out of the way for a few private and church high schools that can at best hope to reach but a few of the children of the people."

[65] *Minutes Baptist State Convention, 1915*, p. 76.

[66] *Ibid., 1921*, p. 104.

the beginning of the century the state has enjoyed educationally, there have been a few instances and areas of conflict between the forces of church and state. Most of them have been relatively unimportant. From time to time charges have been made that the educational tendencies in state institutions constituted "an assault upon the fundamental doctrines of the Christian religion," and that the doctrines of Christ were attacked "boldly and clandestinely in our schools."[67] These were followed by agitation for the teaching of the Bible in the public schools, but the Baptist opposition was too much to be overcome.[68] When the Scopes trial in Tennessee was prominently before the country, an effort was made in North Carolina to forbid the teaching of evolution in the public schools and in the

[67] *Presbyterian Standard*, July 28, 1909.

[68] See above, p. 211. Concerning the Baptist position on this question, which has remained unchanged through the years, the *Biblical Recorder* (Nov. 11, 1903) said: "Baptists stand practically alone in holding that teaching of religion is the work of the churches and not of the State. Roman Catholics do hold somewhat to the same position, but there is the widest difference in this, that the Catholics would use the State as an agency by which they would give religious instruction. Baptists would never do this. Again, Catholics are opposed to free schools because they are not permitted to give religious instruction in them. Baptists are not opposed to free schools and they do not desire to give religious instruction in them. They will give such instruction as they have to give in the home, in the church and in the secondary and higher institutions.

"That the Baptist position is in accord both with the genius of free government and of Christianity we have often written to show. Freedom is not freedom where religion is thrust upon one—as it would be were the state to give religious instruction. Again that is not Christianity which forces religion upon one."

This is followed by a quotation from the *Atlantic Monthly* for Sept., 1903, from an article by Herbert W. Horwill, "The Bible in the Public Schools," which is a strong argument against teaching the Bible in the public schools.

In contrast, the Presbyterians argued: "Religion cannot be taught in our public schools. If the Protestants are in charge the Catholics and the Jews would object. If the Catholics are in charge, the Protestants and the Jews would object. So it goes. In order to offend nobody . . . our schools must be free from religious instruction. How about irreligion? May that be taught? May the Bible be scouted? O yes, there is no law against that. . . . A professor in a State college said to his class, if you propose to study Geology to any purpose you must give up your Bible. Christians are taxed to pay salaries to such professors to teach their children that the Bible is against science, and therefore false . . ." (*Presbyterian Standard*, Dec. 28, 1910).

state institutions of higher learning. The Presbyterians were understood as supporting the Poole anti-evolution bill in the legislature.[69] Other denominations manifested very little concern about it. In fact, the late Dr. William L. Poteat of Wake Forest was predominantly identified with the liberal group which opposed the measure.

Closely related to the anti-evolution agitation was an open attack by a group of Presbyterian ministers of Charlotte upon the *Journal of Social Forces*, one of the leading publications of the University of North Carolina. They protested, in particular, against two articles in the January, 1925, number on the ground that they constituted unwarranted propaganda against religion and for irreligion and infidelity.[70] President Chase disclaimed any responsibility for the views of the publication. His disclaimer, however, did not quite satisfy.[71] The Presbyterian Synod, in the fall of 1925, (1) deplored the "trend of some institutions toward rationalistic theories of morals," (2) requested, where the theory of evolution was taught, that it be presented simply as a working hypothesis and not as an established fact, (3) protested against the apparent connection between the State University and the "unsound views" of the January *Social Forces*, and (4) declared an abiding friendship for the public school system.[72]

Occasionally some institution or denominational group has protested against the state's school policy as imperilling

[69] *Presbyterian Standard*, March 14, 1925.

[70] *Ibid.*, Feb. 25, 1925. The Charlotte Presbyterians also resented the teachings of a professor in the North Carolina College for Women, who came to Charlotte for an extension course for public school teachers. They alleged that he claimed Genesis to be a myth and ridiculed the account of God's writing the Ten Commandments. The editor of the *Presbyterian Standard* (Jan. 21, 1925) wrote: "We . . . wonder if the people whose fathers planted in early days the schools and churches of our State, are willing to allow the money of the State to be used to employ such men to instill their subtle poison into the minds of our young women, and thus touch the coming mothers of the future."

[71] *Ibid.*, March 4, 1925.

[72] Report of Synod's Special Committee on Schools and Colleges, in *Presbyterian Standard*, Nov. 4, 1925.

the existence of denominational schools of all grades.[73] The Baptists, in 1910, registered strong opposition to a proposed bond issue for the benefit of state colleges.[74] And in 1917 they called upon the legislature to require a strict accounting and wide publicity for the way tax money appropriated to state institutions was being spent.[75] In 1919, 1920, and 1921, furthermore, they sought to have the legislature provide scholarships for graduates of all accredited high schools, which scholarships should be valid in all institutions in the state of standard college grade. Their approach was through the friendly offices of State Superintendent Brooks. They did not wage an open fight. The North Carolina College Conference joined the Baptists in this proposal, although nothing came of it.[76] In connection with it, moreover, they also sought to remove the alleged discrimination against graduates of church institutions in the matter of certificates to teach in the public schools.[77] In this they were more successful. A uniform standard of certification was adopted in 1919–20.[78] Rarely has there been open criticism of the conduct of students or the administration's policies within state institutions.[79] The

[73] *Minutes Baptist State Convention, 1909*, pp. 63–64; *ibid.*, 1910, p. 35.

[74] *Ibid.*, p. 48.

[75] *Ibid., 1917*, pp. 24–25.

[76] *Ibid., 1919*, p. 27; *1920*, p. 89; *1921*, pp. 106–107.

[77] *Ibid.*

[78] *Biennial Report Superintendent Public Instruction, 1918–1920*, p. 9; also above, pp. 213–215.

[79] A severe criticism of the University of North Carolina was made by Bishop John C. Kilgo, former president of Trinity College, in 1912, following a fatal hazing episode at Chapel Hill. A lengthy interview published in some of the state papers contained the following interesting statements:

"Among the things which the public ought to learn from our present calamity is to put less confidence in published professions of moral purity to which some schools annually treat it. The habit of hazing in September and sending out resolutions during October is a scheme that should no longer mislead any person, as it has never misled a number of people. . . .

"Two things the public can do to stop hazing. They can cease to furnish money and students to colleges that cannot stop this brutal conduct. I have a notion that when these colleges find themselves thus treated they will develop a genius for government in very few moments. They would not again pull out the tremulo

exceptions to the prevailing good feeling and co-operation abounding since 1900, especially as contrasted with the turmoil and strife of the preceding decade, were so few that the twentieth century may well be characterized as one of conciliation and co-operation.

There is, therefore, at the present time in North Carolina the finest feeling between the educational forces of church and state that has ever existed in the history of the commonwealth. Wherein and why this statement is true has, in a measure, already been answered. It remains to point out additional evidence and to indicate the principal unsettled educational questions the solution of which may require time and the united action of all the best minds of church and state.

The biggest question in the field of elementary and secondary education in North Carolina just now, as elsewhere, is where to get the money necessary to maintain the state's public school system. This is not an issue between church and state. The state has assumed entire responsibility for maintaining an eight-months school term. The churches, except the Catholic, are doing practically nothing in elementary education and very little in secondary education. It is hardly conceivable that they ever shall undertake again to give elementary and secondary education. It is a fact, nevertheless, that the churches are concerned as to what happens to the children's schools under state auspices. Some of them are helping to create a sentiment favorable to a solution of this problem.

Another problem in which the leaders of church and state

---

stops of their voices and say, 'We haven't the support of the students in our efforts to put down hazing.' . . .

"The other thing which the public can do is to require the next Legislature to pass stringent laws against hazing in all forms. . . . True, this would be no compliment to the colleges, it would even be a monumental reflection on them. But about this I am not particular, since the colleges that still have hazing admit that they cannot put it down. . . . This is no time to exchange flattery. We are confronted with a horrible condition of things in one of our colleges, and we should . . . take matters in our own hands" (*Statesville Landmark*, Sept. 24, 1912).

are interested and about which a few are disturbed is that of the religious instruction of children. The churches, through Sunday schools, vacation schools, and extended sessions of one sort or another, are working at the problem. But many of them feel the inadequacy of what they are doing. As has been shown, various experiments have been tried for giving moral and religious instruction in co-operation with the public schools. But as yet no satisfactory or generally acceptable plan has been found. The public school program, including extracurricular and recreational activities, has so appropriated the time of the pupils, even afternoons and Saturdays, that the churches find it difficult, even where they have the leadership, to do effectively what they regard as desirable and necessary.

Concerning teacher training, the combined agencies of church and state are turning out teachers faster than the state can use them. There is in evidence no issue between the forces of church and state concerning the certification of teachers. The good work of Superintendent Brooks, his successor, Dr. A. T. Allen, and Dr. Clyde A. Erwin, the present incumbent, has dissolved the bad feeling which once existed in this area. The one point of difficulty, in this connection, concerns the so-called state teachers' colleges, which, until 1933, charged persons intending to teach no tuition and others only a nominal tuition fee.[80] The legis-

[80] For example, Western Carolina Teachers College (*Catalogue, July, 1932*, p. 20) advertised: "Since the College is supported by the State as a teacher-training institution, there is no tuition for North Carolina students preparing to teach. All out-of-state students pay a nominal fee of fifteen dollars ($15.00) per quarter." Appalachian State Teachers College (*Catalogue 1931–1932*, p. 19), North Carolina College for Women (*Catalogue, 1930–1931*, p. 47), and East Carolina Teachers College (*Catalogue 1931–1932*, p. 14) likewise charged no tuition to those preparing to teach. Tuition at Appalachian State Teachers College was only five dollars per quarter (*Catalogue 1931–1932*, p. 19). The agreement to teach required of those accepting free tuition was rather flexible. For example, note the following from the North Carolina College for Women agreement (*Catalogue, 1930–1931*, p. 47): "I agree, in consideration of free tuition granted me in said Institution, if I can secure employment and my health permits, to teach in the schools of the State, or do other public service for at least two years after I leave the College."

lature of 1933, however, required the trustees of all state institutions to charge fees of all students, except invalids and cripples, sufficient to pay the cost of tuition, room rent, and other services.[81] Athough this change came as a revenue-raising measure in a time of financial depression and not primarily as a concession to church colleges, who were making no special demands at this point, it nevertheless tended to improve a condition admittedly disadvantageous to a number of the smaller church colleges. The fact that it was left to the trustees to determine the amount of the tuition, however, has left the way open for these state institutions to fix their tuition lower than that of most of the church colleges. Some of the representatives of the church institutions, therefore, are feeling that, when there is already a surplus of teachers, it is not only unfair but foolish for the state, under the guise of teacher training, to give practically free higher education.[82]

Then, too, notwithstanding the fact that the organic separation of the public schools from the state institutions of higher learning has been rather firmly established, some ardent agents of state institutions still attempt to use the apparent connection in bidding for high-school graduates interested in becoming teachers, to the disadvantage of church-related colleges. Yet many if not most high-school graduates, even, know that no state institution has appointive power over public school teachers and that many principals and school boards prefer teachers trained in church-related colleges, so that there is little disposition to make an issue of the occasional effort to use a superficial advantage.

With such minor exceptions as have just been discussed, the churches and church institutions are on good terms

[81] Public Laws of 1933, chap. 320, p. 466. This law removed the prevailing practice of granting free tuition to children of ministers and students preparing for the ministry (editorial, "Free Tuition," *Durham Morning Herald*, Feb. 12, 1933).

[82] This problem is brought up frequently in the meetings of the North Carolina College Conference.

with the State University and the other state institutions for higher learning. Beneath the surface there doubtless still remains some trace of ancient animosities, but rarely does it come into prominence. A spirit of comity and a disposition to friendly intercourse are not only presumed to exist between the institutions, but the leaders of both sides are very purposefully and effectively doing what they can to maintain a wholesome, friendly, co-operative spirit and to multiply opportunities for exchange of courtesies.[83] President Frank P. Graham of the State University, a Presbyterian, is doing much to maintain his reputation for broadmindedness and catholicity of spirit and to lift his institution above suspicion of discrimination against even the smallest sect.[84] His stand against no man or party or section or creed or class and for all the interest of all the people of the state[85] seems to be taken at face value. No one is raising the cry of Presbyterian predominance. President Graham has transcended his denominational affiliation; and for the moment at least all the denominations and denominational institutions seem to have come to the position of the late President L. L. Hobbs of Guilford College who never could see the propriety of calling in question the neces-

[83] For example, between the University of North Carolina and Duke University, the two universities in North Carolina whose campuses are only about ten miles apart, there are frequent exchanges of such courtesies as department and community teas. The printed calendar of Duke University contains each week a schedule of some of the principal events of the week at the University of North Carolina for the benefit of the members of the Duke University community who may be interested in these events. Similar publicity is given by the University of North Carolina to Duke University events. The student leaders, moreover, at athletic events and on other occasions, give evidence of ability to rise above pettiness and to put good sportsmanship alongside intense rivalry.

[84] For example, in Sept., 1933, when it came to his attention that the Dean of the School of Medicine was maintaining a rule which limited to four a year the number of Jews who could be admitted to the school, he informed Dean Isaac Hall Manning that, under the statute, he could not fix any limit, and that the law must not be superseded. Manning offered his resignation as dean; and although he had been dean twenty-eight years, President Graham accepted it (*Durham Morning Herald*, Sept. 30, 1933; *Daily Tar Heel*, Sept. 30, 1933).

[85] Frank P. Graham, "Education in North Carolina," *Durham Morning Herald*, Feb. 5, 1933.

sity of all the state institutions from the University down. All the institutions of church and state seem to have about all they can do to take care of the demand for the education of the boys and girls, young men and women, who in increasing numbers apply for admission.

The state, furthermore, has adopted a liberal attitude toward denominational institutions. There is now no disposition to restrict the amount of the holdings allowed church colleges. The charters are amended from time to time to almost any amount requested. The state seems not to fear that the church colleges might ever become too powerful or subversive of the common good. The state seems to recognize that they are relieving the state of the necessity of taxing its people oppressively to provide what, with the churches at work, it is not now called upon to supply.

In short, the present *modus vivendi* is, on the whole, one of friendliness, mutual understanding, and high resolve to carry on for a better state and a happier people.

Bibliography

MANUSCRIPTS

MS History of the University of North Carolina. Author unidentified but presumably K. P. Battle. (In the vault of the Library of the University of North Carolina, Chapel Hill.)

MS Journals of the (North Carolina) Literary Board, 1827–1848. (In Library of State Historical Commission, Raleigh.)

Letters: Alderman, E. A., to Spencer, Mrs. Cornelia P., January 17, 1895.

Atkins, S. G., to the writer, March 3, 1933.

Bailey, J. W., to Kilgo, J. C., July 14, 1897.
—July 16, 1897.
—August 6, 1897.
—November 9, 1897.
—March 24, 1898.

Beck, W. H., to the writer, February 24, 1933.

Branson, E. C., to the writer, October 10, 1930.

Brownlee, Fred L., to the writer, February 21, 1933.

Cotton, J. A., to the writer, February 10, 1933.

Finley, W. E., to the writer, July 5, 1933.

Gaston, J. M., to the writer, February 10, 1933.

Hillman, James E., to the writer, April 19, 1934.

Holden, L. J., to Kilgo, J. C., July 7, 1897.

Holton, Holland, to the writer, February 13, 1931.
—March 12, 1931.

McIver, Alexander, to Spencer, Mrs. Cornelia P., June 5, 1885.

Mebane, C. H., to Kilgo, J. C., January 4, 1897.
—August 17, 1897.

(Letters to Kilgo in Duke University Library.)

Nau, H., to the writer, February 24, 1933.

Patten, Walter, to the writer, April 20, 1934.

Smith, Frank A., to the writer, February 17, 1933.

Winston, G. T., to Spencer, Mrs. Cornelia P., September—, 1894.

Winston, G. T., to Spencer, Mrs. Cornelia P., April 19, 1895.

(Letters to Mrs. Spencer in *Spencer Papers* collection in Library of the State Historical Commission, Raleigh.)

MSS: Letters, University of North Carolina, 1796–1835. (Collection in vault of the Library of the University of North Carolina, Chapel Hill.)

MS: Journal of the North Carolina Conference, Methodist Episcopal Church, 1838–1866. (In Duke University Library.)

MS: Record Book of Davidson College, 1838–1878. (In vault of Davidson College Library.)

MS: Record of Trustees, University of North Carolina.

MS: Reports from the Faculty to the Trustees of the University of North Carolina, 1830–1839. (In vault of Library of the University of North Carolina, Chapel Hill.)

MS: Trustees Record, Davidson College, 1836–1878. (In vault of Davidson College Library.)

NEWSPAPERS AND PERIODICALS

Biblical Recorder—1839–1480, 1853, 1855, 1857, 1873, 1874, 1881, 1885, 1893, 1894, 1896, 1897, 1903, 1904, 1905, 1873, 1890, and 1837–1900 (odd numbers).

Biblical Recorder and Southern Watchman—1837–1838.

Carolina Watchman—1881.

Caucasian—1897.

Charlotte Observer—1894.

Christian Educator—1896–1898.

Daily Tar Heel—September 30, 1933.

Davidson College Bulletin, XXXV.

Durham Morning Herald—January 21, 1933; February 5, 1933; February 12, 1933; September 30, 1933.

Evening Visitor—December 31, 1894.

Guilford College Bulletin—1923.

Guilford Collegian—1889–1903.

Literary Digest—September 2, 1933.

Meredith College Bulletin—January, 1916.

Morning Star—1881–1885.

News and Observer—1885–1899.

North Carolina Christian Advocate—1855, Vol. I; 1858–1921, odd numbers; 1859; 1860; 1861; 1894; 1895–1910; 1921–1934.
North Carolina Journal—1792–1796.
North Carolina Journal of Education—1858–1862.
North Carolina Presbyterian—1860–1898 (odd numbers).
North Carolina State Normal Magazine—1900–1905.
Presbyterian Standard—1899–1925.
Raleigh Christian Advocate—1871–1889 (*Raleigh Christian Advocate*); 1892–1894; 1899–1905; 1907–1919 (combined with *North Carolina Christian Advocate*, June 19, 1919).
Raleigh Episcopal Methodist—1868–1870 (odd numbers).
Raleigh Register—October 13, 1820; June 19, 1837; January 8, 1859; March 19, 1884; February 11, 1885.
Raleigh Star—March 15, 1810.
Religious Education—1927.
Richmond (Va.) Times—December 25, 1895.
Southern Citizen—February 18, 1837.
Spirit of the Age—February 15, 1859.
State Chronicle—1885–1893.
Statesville Landmark—September 14, 1912.
Tar Heel—1893–1900; 1928.
Tarborough Free Press—1824–1851.
Trinity Alumni Register—1915.
Trinity Archive—1894.
University of North Carolina Magazine—1853–1856; 1885; 1893; 1895–1899.
University of North Carolina Record—1896–1900; October, 1925; March, 1937.
Wake Forest Student—1924–1927 and 1929.
Western Carolinian—1820–1824.

PUBLIC DOCUMENTS, PROCEEDINGS, AND REPORTS

Annual Report of Executive Committee of Schools and Colleges of Presbyterian Church in the United States, May 21, 1908 (booklet).
Annual Report of the Superintendent of Common Schools of the State of North Carolina, 1855, 1858–1860.
Annual Report State Superintendent of Public Instruction, 1869, 1873, 1881–1882, 1887–1888.
Biennial Reports of the Superintendent of Public Instruction of North Carolina—1894–1900, 1902–1909, 1914–1916.
Colonial Records—Vols. I, VIII, IX, X, XXIII.

Crowell, J. F. *Annual Report of President of Trinity College to the North Carolina Conference, 1893.* Trinity College Pamphlets.

Journal of the Annual Convention of the Protestant Episcopal Church, Diocese of North Carolina, 1823–1925.

Journal of the House of Representatives of the General Assembly of the State of North Carolina—1825; 1833–1834; 1881; 1885; 1887; 1891; 1893; 1895; 1897; 1899; 1901.

Journal of Senate of the General Assembly of the State of North Carolina—1826–1827; 1833–1834; 1881; 1885; 1891; 1893; 1895; 1897; 1899; 1901.

Minutes of the Annual Conference of the Methodist Protestant Church—1883, 1892, 1896, 1903, 1905, 1914–1918.

Minutes General Assembly Presbyterian Church, U. S. A., 1799.

Minutes of the North Carolina Baptist State Convention—1830–1855; 1857–1858; 1890–1892; 1895–1899; 1900–1905; 1907; 1928.

Minutes of the North Carolina Conference, Methodist Episcopal Church, South—1872–1933.

Minutes of the North Carolina Yearly Meeting of Friends—1847; 1848; 1851; 1853; 1855; 1856; 1860; 1865–1879; 1881; 1883; 1884; 1887–1902.

Minutes of the Synod of North Carolina (Presbyterian, U. S. A.)—1837; 1844–1847; 1849–1852; 1854; 1856–1858; 1861; 1867–1873; 1875; 1877–1913; 1917–1925.

Minutes of the Western North Carolina Conference, Methodist Episcopal Church, South—1890–1930.

Private Laws (of N. C.) *of 1866, 1907.*

Proceedings: Annual Meeting of the Alumni Association (University of North Carolina) Held in the Capitol, Raleigh, N. C., January 26, 1881 (pamphlet).

Proceedings of the Annual Methodist Educational Conference, 1891 (pamphlet).

Proceedings: Inauguration of President Gaines (of Wake Forest College), April 25, 1928 (booklet).

Proceedings: Inauguration of President Walter Lee Lingle, Davidson College, June 3, 1930 (booklet).

Publications of the North Carolina Historical Commission, Vol. I, 1900–1905.

Public Documents (Executive and Legislative), North Carolina—1856–1857; 1860–1861; 1863–1864; 1868–1869; 1873–1874; 1881; 1883; 1885; 1887; 1893; 1897; 1901; 1903.

Public Laws of North Carolina—1871–1872; 1872–1873; 1933.
Public School Laws of North Carolina—1869: Chapter 15 of the Code as amended by the Laws of 1885, 1889, 1891, 1893, 1895, and other statutes.
"Report Central Baptist Association," *Biblical Recorder*, July 15, 1896.
Report of Hon. Kemp P. Battle, President of the University of North Carolina (to Gov. Vance) on the State of the University and the Normal Schools, January 15, 1878 (pamphlet).
"Report of (N. C.) Synod's Special Committee on Schools and Colleges, 1925." *Presbyterian Standard*, November 4, 1925.
State Records, Vol. XIX.
Yearbook of the Churches of Christ (Disciples of Christ) of North Carolina, 1912–1926.

HISTORIES, BIOGRAPHIES, AND OTHER SOURCES

Adams, M. A. "The Plight of Secondary Schools," *Biblical Recorder*, December 2, 1903.
"Address to the People. . . . by Conference of Educators, Held in the Governor's Office in Raleigh, N. C., February 15, 1902." Reprinted in *Guilford Collegian*, 1902.
Addresses and Papers of K. P. Battle: a miscellaneous collection of material, including newspaper clippings (unnamed and undated), Sketches of the History of the University of North Carolina, Chapel Hill, 1889, and other material. (In the University of North Carolina Library.)
The American Catholic Historical Researches, July, 1890.
Anscombe, F. C. *The Contribution of Quakers to the Reconstruction of the Southern States*, Chapel Hill, 1926. (Ph.D. dissertation.)
Appalachian State Teachers College Catalogue, 1931–1932.
Ashe, Samuel A. *Biographical History of North Carolina from Colonial Times to the Present.* 8 volumes. Greensboro: C. L. Van Noppen, 1905–1917.
Bassett, J. S. "Shall a Church Have a College?" *Christian Educator*, May, 1897.
Battle, K. P. *History of the University of North Carolina*, Vols. I, II. Raleigh: Edwards and Broughton, 1907–1912.
Battle, K. P. "Sketches of the History of the University of

North Carolina." Chapel Hill, 1889. (In Addresses and Papers of K. P. Battle.)

Bernheim, G. D. *History of the German Settlements and the Lutheran Church in North and South Carolina.* Philadelphia: The Lutheran Book Store, 1872.

Bernheim, G. D. and Cox, George H. *History of the Evangelical Lutheran Synod and Ministerium.* Philadelphia: Lutheran Publication Society, 1902.

Biggs, Joseph. *A Concise History of the Kehukee Association from Its Original Rise to the Present Time.* Tarborough: Howard, 1834.

Blackmar, Frank W. *The History of Federal and State Aid to Higher Education in the United States.* Bureau of Education, Circular of Information No. 1, 1890. Washington: Government Printing Office, 1890.

Blair, J. A. *Reminiscences of Randolph County.* Greensboro: Reece and Elam, 1890. (Bound with N. C. Pamphlets, Duke Library.)

Boyd, W. K. "The Finances of the North Carolina Literary Fund." Reprint from *South Atlantic Quarterly*, July–October, 1914.

Boyd, W. K. *History of North Carolina*, Vol. II. *The Federal Period. 1783–1860.* Chicago and New York: The Lewis Publishing Company, 1919.

Boyd, W. K. *Some Eighteenth Century Tracts.* Raleigh: Edwards and Broughton, 1927.

Boyd, W. K. "North Carolina, 1775–1861," *The South in the Building of the Nation*, Vol. I.

Brooks, E. C. "Braxton Craven and the First State Normal School," *Trinity Alumni Register*, Vol. I, No. 1, 1915.

Brooks, E. C. "The First State Normal School Becomes Trinity College," *Trinity Alumni Register*, Vol. I, No. 2, 1915.

Brooks, E. C. "How the First State Normal School Became Trinity College," *Trinity Alumni Register*, Vol. I, No. 3, 1915.

Burkhead, L. S. *Centennial of Methodism in North Carolina, Containing the History and Addresses Delivered at the First Centennial Mass-Meeting Celebration, Held . . . in Raleigh, N. C., March 21st to 26th, 1876.* Edited by Rev. L. S. Burkhead, D.D. Raleigh: John Nichols.

Burkitt, Lemuel and Read, Jesse. *A Concise History of the Kehukee Baptist Association from Its Original Rise to the Present Time.* Philadelphia: Lippincott, 1850.

Chamberlain, Hope Summerell. *Old Days in Chapel Hill.* Chapel Hill: The University of North Carolina Press, 1926.

Clewell, J. H. *History of Wachovia in North Carolina.* New York, 1902.

Connor, R. D. W. *History of North Carolina*, Vol. I, *Colonial-Revolutionary Periods, 1584–1783.* Chicago and New York: The Lewis Publishing Co., 1919.

Constitution of North Carolina, 1776, 1868, 1875.

Coon, Charles L. *The Beginnings of Public Education in North Carolina: A Documentary History, 1790–1840.* 2 volumes. Raleigh: Edwards and Broughton, 1908.

Coon, Charles L. *North Carolina Schools and Academies in 1790–1840 . . . A Documentary History.* Raleigh: Edwards and Broughton, 1915.

Craven, Braxton. "Historical Sketch of Trinity College," *Centennial of Methodism in North Carolina.* Edited by L. S. Burkhead. Raleigh: John Nichols, 1876.

Crowell, John Franklin. *A Program of Progress, An Open Letter to the General Assembly of North Carolina of 1891.* Trinity Publication No. 3.

Crowell, J. F. In *Trinity College Bulletin*, Supplement, December 1, 1890, No. 8.

Cubberley, Ellwood P. *Public Education in the United States.* Boston or New York: Houghton Mifflin Co., 1919.

Drake, William Earle. Higher Education in North Carolina Before 1860. Chapel Hill, 1930. (Ph.D. Dissertation.)

East Carolina Teachers College Catalogue—1931–1932.

Erwin, C. P. "Free Tuition," *Christian Educator*, January, 1897.

Flowers, G. W. "A Word of Protest," *Christian Educator*, May, 1897.

Foote, W. H. *Sketches of North Carolina: Historical and Biographical.* New York: R. Carter, 1846.

Gobbel, L. L. The Present Status of Moral and Religious Instruction in the Public Schools of North Carolina, 1927 (unpublished).

Graham, E. K. *Education and Citizenship, and Other Papers.* New York and London: G. P. Putnam's Sons, 1919.

Graham, Frank P. "Education in North Carolina," *Durham Morning Herald*, February 5, 1933.

Griffin, M. I. J. "North Carolina Not An Enemy of Our Faith," *The American Catholic Historical Researches*, July, 1890, pp. 129–132.

Grisson, W. L. *History of Methodism in North Carolina.* 2 volumes. Nashville: M. E. C. S., 1905.

Grisson, W. L. "Some First Things in North Carolina Methodism," *Trinity College Historical Society Papers*, Part 3, Series 9.

Gwynn, P. H., Jr. "The Bible in the Public Schools," *Presbyterian Standard*, October 22, 1924.

Hamilton, J. G. deR. *History of North Carolina*, Vol. III—*North Carolina Since 1860.* Chicago and New York: The Lewis Publishing Co., 1919.

Hamilton, J. G. deR. *Reconstruction in North Carolina.* Raleigh: Edwards and Broughton, 1906.

Hamilton, J. G. deR. "William Randolph Davie: A Memoir," *The James Sprunt Historical Studies*, Vol. VII.

Hamilton, J. G. deR. "North Carolina, 1865–1909," *The South in the Building of the Nation*, Vol. I.

Harris, W. L. The Development of the High School System in North Carolina (M.A. Thesis, Wake Forest—unpublished).

Haywood, Marshall DeLancey. "The History of Queen's College or Liberty Hall in the Province of North Carolina," *North Carolina Booklet*, Vol. XI, No. 3, published by the North Carolina Society, Daughters of the Revolution, January, 1912.

Henneman, J. B. (editor). *The South in the Building of the Nation*, Vol. IV. Richmond: The Southern Publication Society, 1909.

Hobbs, S. H. *North Carolina Economic and Social.* Chapel Hill: The University of North Carolina Press, 1931.

Hooper, William. *"Fifty Years Since"—An Address Delivered Before the Alumni of the University of North Carolina on the 7th of June, 1859.* Raleigh: Holden and Wilson, 1859.

Hoyt, W. H. *The Papers of Archibald D. Murphey.* 2 volumes. Raleigh: Uzzell, 1914.

Hufham, J. D. "How We Got Our Charter," *Wake Forest Student*, 1898.

Hunter, C. L. *Sketches of Western North Carolina.* Raleigh: 1877.

Ivey, T. N. "Address in Behalf of the Methodist Church of North Carolina (on occasion of the inauguration of President Kilgo, Trinity College, 1894)," *Trinity Archive*, October, 1894.

James Sprunt Historical Monograph No. 7.

James Sprunt Historical Publications, Vol. II, No. 2; Vol. XI, No. 2.

James Sprunt Historical Studies, Vol. VII.

Johnson, Livingston. *History of the Baptist State Convention.* Raleigh: Edwards and Broughton, 1908.

Kelly, W. O. An Interpretation of Major Educational Legislation in North Carolina, 1868–1900. (M. A. Thesis, Wake Forest College—Unpublished.)

Kilgo, J. C. "A Ringing Endorsement," *Christian Educator*, March, 1897.

Kilgo, J. C. "An Open Letter to the Friends of Christian Education," *Christian Educator*, September, 1897.

Kilgo, J. C. *Christian Education, Its Aims and Superiority.* Trinity College Pamphlets (Duke Library).

Kilgo, J. C. "Dogmatic Criticism," *Christian Educator*, February, 1897.

Kilgo, J. C. "Education and Crime," *Christian Educator*, October, 1896.

Kilgo, J. C. "Education of the Poor Boy," *Biblical Recorder*, December 9, 1896.

Kirby, G. F. "In Defence of Dr. Kilgo," *Christian Educator*, November, 1898.

Klain, Zora. *Quaker Contributions to Education in North Carolina.* Philadelphia: Westbrook, 1925.

Knight, E. W. *Public School Education in North Carolina.* Boston and New York: Houghton Mifflin Co., 1916.

Leonard, J. C. *History of Catawba College.* Published by the Trustees of Catawba College, 1927.

Leonard, J. C., *et. al. Historic Sketch of the Reformed Church in North Carolina.* Philadelphia: Publication Board of the Reformed Church in the U. S., 1908.

Letters and Papers of Governor Cameron Morrison, 1921–1925. Edited by D. L. Corbitt. Raleigh: Edwards and Broughton, 1927.

Martin, Francis-Xavier. *The History of North Carolina from the Earliest Period*, Vol. II. New Orleans: A. T. Penniman and Co., 1829.

Mebane, C. H. "Statement of the Superintendent of Public Instruction," *Biblical Recorder*, March 17, 1897.

Moore, John Wheeler. *History of North Carolina: From the Earliest Discovery to the Present Time.* 2 volumes. Raleigh: A. Williams and Co., 1880.

Nash, Frank. "The North Carolina Constitution of 1776 and Its Makers," *James Sprunt Historical Publications*, Vol. II, no. 2.

Newbold, N. C. "Common Schools for Negroes in the South," *The Annals of the American Academy of Political and Social Science.* Philadelphia, 1928.

Nixon, J. R. "German Settlers in Lincoln County and Western North Carolina," *James Sprunt Historical Publications*, Vol. XI, No. 2.

Noble, M. C. S., Jr. *A History of the Public Schools of North Carolina.* Chapel Hill: The University of North Carolina Press, 1930.

North Carolina College for Women Catalogue, 1930–1931.

Papers and Letters of Governor Angus Wilton McLean (1925–1929). Edited by D. L. Corbitt. Raleigh: Edwards and Broughton, 1931.

"The Paradoxes of the Centuries," A Sermon Preached in the Second Presbyterian Church, Charlotte, North Carolina, December 30, 1900. Published in *Presbyterian Standard*, January 9, 1901.

Paschal, G. W. "Public School Advancement in North Carolina," *Wake Forest Student*, November, 1929.

Paschal, G. W. *History of North Carolina Baptists*, Vol. I. Raleigh: Edwards and Broughton, 1930.

Paschal, G. W. "History of Wake Forest College," *Wake Forest Student*, 1924–1927.

Phillips, F. M. *Statistics of Universities, Colleges, and Secondary Schools*. U. S. Bureau of Education Bulletin, 1929, No. 38.

Randall, J. H. *The Making of the Modern Mind*. Boston and New York: Houghton Mifflin Co., 1926.

Raper, C. L. *Church and Private Schools in North Carolina, 1898*. Greensboro: J. J. Stone, 1898.

Reeder, W. G. "State Control of Private and Parochial Schools," *School and Society*, No. 17, April 21, 1923.

Reep, A. R. The Educational Influence of Methodists in North Carolina. (M. A. Thesis, U. N. C., 1925—Unpublished.)

Shaw, Cornelia. *Davidson College (A Compilation of Records)*. New York: Revell, 1923.

Sherrill, L. J. *Presbyterian Parochial Schools, 1846–1870*. New Haven: Yale University Press, 1932.

Sikes, E. W. "The Genesis of Wake Forest College," *Publications of the North Carolina Historical Commission*, Vol. I, 1900–1905.

Sikes, E. W. *The Transition of North Carolina from Colony to Commonwealth*. Johns Hopkins University Studies in History and Political Science. Baltimore: The Johns Hopkins University Press, 1898.

Slater Fund Educational Papers, Nos. 3, 5, 9 (on Negro education in North Carolina).

Smith, C. Alphonso. "Presbyterians in Educational Work in North Carolina since 1813." Reprint from *Union Seminary Review*, December–January, 1913–14.

Smith, C. L. *History of Education in North Carolina*. United States Bureau of Education, Circular of Information, No. 2, 1888.

Spillman, B. W. "Who Proved Themselves Friends to the Public Schools?" *Biblical Recorder*, March 17, 1897.

State Department of Education, *Educational Publication No. 76*, 1925.

Stewart, John. *The Organization of Education in Edinburgh*. Castle Terrace, Edinburgh: Education Offices, 1925.

Taylor, C. E. *How Far Should a State Undertake to Educate? or, A Plea for the Voluntary System in the Higher Education*. Raleigh: Edwards and Broughton, 1894.

The South in the Building of the Nation, Vol. I. Richmond: The Southern Publication Society, 1909.

Trinity College Bulletin, Aug. 5, 1896.

Trinity College Bulletin No. 8, Supplement, December 1, 1890.

Trinity College Historical Society Papers, Part 3, Series 9.

Trinity College Publication, No. 3.

Trowbridge, C. H. Functions and Limitations of Denominational Secondary Schools. (M.A. Thesis, University North Carolina—Unpublished.)

Tuttle, Harold S. *Character Education by State and Church.* Cincinnati: Abingdon Press, 1930.

Ware, C. C. *A History of the Disciples of Christ in North Carolina.* St. Louis: Christian Board of Publication, 1927.

Weeks, Stephen B. *The Beginnings of the Common School System in the South: Calvin Henderson Wiley and the Organization of the Common Schools of North Carolina.* Washington: Government Printing Office, 1898.

Weeks, Stephen B. *Church and State in North Carolina.* Baltimore: The Johns Hopkins Press, 1893.

Weigle, L. A. *American Idealism*, Volume X, "The Pageant of America Series" (Ralph H. Gabriel, editor). New Haven: Yale University Press, 1929.

Weigle, L. A. *Religious and Secular Education* (tract). New York: American Tract Society.

Weigle, L. A. "Why the Principle of Public Responsibility for Education Has Prevailed in the United States," *Religious Education*, June, 1927.

Western Carolina Teachers College Catalogue, July, 1932.

Wheeler, John H. *Historical Sketches of North Carolina from 1584 to 1851, with Biographical Sketches of Her Distinguished Statesmen, Jurists, Lawyers, Soldiers, Divines, etc.* Philadelphia: Lippincott, Grambo, and Company, 1851.

Wiley, C. H. *Alamance Church, A Historical Address Delivered at the Dedication of Its Fourth House of Worship.* Raleigh: Edwards and Broughton, 1880. (In N. C. Pamphlets, Duke University.)

Wiley, C. H. "History of the Common Schools of North Carolina," *North Carolina Educational Journal*, 1881.

Wiley, C. H. *North Carolina Reader, Number III.* New York: A. S. Barnes and Co.; Raleigh: W. L. Pomeroy, 1859. Prepared with Special Reference to the Wants and Interests of North Carolina, under the Auspices of the Superintendent of Common Schools Containing Selections in Prose and Verse.

Wood, Marquis L. *History of Methodism in the Yadkin Valley.*

Yoder, R. A. "Views from Different Sources," *Christian Educator*, October, 1896.

INDEX